J.P. McCarthy ♣

Just Don't Tell 'Em Where I Am

Michael Shiels

 SLEEPING BEAR PRESS

Sleeping Bear Press   Sleeping Bear Ltd.
121 South Main   7 Medallion Place
P.O. Box 20   Maidenhead, Berkshire
Chelsea, MI 48118   England

Printed and bound in the United States.

10 9 8 7 6 5 4 3 2 1

Cataloging-in-Publication Data on file.

ISBN 1-886947-24-4

Contents

Foreword

When my good friend Michael Shiels called me up and told me he was writing a book about my father, Joseph Priestley McCarthy, my reaction was simple: there couldn't be anybody more qualified! He humbly accepted the compliment and the conversation ended.

Five minutes later the phone rang: "It's Mike again. How would you like to write a foreword or a dedication describing who J.P. McCarthy was to you?" My reaction wasn't quite as simple as it was to the first phone call, but here's what I came up with:

J.P. McCarthy was . . .

The man whose picture should have been next to the word "inquisitive" in *Webster's Dictionary of Comparative Illustrations.*

A little Frank Sinatra, a little Bing Crosby, and sometimes a lot of Dean Martin.

A magician of the English language, who, like most fathers, was never wrong . . . only, he never *was* wrong! I know, because he was always on the other team in Trivial Pursuit!

The man who made everybody and their mother from every race, creed, and color come together for one day, only to make them Irish . . . he was twisted, too!

The man who went out of his way to help just about every charitable organization that was ever created for the betterment of mankind, and is still doing so through the J.P. McCarthy Foundation.

A man who loved movies so much he built his own miniature home theater with a sound system so high-tech that the rest of the McCarthy family is currently speaking in sign language.

A father whose technique of parenting was much like "Mr. Miagi" in *The Karate Kid*. We weren't just outside "painting fence" just to "paint fence." We were outside "painting fence" so he could get some sleep! Seriously, there was always a lesson involved with my dad.

A father who never wanted his sons to be mama's boys, but expected them to have the utmost respect for their mother.

The type of father that expected greatness but certainly accepted the 'C' student. The McCarthy boys didn't give him much of a choice—although it's said 'C' students run the world.

A man who respected those who came from nothing and worked their way to the top . . . much like himself. Although he said, himself, he never had a real job, I'm currently doing some radio and I can tell you that to be good requires lots of hard work.

A man who when at sea was considered as "salty" as they come; of course, this was in his own opinion. The reference is from an occasion when I was boating with him and I could not tie a simple knot. We connected much better on the links.

A man who might shoot 88 with his friends on Saturday, but always shot a 75 against his sons on Sunday.

A man who practiced what he preached, worked hard, played hard, and always answered the bell.

A man who, for every 24 hours he lived, became that much closer to omniscience.

The one and only "Great Voice of the Great Lakes."

Foreword

A man who knew who he was, but never took advantage of it.

A man who loved Detroit, and did everything in his power to make it a better place, believing Mayor Dennis Archer could turn it around.

A man who was intimidated by no one, but treated all with equal respect.

A man who was old-fashioned in his beliefs, yet never forgot the concept of change . . . probably why he was number one for so long.

Not a Republican or a Democrat, but certainly kept everyone guessing.

A tough man with a very big heart.

A man who despised the lackadaisical and praised the over-achiever. As his son, you wanted to be the latter.

A man who loved his wife Judy and his children, John, Susan, Diane, Kathleen, Kevin and Jamie to no end.

A man who lived each day as if it were his last, and when his last day did come, said to me, "I am a very lucky man, son. I've done everything I ever dreamed of doing and a lot more. I've had a great life."

He was my father, my mentor, my hero, and my friend.
The greatest man I have ever known.

— Jamie McCarthy

Introduction

J.P. McCarthy was my professional idol. He was my leader, my boss, and my friend. He treated me like a son. Working as his radio producer for the last five years of his career and life, I learned from him things he didn't even know he taught me. He showed me style, displayed sincerity and dignity, gave me an example of how to treat people, how to make small talk, how to make things happen, and how to have a lot of fun. He knew sometimes you had to just break away.

When we took the show on the road, he would make sure we investigated the "local lifestyle and culture" by disappearing for a few hours to "hoist one, by God" at watering holes in places as diverse as Tokyo's Imperial Palace Hotel, so we could "drink where MacArthur drank," and the chic "Fouquets" on the Champs Élysées in Paris, so we could "carefully note the Parisian fashion choices," or "just one" at the Pegasus in the Fisher Building.

J.P. always prided himself on figuring out the complex subway systems of these world cities. More often than not, his efforts would result in "seeing more of the town" and nearly missing the start of our remote broadcasts, in which he would interview ambassadors, politicians, business leaders, journalists, and others.

He taught me that it takes, indeed, a whole day to celebrate St. Patrick's Day properly, and that when singing Christmas carols outside in front of two thousand people, you'd better make sure your voice is properly lubricated. He was an incredibly smart and humble man who taught me little lessons like "you can never go wrong with a blazer" and "make sure you transfer that weight back to the left side through your downswing."

He gave me the break of a lifetime when I worked at WJR in 1990. I worked for Jimmy Launce then, but word was J.P. might soon be looking for a new producer. When I received a dream job offer from the PGA Tour in Florida, I was faced with a dilemma. I sheepishly contacted J.P. for advice. He told me, "Rest assured, you will produce my show someday. For now, go on down to Florida and beat winter. It sounds like a lot of fun. I'll call you when I'm ready!" He didn't make me choose, and when he did call he humbly asked, "Do you think you still want to come back?" I promised him loyalty . . . he changed my life.

He introduced me to some of the highest quality people in the world. People who immediately joined him in putting their arm around me and teaching me about their given specialty in life or providing priceless advice and counsel. The respect and consideration shown me by these giants of industry, just because I was J.P.'s producer, was most flattering, and I hope to do them and all of J.P.'s loyal listeners proud.

When we worked together, J.P. could be very demanding. During the four hours that made up his show, he would bark out commands and tell me the names of some people he wanted me to contact. I didn't bore him with the process, but I delivered, though they were sometimes hard to find! As a test, he would challenge me with names even he thought I couldn't reach. He once badgered me every ten minutes all morning about finding General Chuck Yeager, and was then surprised to find him waiting on hold, ready for an early morning phone conversation. "You mean you got Chuck Yeager?" he exclaimed.

What he didn't realize is that he made my job easy by his years of accomplishment and his reputation for treating interview subjects with respect and thoughtfulness. His name opened doors. He wasn't "the media" . . . he was J.P.!

In our last phone conversation, he told me how proud he was that his show was always making news. "It's nice of us to provide the news department with so much material," he told me. Unfortunately, the last phone call I set up for J.P. was a call from Cardinal Adam Maida to his room at Sloan Kettering Hospital in New York. The Cardinal said they spoke of God, and that J.P. was at peace.

Joseph Priestly McCarthy lived a very full life. He *loved* life! I've never met anyone who had done so much, but had so much more yet to do. I was in the process of arranging an interview between J.P. and Pope John Paul II at the Vatican when the pipes called him. J.P. and I were also poised to be partners in our own production company and to syndicate his radio show all over the country. Stations all over Michigan were ready to start the network immediately. It was his #1 new interest.

As I was closer to his children's age than his, I am to this day mystified by why he chose me, and why he chose to make so many good things happen for me and give me so many opportunities. He would tell me jokingly that it was because he wanted to work with someone his own age!

Seriously, as a child, I remember skipping school each year the day before the Michigan–Ohio State game so I could listen to J.P.'s famous "tailgate show" with Ron Kramer. When I told J.P. how neat it was to now produce that special show with him, he'd tell me, "My boy, I have socks older than you!"

He regaled me regularly with stories of days gone by, and I hope that I learned from him. He watched out for me, and I did my best to take good care of him.

The morning after J.P. died, I gave him his show one more time. I replayed some of his greatest moments on tape. I hung his headphones on the microphone, placed his glasses and coffee where they normally waited for him, and left his chair empty. When the last few seconds of his theme song faded out at 10:00, I knew "The J.P. McCarthy Show" had come to an end, and it caused me to shudder. It was an era made of voice, ushered out in silence.

I loved him, and if he knew I was writing this book, I'm quite sure he'd utter his famous regular quip. He'd say "Michael, mention my name in the book . . . just don't tell 'em where I am!"

Michael Shiels

In His Own Words

by J.P. McCarthy, 1984

The fact is, I am still surprised that I get paid for doing what I do—climbing into the WJR playpen every day and having more fun than a kid on his first day at Montessori School.

Five mornings a week, I have 50,000 watts of power, a microphone, a telephone . . . and close to 6 million playmates in three states and the Province of Ontario. (More than that, if I can count WJR's national audience in the early hours before other signals jam me). Who could ask for more than that?

With WJR footing the considerable phone bill that I run up, I can wake up Howard Cosell, Billy Martin, and ex-President Jimmy Carter . . . and have! I can chitchat with Monte Clark, Sparky Anderson, and Mike Downey . . . to argue with Roger Stanton, bow to Bo Schembechler, and quiz Russ Thomas.

I can also call Beirut, Lebanon, Londonderry or Grenada to connect us to what's happening in the world . . . even before (in some cases) the rest of the world knows it's upon it. Case in point: The morning of the Grenada invasion . . . I happened to get the Grenada overseas operator, who screamed at me . . . "I can't talk to you now . . . we are being attacked! We have been ordered to our battle stations!" Now, *there's* a hello to wake you up!

Maybe I've never grown up . . . but it's more fun than I can tell you to call Buckingham Palace (and get through to the Queen's Lady-in-Waiting) . . . dial the White House and be put through to a Presidential assistant who says: "President Reagan is brushing his teeth and cannot be disturbed." Or call the Pentagon and have a major general call me "Sir"! That to a former Air Force airman second class. Wow!

The same holds true for my "Focus" show at noon when the major names in show business, the arts, business, industry, and government troop into Studio D . . . to be interviewed by me— the kid from the East Side of Detroit. I'm still awed by a Roger Smith, George Bush, Lauren Bacall, Alan Alda, General Westmoreland, Lee Iacocca, James Michener, or Charlton Heston.

When I began in radio—up in Anchorage, Alaska (while in the service)—I did aspire to come home to WJR Radio . . . but, I'm not sure that I saw myself in Studio D with the late, great Lowell Thomas, or Chet Huntley, or Margaret Mead. I might have fainted at the thought of sitting down with Arthur Fiedler, or Antal Dorati someday.

See what I mean? My job is never quite the same . . . in the morning or with "Focus." And it's always a little scary, challenging, and above everything else . . . exciting! It's truly like going to school every day . . . with the best teachers in the world telling you everything you've ever wanted to know. Or, sitting down with the most knowledgeable and fascinating people in the world, who will graciously answer any dumb question I pose to them . . . and even tell me how much fun it was talking to me! Sometimes, I have to pinch myself to see if I'm real!

Imagine sitting a timestep away from Fred Astaire. Imagine being verbally spanked by Gore Vidal. Imagine staring into Candace Bergen's pale blue eyes for forty-five minutes!

Get the picture? The greatest job in the world, right?

Aside from the obvious thrill of just getting to meet people like Dustin Hoffman, or Alex Haley, there is the great satisfaction that goes with learning that they are all where they are because of what they are: substantive and sensitive people. I have learned that even flamboyant celebrities like Muhammad Ali or Joan Rivers are, beneath the bravado and image, very real and warm people, and I feel that I have learned from all of them the demands that go with celebrity status. It's a price not all of us would like to pay.

Amazingly, I have had "Focus" guests whom you would have assumed were close friends or associates meet one another for the first time in Studio D . . . like the first meeting of portrait photographer Yousuf Karsh and *Life* photographer Alfred Eisenstadt.

Then there have been startling moments when major names have (literally) made news on "Focus"—as female jockey Debby Hicks did . . . when she casually blew the whistle on race track irregularities! Controversial Admiral Elmo Zumwalt also told "Focus" listeners that it was all right for sailors to wear their hair long if that's what they wanted . . . and found himself in a hairy battle with the Pentagon and the White House.

Never a dull moment! And I get paid for this! Only in America, I suppose!

Still another exciting facet of my job is hearing from you— my audience. Between 6:15 and 10 a.m., my phone never stops ringing, nor does my producer's ear. You are the ones who give me my "Winners & Losers" of the day; give me "what for" when I've blown a name or a date; tell me who played second base for the Detroit Tigers in 1938; or when the last Model A rolled off the assembly line.

You also give me my best ideas of who I should call and what you want to know. You, the audience, also tell me when I should "Make it . . . or break it" when a new record spins for the first time. You tell who's in, and who's out . . . what's hot and what's not . . . and in no uncertain terms.

You also worry about the other personalities on the station; who has a cold, who's on vacation, and where is Bud Guest or Jack Harris these days? (The latter was last heard answering a page at The Polo Lounge at the Beverly Hills Hotel.)

What can I tell you? When I was a kid, did I aspire to become a disc jockey or radio interview host? You can bet your socks I didn't. I wanted to be President of GM or Ford or Chrysler or AT&T—and I definitely haven't given up the idea of playing second base for the Detroit Tigers.

Not only that, if they don't throw this column into the wastebasket, and it makes it into print, I may just want to take a shot at writing a column for somebody! Pete Waldmeier, watch out! Bob Talbert, eat your heart out!

But Man, ♣ That Cat Could Sing

This is the story of a frustrated singer and would-be television personality. If only he hadn't been so damned good at radio.

This "disc jockey," you see, had tremendous passion and intellect. He was schooled by Catholic nuns at Annunciation prep school in New York until one day the eighth-grader came home and told his father Priestley, "That's it. I'm not going back there."

J.P. McCarthy completed high school in Detroit with the Christian Brothers at De La Salle Collegiate and took his photographic memory to the Jesuit Priests at the University of Detroit with the intent of becoming an engineer and a draftsman.

J.P. was drafted in the middle of his studies, and the Air Force sent him to Alaska by way of Seattle. "You take things in stride, but it breaks your heart to have your child go so far," his mother Martha says. "You think about faraway places and you can't see him, but Joe was brave about going in and he always wrote to us and sent pictures."

That's where it happened. It happened on maneuvers in the middle of the desolate, barren Yukon. That's where the gift— "the magic"—first came in handy.

"Out on a troop ship during maneuvers, in order to stay awake, Joe had to recite with his buddies and sing and keep talking," explains Martha McCarthy. "One of the brass overheard him and thought, 'He's just right for the air!' Joe had always been around adults, so he knew how to speak up and he knew the right things to say. The next thing he knew he was on the radio talking about the army," says Martha.

Joseph McCarthy hit the air on the Armed Forces Radio Network, and in Fairbanks, Alaska with a part-time job at KFAR. When he was released from the service, he came right back to Detroit and began working nights at WTAC Radio in nearby Flint. Martha says, "I don't think Joe and his boss in Flint jived. That boss was so wrong, wasn't he?" she proudly asks.

♣

J.P. returned from Alaska with not only his radio ambition, but with his first wife and young baby, too—Sally Thompson, now Mrs. Joe McCarthy, and little John Priestley McCarthy. "He sent us a letter to tell us he got married," says Martha. "She was an auburn haired young chorus dancer who swept him off of his feet. When you're away from home and lonely, you fall in love, and it happened to Joe." McCarthy's first marriage produced five children: John, Diane, Susan, Kevin, and Kathleen.

J.P. and Sally lived with Martha and Priestley while J.P. tried to make a go of his radio career. "He had high hopes and he believed in himself," Martha beams. Joe Pemberthy, a staff announcer at Goodwill-owned radio station WJR, remembers McCarthy's efforts to make it to the already legendary "Great Voice of the Great Lakes":

"McCarthy used to come up to the station to audition and see chief announcer Charlie Park about trying to get a job," recalls Pemberthy. "We had nine announcers on staff then, and I

2

was one of the nine, and I used to sit in on auditions. J.P. was a young guy and we used to call him 'the kid.' We'd say, 'the kid is up again!' He was a skinny kid working in Flint who was awestruck."

The ambitious "kid" auditioned over and over, along with other rising stars. One auditioner that never made the cut was Soupy Sales. "That wasn't Soupy's gig," says Pemberthy. "An announcer's position was very structured and staid serious announcing."

The nine announcers on staff would read station breaks, introduce shows, and read commercials, in what was basically radio's entry level position. Paul Carey, who would later broadcast Tiger play-by-play, started as a staff announcer.

"Charlie Park liked him," Pemberthy continues, "and he was on top of the hire list for some time. Some people accused J.P. of being cocky, but he wasn't cocky—he was self-assured, confident, and pleasant to be around."

So now, "the kid" just needed a break. Six months after J.P.'s first audition, Joe Pemberthy walked into Charlie Park's office. "I handed Charlie my resignation letter," says Pemberthy, "and he tore it up. I said, 'Dammit, I'll just have to write another one, because I ain't going to stay. I'm leaving in two weeks.'

"So I wrote another letter and this time he accepted it and said, 'Well, I'll have to find somebody to take your place,' and I said, 'Well, this would be a good chance for the kid.'

"Yes, I guess it is," came Park's reply.

"They called J.P., and on October 1, 1956, he started work as a staff announcer on WJR," states Pemberthy.

♣

What was McCarthy's morning announcing shift like? It was workmanlike. He did nothing but "announce." He would sign the station on the air at 5 a.m., then introduce Marshall Wells with "The Farm Report." After that, he would introduce Charlie Park, who had a letter-reading show from 6 a.m. until 6:30, because in those days, the Federal Communications Commission did not allow telephone calls on the air. An introduction of "The Music Hall Show" followed until it was time to introduce the

8 a.m. news and Bud Guest's Show from 8:15 until 8:30, when "The Music Hall" would take over again. Then he'd introduce Jack Harris, who would sing his way with the Jimmy Clark Five live in the studio from 9:00 until 9:30, when "Mrs. Page"—whose real name was Aggie Clark—would do her recipe show until the end of his shift.

Not exactly what you would call glamour or artistry. Pemberthy says that McCarthy was probably hired in for about $5,000 per year, "which was a pretty good number—as much as they could pay him," he says. At the zenith of his career, McCarthy would earn that amount per day!

"There was an 'announcers' lounge' where we'd all sit around and wait for our shifts," says veteran WJR personality Mike Whorf, who also started as an announcer, and later went on to win the prestigious Peabody Award. "It was quite a big announcing staff, so we did more sitting than announcing," he explains, "but we'd sit and dream and talk about what our desires were and what we wanted to do in broadcasting. Joe was always so dapper and pleasant, with a certain cockiness, which I attributed to confidence."

While McCarthy quickly outgrew his announcer position, Marty McNealy hosted the WJR morning show, then called "The Music Hall." "Marty was a nice, humble guy who played records—elevator music and big band stuff," says Pemberthy.

> *"Good morning, about 8:31 here in Detroit, the second call to the Music Hall for this Thursday morning, December the 9th. This is Marty McNealy, We'll be around with recordings by Sarah Vaughn, Joan Webber, Pee Wee Hunt and his Dixielanders, and Perry Como, with a brand new song that's brand new over here, although it's one of the top selling songs in England at the present time. Here to lead things off, the Crew Cuts with 'Dance, Mr. Snowman, Dance!' . . ."*

After Marty McNealy lost the #1 rating, he left WJR to become a newsreader at WBBM in Chicago. The pressure was now on operations manager Jim Quello—who would later go on to become FCC Commissioner—to find a winning replacement. "I suggested J.P.," says Quello, "because he had a good voice and he was a Detroiter."

So J.P. ascended from his announcer's position to become WJR's new host of "The Morning Music Hall." It was not a decision made without controversy. Station General Manager Worth Kramer and Vice President of Sales Elmer Wayne approached Quello after hearing McCarthy and said, "Jesus, is that the best you can do?"

"I called J.P. in to my office," recalls Quello, "and I said 'Joe, there are two things on trial here. Your talent, and my judgment!'

"They really put the two of us on the spot, so what we did was promote J.P. not only in the newspaper, but all over the station," Quello explains. "We had Mrs. Page give J.P.'s favorite recipe on her show, and the sports people gave J.P.'s sports predictions, and the other shows played J.P.'s favorite records. J.P. had the voice and talent to make it, but the promotional campaign helped, and he instantly became the #1 rated show in Detroit," says Quello, who says McCarthy called him years later to reminisce. "J.P. asked me if I remembered when I hired him for $14,000," laughs Quello, "then he told me he was making a million. I told him, 'You've earned it and you deserve it!'"

Fourteen thousand dollars was awful low pay, says Quello, who explains that station management convinced talent to work for low salaries by telling them they were lucky to be on a 50,000-watt, clear channel signal. "We had that theory down almost to a fault," says Quello. "We didn't pay a helluva lot."

♣

Although J.P. enjoyed his rookie command of "The Morning Music Hall" and his hometown success, money would, for the only time in his career, eventually become a divisive issue that would separate J.P. from WJR.

"He wanted to get permission to do Stroh's Beer commercials," explains Quello. "For about three hours of work he would have received about $10,000, which was a lot of money in 1962. I couldn't get him permission. The board was against it, the company president was against it, so I had to say 'Sorry, Joe. We want you to devote all your time to WJR.'

"He said 'This riles me. Why can't I do it?'"

"I personally felt 'Why not let him do it?' He can make money on the side, and it doesn't interfere with his performance on WJR. I think the board's feeling was that he shouldn't identify himself with one client to that extent," guesses Quello, who figured a happy and well paid McCarthy was likely to be a good performer.

An annoyed McCarthy left WJR, bound for KGO Radio in San Francisco, and took the Stroh's freelance business with him. WJR management replaced him with a man named Dale Barger, but they quickly changed his name to "McCaron" in an attempt to hang onto the McCarthy audience.

In San Francisco, J.P. and his growing family lived in a house on stilts, and McCarthy took the morning show from #6 to #3 in the ratings, but it would never be #1 because San Francisco already had their morning favorite in Dick Whiddinghill, whom McCarthy knew would always hold the spot.

Young John McCarthy, then nine years old, remembers seeing billboards with his father's picture and the pictures of KGO's comedy team, and his sister Susan recalls the sweeping vista of the Golden Gate Bridge, and swimming in the ocean with dad.

♣

Meanwhile, back in Detroit, WJR AM 760 was sold to Capital Cities Inc. in 1964, advertisers were still complaining about the loss of McCarthy, and the new ownership questioned Quello about strategies for the station. New president Dan Burke, who would go on to become Chairman of ABC, asked Quello why he thought so highly of J.P. McCarthy.

"I think he's the best we've ever had," answered Quello.

"Why did he leave?" Burke inquired.

"He left because of a rule I couldn't understand and could never get overturned," Quello explained. "They said he couldn't do commercials."

"How do you feel about it?" Burke asked.

"I think we ought to get him and let him do any commercial he wants."

"Can you get him back?"

"I'm quite sure I can," Quello responded.

With that, Quello was off to San Francisco, where he took McCarthy to lunch and described the new, enlightened management. He told J.P. that he could come back home where he belongs and be #1 again hosting both the morning and afternoon drive shows.

"He plied me with drink and promises," McCarthy would later say.

"Capital Cities was more forward-thinking on compensation overall," says Quello. "They paid the talent very well, and J.P. came back for more money than he was originally making at WJR, plus he was allowed to make his commercials!"

McCarthy would do lucrative commercial work for the rest of his career for major national clients. J.P.'s voice would be heard all over the country advertising for products like the Ford Mustang, Dodge, and Kelly Services. At the height of his popularity, he could earn up to $1,000 for simply recording a 60-second piece of copy right from Studio D just after his show, or sometimes during newsbreaks. He rarely did more than one take, and sometimes even refused to do a second take—"just 'cuz," "nah, I don't think so," or "maybe tomorrow."

On December 7, 1964, McCarthy came back to Detroit with a big "welcome home" reception and, alas, another critical sales manager, who complained to Quello that J.P. talked too much, and should just play the records and commercials. This time Quello put the meddling sales manager in his place. "People don't listen because he plays the same records everyone else does," Quello told him. "They listen to him because he has some information and a great way of presenting it!"

Burke was, in fact, worried about McCarthy after his splashy homecoming. "He was a little off stride the first couple of weeks, and I was concerned," says Burke. "He seemed a little nervous to be back and not as relaxed until he finally calmed down. He was very excited to be back, and he became very powerful and influential," Burke says.

J.P. McCarthy

"Here's a man who stole Marc Avery's show, Marty McNealy's voice, and Lou Gordon's hairpiece, and out of it fashioned the finest radio talent any of us have known."
— Dave Diles, "J.P. McCarthy Charity Roast,"
June 13, 1994

While McCarthy never again had to slug out a compensation dispute, he did have to negotiate and sign employment contracts with WJR over the years. CPA Tony Frabotta remembers one occasion:

"In the early '80s his contract was up, and he wasn't sure whether or not he needed assistance in negotiating his new contract. We met at the bar at the Fox and Hounds in Bloomfield Hills.

"I said 'Joe, what do you want this year? Let's sit here and talk about it so we can outline it on a piece of paper.' We got a bar napkin and I asked him how much he wanted to make and what was important to him. The most important thing to him was time off. He wanted more time off.

"I asked, 'How many weeks do you want off?' and he rattled off a number of weeks.

"I asked, 'How much money do you want to make?' and we wrote that down.

"We then wrote down some retirement issues, and he told me he wanted to phase out of hosting the "Focus" show. He felt that he had interviewed everybody and that the show was getting stale. So we wrote these things down on a bar napkin and I suggested he take the napkin and approach the people at Capital Cities/ABC and just explain to them what he wanted.

"The next day he called me and said, 'Guess what? They gave me all of it!'

"I said, 'That's great!'

"He said, 'I think so, but maybe we didn't ask for enough!'

"He was joking, but he was very pleased because he got everything he asked for. I knew he was their top commodity, and he could ask for anything he wanted, but I was still amazed," says Frabotta.

"I remember him telling my mother, 'This is what they're offering me! Can you believe it! I'm not worth that,'" says J.P.'s son Jamie. "He was so humble that he always thought he was overpaid. In truth, he could easily have asked for a lot more, but he was always shy about the money thing," says Jamie.

♣

Another McCarthy confidant, attorney John Schaefer, discussed McCarthy's compensation situation with him in March of 1993:

"We were on a flight to Florida," recalls Schaefer, "and I said to him 'Okay, look at this:

"'Hypothetically, you play fourteen commercials an hour, right? At $600 dollars per commercial, that's $8400 dollars. You are on the air for four hours, so that's $33,600, times five days is $168,000 per week, times fifty weeks makes $8,400,000 dollars per year. That doesn't even include "Focus," and the rest of the station shows are driven by you because advertisers buy commercials on other shows to reduce the unit costs.'

"So I told him, 'Conservatively, you are one-half of WJR's twenty-one million dollars in sales. So therefore, Stupid, your value is somewhere between two and a half and three and a half million dollars a year!' I asked him, 'Why don't you turn me loose on them to get you a better deal?'

"He said, 'Boy that's . . . gee, let me think about that.'

"About two days later we were walking on the beach and he said, 'They've been so good to me, and I think there's probably more to this than money. Dan Burke is thinking of making me a Vice President of Capital Cities, and that will dramatically impact my pension plan. I know you would handle it diplomatically, but there's been a rule at the station for so long that if you bring in a lawyer they'll cut your throat.'

"That was it. End of story," remarks Schaefer.

♣

"One time his salary came out in the newspaper," recalls Jamie McCarthy, "and he was so embarrassed."

Humble as he was, J.P. McCarthy made a lot of money and became a standard by which all radio performers would be measured, not only for his performance, but for his understanding of the medium and the way he made it his own. The secret of his performance was his sheer *lack* of performance. It was information, opinion, humor, analysis, warmth, and concern—not *presented* but rather *communicated.* Any hint of performance was always done in a campy, whimsical fashion that poked fun at the "show biz" nature of broadcasting.

How a man could be so breathtakingly good at communicating is a mystery, but we can be reasonably sure that it cannot be taught, learned, or imitated. The ability to be completely real, sincere, informed, and likable while operating the hectic high-wire act of a major market radio "diary" of an entire region can only be called "the magic"—the ability to sound so interested yet casually unconcerned, respectful to his guests, yet somehow superior at the same time.

It always came back to J.P. Listeners heard newsmakers break stories on his show, but their interest was in what J.P. would say about it or how he would handle it.

Did he know his audience? He knew what he was interested in, and if he was interested in a subject, listeners were too. If J.P. was confused by an issue, listeners pulled up a chair and we all learned together, because J.P. wouldn't let us down. He'd get to the bottom of it.

J.P. protected his listeners from the formulaic clutter and hyperbole that screamed at listeners of other shows. He even resisted contests and giving prizes away to his listeners. After all, was it really that exciting to get a couple of free concert tickets or a piece of jewelry? Sure, it was exciting to the winner, but he was dealing with a vast number of people who didn't listen to him to hear "Gerri from Warren" collect a free dinner in the suburbs or a junket to Florida. Besides, such a high percentage of those listeners would never call a radio show anyway, and most young moms or corporate executives were too busy to be bothered with speed dialing to get through six lines of contestants.

This was indeed a performer who believed in the soft sell, often editing boastful or sensational promotional copy to make it more dignified and less braggadocious.

After all, as J.P. might have said, "It isn't the end of the world, man. It's a radio show."

"He was an interesting guy, so his show was interesting," says longtime McCarthy friend and listener Hoot McInerney. "I don't think Bill Blass or Armani go out and ask women what kind of dress they want when they know how to create it themselves. That, you're born with. You can't teach it," McInerney explains.

♣

Meanwhile, J.P.'s underground "singing career" plowed ahead. The crooning began early in his life. "He studied music, he was an altar boy, and he sang," Martha McCarthy reminds us. "He had a good voice and words came easy," she says.

In McCarthy's early days at WJR, a live orchestra supplied music daily at WJR. He was once the guest singer with Jimmy Clark's band on "The Jack Harris Show," knocking out "How Time Slips Away" and "Who Takes Care of the Caretaker's Daughter?" It was easy to hear how much he enjoyed singing.

In 1968, he recorded "It's a Lot of Fun to Go to a Ballgame," a jazzy pep song for the Detroit Tigers that became an Opening Day standard on WJR. McCarthy would introduce it by kidding that it sold four copies, and he had three of them.

Oh it's a lot of fun to go to a ballgame when the fighting
  Tigers play
No clouds in the sky, the sun is up high and it looks like a
  beautiful day
I like to hear the crowd stand up and cheer when a Tiger hits
  that ball
Here they come with another home run, well it just went over
  the wall
I get a thrill when we beat those damned Yankees, I'm the
  first to shout "'hooray!'
'Cause it's a lot of fun to go to a ballgame when the fighting
  Tigers play!

While J.P. never sang the national anthem at a Tiger game, the Tigers did invite him to sing "Take Me Out to the Ballgame" from atop the dugout during a seventh inning stretch. Mike Ilitch had just bought the team and was looking to add some extra pep to the stadium and game presentation.

J.P. stuck his head in my office before he got ready to leave for the afternoon game at Tiger Stadium. "You want to go to the baseball game with me?" he asked, then followed it up with, "Ah, probably not," to offer me a quick out. I knew he was singing, and there was just a touch of performance anxiety.

"Of course I'll go. It'll be fun," I answered.

J.P.'s close friend Tim Johnson, who sang with J.P. at University of Detroit college parties, went along. "Tim won the 'Arthur Godfrey Talent Search,'" explains automotive plastics mogul Tom King. "Tim was small, so he used to stand behind Joe and whisper the words to Joe!" We went into the stadium after a quick lunch at Nemo's. Another pal, Tony Frabotta, met us in the on-deck circle seats. As the seventh inning approached, J.P. was visibly nervous, bouncing his knee through innings he was never usually still at the park for.

With two outs to go in the top of the seventh, we received our instructions from McCarthy: "When I get off that dugout and back to these seats, we leave with no delay. I won't even sit back down, so be ready!"

The inning ended, and McCarthy climbed on top of the dugout and warmed up the crowd as he waited for the organ to start playing.

That's when the trouble started.

The organ began to play the opening notes to "Take Me Out to the Ballgame," before he finished talking to the crowd. The little "preamble" notes that lead up to the verse echoed through the stadium, and there was a slight delay in the amplifier system. By the time J.P. realized what was happening and began to sing, the organ had restarted the verse, and the two were completely out of synch. McCarthy, doing his best, crooned along in his own key while the organ fumbled to get back in the flow in another.

The result was less than spectacular, and there was some pain involved as we listened to the ode. When it was mercifully over, McCarthy came back to the seats and we immediately rose and filed out of the park behind home plate, right in front of the WJR radio booth. Tiger announcer Rick Rizzs told the listening audience that "J.P. and his entourage were making a fast get-away." Needless to say, that was J.P.'s version of a Tiger pep song that was never recorded or sold.

Another Tiger radio announcer that understood McCarthy's appreciation for music was Ernie Harwell, who also spent a lot of time as a songwriter. "When I was first starting out I had written a couple of songs and was playing the organ," Harwell explains. "You know how songwriters are. They want people to hear their songs. I invited J.P. over and he sat there while I played some of my songs for him on the organ. It was the ultimate in someone being nice to me, because I hit a few clinkers on the organ and he just sat there and let them go by and wasn't too critical of them," laughs the Hall of Fame announcer. "He played my songs on the radio and would call and give me a little comment or interview me about the songs. That's all any songwriter can ever ask is to get a little exposure, even if it's indecent!"

♣

Larry Santos was another local talent who appreciated McCarthy's support. "I came to Detroit in 1972 and started singing commercials and performing in clubs with a three-piece band making $800 per week," recalls Santos. "I was hot as a cabaret singer in places like the Apartment Lounge, the Hourglass, the Tender Trap, and Duffy's at Union Lake. He happened one night to come and see me perform, and we talked, and I told him I was putting records out, and he said, 'Whenever you put a record out, let me know. I want to hear it.' From that point, whenever I put a record out, he usually gave it a spin or two and was always willing to listen to it," says Santos, who would become one of the most successful "jingle singers" in the commercial business as the voice of Budweiser, GMC Truck, McDonalds, Whirlpool, 7-Up, and others.

It was a special Santos song known as "the Bubble Gum Song"—actually called "I Love You More Than Anything"—that caught McCarthy's fancy. "He played it three times a week," says Santos, "and made the record sell like crazy in Detroit."

13

It shouldn't be a suprise that McCarthy was interested in Santos' tunes and Harwell's at-first novice efforts. Although his favoritism for Frank Sinatra and boozy crooners was obvious, his days as a "disc jockey" served to widen his appreciation, and he knew that there was always room for a new hit.

"Joe knew he had to play The Four Tops or whatever was in vogue," says Whorf.

"He knew I had a suite at the Palace of Auburn Hills," laughs Tom King, "and so one day he called and insisted that we go see the Madonna concert! He was always curious about the hottest thing. He wanted to see what was going on," King explains. "Our seat was 'right on the 50,' so he could even see her beads of sweat. He loved it, and he was then able to talk to his listeners about a popular event because he was right there."

Singer Bobby Short with J.P. McCarthy, "Focus" show, 1985

"Bobby Short, you've been associated with the old songs. Mitch Miller was in town this week and I asked him what he thought of today's music and if he ever watched 'MTV,' and Mitch gave me a ten-minute diatribe on how all of that is basically garbage. He asked 'Where's Gershwin? Where's Porter? Where are Rogers and Hart?' Bobby Short plays it at the Carlyle, that's true. That's your stock and trade. Are there any new talents around of the stature of those people?"

"I don't think it's a matter of stature. I think that the new talent is taking a new direction altogether. I think today's record is next week's garbage. It's over and done so quickly."

"But you know, Bobby, they used to say, twenty-five years ago, the same thing about Elvis Presley. They said the same thing about the Beatles, and that's not true. Those are standards today. Difficult though it may be to believe, it's true!"

♣

J.P. was always proud that he was the very first radio host in the country to debut a new song that would rocket to the top of the charts in 1991. It was an old standard blended with the performance of a young Natalie Cole called "Unforgettable." Nat King Cole's mellow and unmistakable voice was dubbed in to form a virtual duet that was first heard over the air on J.P.'s show. An old song in a new form. McCarthy was also fond of Harry Connick, Jr., who made the old songs new again, and was popular with younger listeners. Connick even visited J.P. on his "Focus" show.

So McCarthy blended hits with his old favorites, and always personally picked the music he played on his show, as Whorf explains: "We weren't allowed to play 'rock and roll,'" says Whorf. "We didn't even play the Beatles, but J.P. would sneak one through, and then management would take him aside and tell him not to do that," laughs Whorf.

A station program director also once decided that Neil Diamond's "Cherry Cherry" was never again to be heard on WJR. The problem was, no one wanted to try to tell McCarthy what he could and could not play on his show, so the program director sternly ordered J.P.'s producer, Hal Youngblood, to break the news to him. "I responded by saying, 'Why don't *you* go in there and tell Joe you don't want it played again,'" recalls Youngblood, "but they insisted that it was *my* job to do so!"

So Youngblood entered Studio D during the show and relayed to McCarthy the management directive that he never play "Cherry Cherry" ever again.

"Have you got it on the turntable?" J.P. queried.

Before Youngblood could answer, "Cherry Cherry" was ringing out of the station hallway speakers and over WJR's 50,000-watt signal.

♣

Youngblood says he and McCarthy fought almost every morning over music selections for the show. "I had a stack of two-hundred 45s waiting for him, and when Joe came in I said to him, 'Let's open the show with the Mamas & the Papas.'

15

" *'Nope.'*

" 'Oh come on, you'll love it!'

" *'No.'*

" 'Okay, what do you want then?'

" *'I don't know. I want something good.'*

"I named off ten titles," Youngblood continues.

" *'No, no, no, nope, no.'*

"I'd say 'C'mon, there are one-hundred and fifty records right in front of you. Pick one out.'

"He then picked up the stack of 45s and began to use them like Frisbees, spreading them all over the studio.

" 'You're going to pick those up,' I said.

" *'Wanna bet?'* "

♣

I can imagine Youngblood's frustration, because I knew McCarthy to sometimes display that same impish crankiness. Once when preparing for an interview with the Four Freshman, I was looking through the music library cards for a selection to play, when J.P. barked, "You'd better bring all the cards to me because whatever you pick it will be wrong!"

Sometimes, McCarthy had special, inexplicable reasons for carefully choosing his musical selections. "He had a song he'd play just for me," Judy McCarthy swoons. "He'd play 'That Face, That Fabulous Face' every day for me as I was driving to work. It was our little secret thing," she whispers. "He'd just say, 'This is my favorite song' so that no one would think he was being drippy," she explains.

In fact, even after she was no longer driving to work each morning, she still listened faithfully to her husband. "I had to pass a test every day," she laughs. "He'd come home and say,

'Okay, did you hear me with so and so? What did you think about that? Okay, who came after that?'

"I'd have to say who it was.

"'What did you think about that?' he'd ask.

"He tested me just to make sure I listened, and if he thought I'd missed some of it, he'd say, 'Did you go back to bed? Did you go to sleep?'

"I'd say, 'No,' but a couple of times I had to fake it," Judy laughs. She appreciated her husband's interest in her feedback. "He really valued my opinion," she says.

J.P. also carefully selected his own theme music over the years, including "Holiday for Flutes" and "Put on a Happy Face," finally settling on a big band version of "Have a Nice Day" that opened his show each morning:

J.P. and a listener, "The J.P. McCarthy Show," December 7, 1984

"Yes madam. You have a question for the 'answer man'?"

"We moved into the area twenty years ago. I don't remember life without J.P. McCarthy in the morning!"

"Me either!"

"I remember the morning you were going to pick a new theme song. You had a few that you were considering. Why did you choose the one you did?"

"I picked the one that I use now, which is called 'Have a Nice Day,' frankly because it's just a great tune. It gets your blood coursing through your body, and it's also five minutes long!"

"Maybe that's it. It gives you time to get your coffee before you sit down."

"I can be driving in on the freeway and hear it start and still make it!"

"I know every morning when you're late, too."

"What? I've never been late, madam! Thank you very much for calling."

♣

"When he was late I'd play the full, elongated opening theme music," says Youngblood. "If the theme music ended, I'd jump on and do a few words in my J.P. impression. At that hour of the morning, not everyone could tell the difference. Then we'd play two commercials, and the newsman would come in and do a little news report, then we would go directly to John McMurray, who had been warned, and he would open his weather report by saying, 'Joe, the weather today . . . .' We'd fake it as long as we could," Youngblood reveals.

"Of course, I'd get a phone call from somebody like Hoot McInerney, saying, 'He's not in yet, eh?'" Youngblood continues. "I'd say, 'Well, he just called and his throat sounds awful.' Hoot would say, 'Oh, of course it does, he's got the flu. The kind of flu you catch from the lip of a scotch bottle. I was with the son of a bitch until 2:30!'"

"He was always in a hurry in the morning," explains Judy McCarthy, "and Dan Burke would go nutso when Joe was late. He really had a temper!" Jim Quello was again charged with finding a remedy to the situation. "They'd be playing records over and over waiting for him, and I'd call and raise hell," Quello recalls. "So at last I called McCarthy into my office and I said, 'Joe, this is embarrassing. You're a grown man and I'm a grown man. Just write out a check for $2,000, and the next time you're late we'll cash it and have you write another one. This way we don't have to get into this immature argument.' After that, I don't think he was late for two years!" Quello laughs.

"$2,000 was a lot of money to Joe and me at the time," says Judy McCarthy. "It was all that we had in our savings," she says, and Judy insists that the next time McCarthy was late, it was with good reason.

"I always got up with Joe at 4:45 a.m.," explains Judy. "He'd always have a glass of fresh squeezed orange juice, and a bowl of cereal, and he'd take a coffee with him. Well, one morning after he'd gone, I was still in the kitchen and he came running back in the kitchen yelling, 'Judy! Judy! Judy, goddammit, come here quick!' He takes me to the front door and on our porch is a horse from the neighbor's farm. It was a really big horse and it was blocking the door and snorting and pawing at Joe!

"Joe liked horses to race and bet on, but not to ride or get close to. I knew horses and had been taking the girls for riding lessons, so he said, 'Get this goddamned horse off the porch so I can get out!' I'm yanking and pulling and this horse was not going to budge. The horse came up the steps on the porch, but it wasn't so sure it wanted to go down those steps," Judy continues.

"So I searched through the refrigerator trying to find a carrot, and Joe knows he's got to get on the road to make it to work on time! I pushed the screen door open just a bit and the horse was nipping. I finally got a carrot, pulled the horse away, and Joe snuck out to the car and took off," she laughs.

♣

J.P.'s morning routine, although hurried, was very deliberate. "When I woke up with him, I never spoke," explains Judy, "because it was too early. I think he liked to talk to get his voice ready for the show. He'd do all of this talking and I'd just go 'Mmm-hmm.'"

McCarthy pal Barry McGuire remembers riding in with J.P. one morning. "He was singing all the way there. Singing and singing to get his voice ready and cleared up," recalls McGuire. "He'd sing anything, but a favorite of his for morning singing was 'See You in September.'"

J.P. with Mary Wilson, on the "Focus" show, October 28, 1996

"I write about the good old days in my book. Growing up in Detroit and being two blocks from here at 'Hitsville' when we were fifteen years old, knocking on the door of 'Hitsville' asking for an audition. Berry Gordy gives us an audition but says, 'Four young girls. What am I going to do with four young girls?' So he gives us the brushoff. He says, 'I like the way you girls sing, but can you come back and see me after you graduate from high school?' That was his way of brushing us off, but we didn't wait until after high school."

"What high school?"

"I went to Northeastern High. Diana went to Cass Tech. She was the brainy one. We'd hitchhike to 'Motown' every day after school. That's how eventually they signed us up."

"But somebody liked you. Somebody said, 'Hey, these girls have talent!' Who was that?"

"I think by going there every day, our persistence paid off. We knew we were good. Diana, Flo, Betty, me, we all met in the projects and we were all in the Bishop Elementary School talent show as individual acts. Afterward, we got together and said 'Everyone's forming a group. Why don't we think about that, and if someone wants to put one together let's remember each other.'

"Three months later someone asked Flo if she wanted to join a group. Someone asked Diana, who lived across the street from me, if she wanted to join a group, and that's how we came together. The two people who asked us were Eddie Kendricks and Paul Williams, who later became the Temptations. They put us together, and we immediately began doing sock hops."

"You went on to become the Supremes, and out of this tight little nucleus, superstars were born, and the 'Motown' legend lives on."

♣

"He really thought he could sing," says football great and McCarthy pal Ron Kramer. "I'd tell him not to quit his day job, but he'd try to sing everywhere," Kramer laughs.

"He was so concerned about his image that he'd only sing songs he'd practiced," insists Tony Frabotta, a McCarthy friend who often heard J.P. sing. "As soon as he got a little loose he'd say, 'I'm not singing. I'm not singing.' Then he'd sing," laughs Frabotta.

McCarthy's standard songs were "Teach Me Tonight," and Matt Denis' "Everything Happens to Me." Every once in awhile after hearing him sing while out the night before, I would suprise him and slip an instrumental version of one of those songs as closing music during the morning show. He'd look up over his glasses and give an appreciative, knowing grin, but never make any reference to it on or off the air.

I make a date for golf
and you can bet your life it rains.
Try to throw a party
and the guy upstairs complains.
I guess I'll go through life
catching colds and missing trains.
Everything happens to me.
I try to sing a song
and the conversation flows.
So I sing a little louder
and the whirring mixer goes.
Then to top it off
Somebody blows his nose.
Everything happens to me.

Dr. Bob Nestor remembers McCarthy singing a duet with Oakland County Executive L. Brooks Patterson at Nestor's wedding. "I was amazed," says Nestor. "He was a very, very good singer!"

"All Irishmen can sing," says Larry Santos in a critique of J.P.'s voice. "He could carry a tune. Had he cultivated it when he was younger, he could have been a cabaret singer. It was an uncultivated voice because he had never really worked on it, and singing is something you've got to practice with a band or work on just like you're swinging a golf club," continues Santos. "It was a natural good quality, a tonal quality. He had a pretty good ear for notes. Based on a rating of ten, he was an eight, and great singers are a twelve. He had a nice Irish voice, and with his personality could have been a Jack Jones type singer," Santos speculates.

J.P. McCarthy

"Sometimes he was very good, and sometimes he was not so good," recalls Ed Oldani, who heard J.P. sing with the piano player at Little Harry's bar in Detroit. "He loved Matt Denis songs," Oldani continues, "and had he devoted his life to singing, he would have been a very popular singer. I think he envisioned himself as a touchable Frank Sinatra."

"Joe loved Frank Sinatra," Hoot McInerney agrees. "One time we went to see Sinatra at Caesar's in Vegas. We had it all set. We went in the back way through the kitchen and met Jilly Rizzo! Joe loved the showbiz of it all," says McInerney.

McCarthy never hid his enjoyment of Sinatra from his audience, often interviewing Frank Sinatra, Jr. On Sinatra's birthday, J.P. would often play only Ol' Blue Eyes selections, like "Summer Wind" and "I Get a Kick Out of You."

Kitty Kelley, author of His Way with J.P. McCarthy on the "Focus" show

Frank Sinatra tried to stop Kitty Kelley from writing his biography. She resisted the legal pressure, won the battle, and now has a bestseller on her hands. Let us examine this Frank Sinatra. The 'Ring a Ding Ding' king. The man called the greatest purveyor of popular songs in American music history. The man about whom Tommy Dorsey once said, 'He's the most fascinating man I've ever met, but don't put your hand in the cage.'

"We're with Kitty Kelley, the author of 'His Way,' the unauthorized biography of Frank Sinatra. Boy, is Frank mad at you! Have you ever talked to him?"

"No. I've tried to talk to him, J.P. Instead of talking to him I've had to talk to eight hundred and fifty-seven other people to do this book. I think that's why it took so long to write."

"You know people who read your book are going to change their minds about Frank Sinatra if they were fans of his. He is, indeed, one of the great singers of American popular music."

"Oh, absolutely, and he's still my favorite."

22

"Yet, can you love the singer and despise the man? I don't know. What about Kitty Kelley? Do you like Frank Sinatra after having spent three years writing about him?"

"I love his singing. I really do love his singing."

"What about Frank Sinatra, the man?"

"No."

"He is reprehensible in his behavior?"

"He is reprehensible in his behavior. There are two schools, you know, J.P. Someone like Sammy Cahn says that he can forgive Frank Sinatra anything when he hears him sing. Someone like Mitch Miller says that he doesn't care how well Sinatra sings, he has no right to treat human beings the way he does."

"Will you go to a Frank Sinatra concert the next time he's in the neighborhood?"

"First chance I get."

♣

"J.P. was a big Sinatra fan," says Oldani, "and Sinatra used words well. I think one of the reasons Sinatra lasts so long and maintains his popularity for so long is his sense of subtlety and the nuance of the English language. J.P. agreed with me, and ironically, this is one of the reasons J.P. was so good," Oldani continues. "He had that trait that Sinatra has: a tremendous grasp of subtlety and the nuance of the English language."

There's no doubt J.P. McCarthy carried an aura of Sinatra-like stardom with him. It wasn't exactly the tuxedo Vegas type style of Frank. It was more the "nice 'n easy" electricity that he brought to a room. It was the way an event was validated by his presence. It was the way he'd do his show in a tilted cap and never take orders, but only accept "suggestions." It was the way he was in complete command of his on-air performance, and the way he rarely talked about "the act." It was the way he could order a scotch, have a beer with the boys, or thoughtfully sample a red wine. It was the way he could be a chauvinist and still charm all the ladies at the same time. He could be tough one minute, and he could be an old softy the next. Mostly, it was the way J.P. and Sinatra held their listeners' attention because there was weight to what they said, and there was a genuine mystery in what they might say next.

J.P.'s style was decidedly his own, and he stuck with it.

♣

If J.P. McCarthy was a "touchable Sinatra," like Oldani says, you can bet, like Frank, J.P. was always at the center of his own "rat pack." This group of close friends always accompanied McCarthy to his famous WJR/Detroit Free Press Christmas Sing each December.

While throngs of bundled and spirited carolers and McCarthy fans would gather in front of the Hart Plaza stage, J.P. and the boys would meet early to warm up their throats with a "spirit" of their own. When the event was at Hart Plaza, they'd gather before at Galligan's bar or Don Vargo's 1940 Chophouse. CPA Tony Frabotta, automotive plastics king Tom King, meteorologist John McMurray, Fat Bob Taylor, lawyer Nino Ciaravino, crooner Tim Johnson, and Larry Santos celebrated the annual event with McCarthy.

"Usually we'd have a drink before the show," recalls Santos, "and J.P. was getting in an up mood about Christmas and he realized what a nice thing this event was for the people."

When McCarthy and the gang hit the stage around 7:30 p.m., Hart Plaza—or later, New Center Park—was filled with fans. I served as floor director, giving J.P. his cues, but more importantly, providing McCarthy and the rat pack with "coffee." I visited each of them with my thermal pot and Styrofoam cups, pouring what would become my famous coffee, which was usually brewed with Dewars scotch or Christian Brothers—minus the coffee! Needless to say, it was a hit!

Song booklets were distributed to the crowd, and McCarthy would simply call out the number of the song he wanted to sing next. The joke was to call for "old number seven" at least three times in the hour, because one year, after a few too many sips of

24

coffee, McCarthy repeatedly called for number seven, "Winter Wonderland," forgetting that they'd already sung it!

J.P. would also ask the crowd to shout out their hometowns and invite Santa Claus to join him on stage. Usually he'd also ask Larry Santos, who was a very successful commercial singer, to tickle the crowd by singing his famous Budweiser jingle. Larry would also sing a solo carol, as would Fat Bob Taylor. It was absolutely a wonderful night to be in the city, and a long-running tradition.

After the singalong ended, McCarthy and his pals would climb into the limousine and head for their own personal after-glow, held in later years at Sam Lochricchio's Arriva Restaurant in Warren, where McCarthy could sing jazzy standards with the piano player. "He loved Arriva because it was the only nightclub left in town," says Tom King.

McCarthy even had plans to perform in Arriva's dinner theatre in 1995. "I think bandleader Johnny Trudell talked to him about putting a band together and doing a show," says Santos, who has also performed at Arriva. "J.P. was going to sing Tony Bennett type songs, and he called me one day and asked me 'Larry, do you think I can do this?'"

Santos says he encouraged McCarthy to do the show and told him he would be well accepted. "I told him it was a lot more work than he thought it was going to be, though," says Santos. "It's going to be rehearsals, knowing the songs, and having it down cold with the orchestra. You're going to do a ton of work and then get out there and perform for an hour and maybe do two or three nights, but go try it," Santos told J.P. "It's a shame he never got to do it, because he would have got such a thrill out of being in front of a big band and performing," Santos laments.

♣

J.P. did find himself recording with Larry Santos on one very special occasion. "He came into my studio with his son Jamie," recalls Santos. "Jamie was an aspiring singer, and he wanted Jamie to sing a few songs. Jamie sang, and then I asked J.P. to get on the microphone and sing one. He resisted, and I convinced him to do it. He finally got down on the mike and sang 'White Christmas,' and it was absolute magic," says Santos.

The recording never resurfaced until after McCarthy's death, when his "rat pack" and WJR audience gathered once more at New Center Park for the annual Christmas singalong. The scene was the same, the location was the same, the "coffee" was the same and the format was the same, except the host, the leader, was not there. The crowd gamely carried on with the singing tradition until it came time for the final song, when the recorded version of McCarthy's "White Christmas" was pumped through the loudspeakers in the park and over the airwaves.

The stunned crowd listened in silent respect, and many were even moved to tears. Some fans lit lighters as McCarthy's voice echoed over the city blocks that he drove through every day on his way to work. By the second verse, they joined in and sang with him, in a most moving reunion of the man and his listeners. With his voice leading the crowd one last time, those of us on the stage were overcome with indescribable emotion.

♣

The singalong was also missing two of McCarthy's "rat pack" friends. Tim Johnson, the mellow-voiced, witty, and charming pal J.P. had known since college, had suffered a stroke the previous spring and was unable to attend, and Robert Taylor had suffered a stroke and passed away in the same summer as McCarthy. Fat Bob Taylor was one of J.P.'s nearest and dearest on-air cronies.

It was 1967 when "the singing plumber" called J.P.'s show to complain about a version of "Vesti La Giubba" McCarthy played on his show. When J.P. challenged Taylor to do better, Fat Bob belted out a stunning version that knocked all of WJR's audio meters into the red! In that moment, Fat Bob Taylor—"the singing plumber"—became a character all his own and a regular contributor to J.P.'s show who would then go on to himself become a radio host on WJR.

After Fat Bob's phone call to McCarthy, his next move was to show up at a charity golf tournament McCarthy was playing in. Each time J.P. set up to hit a shot, he heard a vaguely familiar voice heckling him mercilessly from the gallery. Sure enough, he finally recognized the man in blue jean overalls carrying an oversize plastic wrench and causing a scene. Fat Bob, the singing plumber, was then invited to make his real radio debut, face to face with McCarthy on the "Focus" show:

Fat Bob Taylor with J.P. McCarthy, the "Focus" show, 1967

"From time to time you have mentioned to me on the air—I assumed that you were kidding—that you won the Metropolitan Opera Auditions last year. Are you a fraud, sir? Is that true?"

"No, that's true! I started studying opera three years ago. In the second year I entered the Grinnell Contest, which I did not win, but I was able to go to Cleveland, where we had a nicer judge, and I won the regional in Cleveland. I went on to sing at the old Met before they tore it down."

"What happens when somebody wins the Metropolitan Opera audition? I just assumed you'd work for the Met."

"You become a plumber! There were jobs offered and, unfortunately, they can't meet plumbers' wages."

"Are you serious?"

"I'm dead serious, Joe. They did come up with some money, but I'll regroup in the hope that I'll get better and someday make another stab at it."

♣

Fat Bob Taylor was born in Leamington, Ontario, and moved to the United States in 1941. He spent a year attending Michigan State University, and then joined the United States Air Force, where he began singing. After the service, his nightclub appearances were too far and few between, so Taylor earned his master's plumbing license, and eventually formally studied music under Millard Cates at the University of Michigan.

J.P. McCarthy

In addition to his appearances with J.P., Fat Bob appeared on the nationally televised "Mike Douglas Show."

Fat Bob was indeed an accomplished singer, and went on to sing concerts, weddings, and the National Anthem at twenty-four consecutive Tiger Opening Day baseball games. In fact, he would announce on McCarthy's show that he was available for hire each Valentine's Day to call and sing a love song to listeners' loved ones. For twenty dollars, you could hire Fat Bob Taylor, the singing plumber, to give your wife a suprise phone call. He'd spend his entire Valentine's Day singing "Let Me Call You Sweetheart" over and over and over to delighted women on the telephone.

Fat Bob Taylor was an eccentric and very, very funny fellow who raised llamas on a farm near Ann Arbor. Off the air, he told the saltiest, dirtiest jokes I've ever heard, and if he'd done them on the air he would have been radio's original "shock jock." Instead, he would call J.P. during commercial breaks and make funny comments and ribald observations of how the show was going. Then one day, a lively old woman named "Mrs. Pennyfeather" telephoned J.P. during his show. Before putting her on the air, McCarthy asked then-producer Hal Youngblood, "Who is that?"

"I think it's Fat Bob," groaned Youngblood.

"Let's roll with it," ventured McCarthy. "It sounds funny!"

So there was the birth of another McCarthy regular. The popular "Mrs. Pennyfeather" was really Fat Bob Taylor. Mrs. Pennyfeather had a very droll and biting sense of humor, and when Fat Bob was moved to call the show as Mrs. Pennyfeather, there was never a script, and it was never planned. "He would dance right on the head of being dirty," says Youngblood, "talking about 'Mr. Longhammer' and 'Mrs. Goodmore's Elixir.' 'Old folks just love her elixir! It makes them feel so good,'" Youngblood recounts.

While "Mrs. Pennyfeather" always called from the "Blue Star Home," Fat Bob invented other characters like "Luigi from the car wash," and a composite of Irish pastors. There were many politically incorrect voices he called and performed for J.P. off the air, too. He listened to the show every day, and was a very kind and funny man, who would sing anytime J.P. asked him to, including St. Patrick's Day, when he would show up in a kilt to belt out "Danny Boy."

Fat Bob Taylor went on to do his own radio shows at WAAM in Ann Arbor and at WJR. He had an old style penchant for calling female listeners "dear," and "darling," and political correctness never bothered Fat Bob Taylor. His laid-back style always seemed to have an edginess to it, and his ability to break into song at any moment made him a very unique radio performer. He could also deliver salty innuendo with the best of them, and off the air would always offer the dirtiest jokes ever told.

Fat Bob Taylor also hosted a syndicated cable television show called "Fat Bob's Kitchen," which was produced in Dearborn and seen on Southeast Michigan cable systems. The show was a homespun cooking show featuring noted area chefs, and won the Cable Ace Award on more than one occasion. Even after Taylor's death, the show continued under the name "Now You're Cooking," with chef Vera Ambrose, who was a frequent Fat Bob guest.

Fat Bob and J.P. remained close, and their on-the-air "Abbott and Costello" type rapport was really indicative of their mutual admiration. They also shared a mutual admiration for the composers, writers, and performers of heartfelt classic American song.

♣

Music remained a very important part of "The J.P. McCarthy Show," even in later days when he played only one song per hour. At one point, programmers urged him to take music out altogether, saying that research showed it was an element that didn't attract listeners but didn't chase them away either. Research seemed to show that listeners tolerated the music, waiting to hear J.P. So McCarthy tried doing his show without opening with song for a few months, and slowly but surely he went back to opening his hour with a tune of his choice. The age of a song had little relevance to J.P. He knew that quality standards held up forever, and he appreciated excellence in music past and present.

J.P. McCarthy

Henry Mancini with J.P. McCarthy, the "Focus" show, 1992

"We live in an era where nothing goes away. Nothing is old. Your 'Pink Panther Theme,' which was done twenty-eight years ago, is still around, still fresh, and still played. The 'Pink Panther' movies are still on. Nothing ever goes away, and it's always with us."

"Well, that happens when you put a visual with the sound, and if you do it right, which isn't easy to do, and you get an image up there with the sound of the music, then you've kind of got it etched up there for a very, very long time."

"Forever. You've been doing that most of your career—that is, putting music to visual images. I don't know if 'Peter Gunn' was the first, but it was one of the first and most successful for Henry Mancini."

"That was the one that took me out of my little room where I write music all the time. It was a big '58—1958, the season of '58—on TV."

"An enormously popular TV show, a very hard-driving, jazzy theme that established you but didn't corner you in terms of style because you've done many, many different kinds of things after 'Peter Gunn.'"

"It's funny. That was the one that was the most successful, but I think the one that set up this romantic image that I have, you know, the sophisticated kind of guy, was 'Breakfast at Tiffany's.' That was the one with 'Moon River.' Then came 'Charade' and these romantic comedies. Kind of romance and sophistication."

"Romantic, sassy music, though. You could fall in love to it, but you could smile to it, right?"

"I guess that's the best way to go, given a choice!"

♣

Radio listeners and friends all knew that J.P. loved the movies.

"Eddie the Actor" Oldani, as he was referred to by McCarthy, can remember sitting at the bar with J.P., passing the afternoon by acting out lines from great Hollywood movie scenes. "*Casablanca* was a favorite of his and mine," says Oldani. "J.P. loved doing the Bogart lines. We'd be in various places, doing lines, and people would gather around and seemed to enjoy it!"

Hoot McInerney remembers a time McCarthy really got into the Bogart role. "Joe loved Bogart," says McInerney, "and he went to a party dressed as Rick from *Casablanca*. He had the white coat on and everything, but Ron Kramer still picked him up and threw him into the pool!"

Oldani says McCarthy gave him the pet name "Eddie the Actor" when Oldani ran into J.P. and actor Cliff Robertson in the elevator at the Fisher Building. "Robertson just happened to have seen a play I did in Santa Monica three weeks earlier," laughs Oldani, but I'm not sure he remembered my last name. So when J.P. tried to introduce us, Robertson said, 'I know Eddie. Eddie the actor. Eddie!' McCarthy couldn't believe it, so from then on my nickname was 'Eddie the Actor.'"

Oldani became a regular guest on J.P.'s show, talking about movies, television, and stage plays. Whenever Oldani had a part in a film, as he did in the infamous *Detroit 9000*, McCarthy would have Oldani, a hometown actor, on his show. "In *Detroit 9000*, I was involved in a long chase scene," explains Oldani, "and I was the last bad guy in the movie to get killed. During the shooting, they had me running for days. I was running down railroad tracks and over expressway viaducts and every day I'd show up on the set and say to the director 'Are you going to kill me today, for God's sake?'"

Oldani remembers a bit of an acting turnabout he and McCarthy encountered one day. "I had been at WJR guesting on the 'Focus' show, and J.P. and I had a drink or two after the show in the Fisher building before we decided to head downtown for a few," Oldani recounts.

"We went to the Lindell AC and a few other places before we ended up at an establishment in the Warehouse District, where many of the people were dressed up to celebrate the Mardi

Gras. We ordered a drink, and a waitress slides up to J.P. and starts talking to him. She was somewhat attractive and brought us another drink and we were carrying on and talking about sports when suddenly J.P.'s eyes go wide and he says to the waitress, 'Excuse me, but what is your name?'

"The waitress says, 'Skippy,' and walks away.

"Then J.P. whispers to me, 'Don't look around. These are all guys dressed like women! Let's get the hell out of here!'"

♣

Oldani and McCarthy could spend hours "talking movies" when they got together for afternoon sojourns after the "Focus" show, and on one occasion, they allegedly spent the afternoon toasting great films in a bar in the basement of the Fisher Building with producer Hal Youngblood, who was himself a student of the arts, and a producer of stage plays. There were many great films to toast, and as the afternoon went on, Youngblood decided he needed to go up to his WJR office for just a minute to make a quick phone call.

Over half an hour passed, and Youngblood had not yet returned, so J.P. and Eddie decided to go up to the office and see what had happened. They called the elevator, and the doors opened to reveal Youngblood asleep on the floor of the elevator! They sent the elevator up to the 28th floor and waited for it to come back down, only to see the doors open and find the exhausted Youngblood still sleeping in the lift. Now barely able to contain their laughter, they got in the elevator with Hal and rode up and down pretending not to know him, and observing the varied expressions of elevator riders who got on and off at their floors!

♣

"Joe didn't miss many movies," says friend Tom King, "and in fact, he had a special room in his home where he installed a big TV with great speakers and a video disk player. He took me in there to show it to me, and put in *Top Gun*. He turned it way up and was like a little kid with planes flying and shots blasting and he was sitting right on the front of his leather chair shouting 'Wow!'"

Susan Stark, the acclaimed *Detroit News* film critic, became a regular guest on J.P.'s show, as well as a personal friend. "I was a New Yorker, hired originally by the *Free Press,* and I wasn't two weeks old in this town in 1968 when J.P. called me to come up and be a guest on his "Focus" show," Stark recalls. "As we talked, I realized that I was dealing with a major person. A human being who was of major intelligence and someone I could have a lot of fun with and someone that I could have very, very intellectually substantial conversations with," Stark remembers fondly.

Apparently, McCarthy felt the same way, telling Stark, "I just love to discuss movies, I love movies, and I love to talk about movies and look in your eyes, and when I see that love that you have for movies, I know I'm with the right person. I want the best. You're the best, and I want you on my show every week and we're going to pay you."

Susan did a telephone interview and movie review with J.P. every Friday on his show. "I did this for fifteen years in my nightgown from my kitchen," Stark laughs.

When told of J.P.'s afternoon "acting skits" with Ed Oldani, Stark says "I don't think J.P. would have been a good actor. His honesty, what he really felt or thought, even when he took the 'devil's advocate' side, always showed through. He never struck a pose for any reason," she insists. When pressed, Stark admits, "He did the best Dracula imitation I've ever heard."

♣

While Stark and McCarthy developed a very friendly banter and warm rapport, she says it was an unspoken "good cop/bad cop" routine on the air. "He wanted me to do what I do," she explains, "which is to do, I suppose, 'high middle end criticism,' which is to say I like movies with substance, ideas, a little challenging, and a little odd."

Stark would recommend certain films, and McCarthy would exclaim, "Ah, another of your 'artsy-smartsy' movies, Susan!"

"Take a chance, J.P.! Take a chance," she would implore.

"It was always a little game we would play on the air, but he knew his audience very well," Stark says, "and he knew what made his audience comfortable. He had to bring me down many times. Bring me to 'middle of the road' thinking, and still give me absolute freedom to speak my opinion."

While McCarthy may have initially squawked at seeing controversial films or films with subtitles, Stark says she'd chip away at his resistance by telling him to "see it for Judy," and in many cases he'd take her advice, see the movie, and end up thanking her for the recommendation.

Judy McCarthy, who held hands with her husband through many afternoon movies, agrees. "Joe had a great relationship with Susan Stark, whom he really liked a lot and respected," says Judy. "He'd come home after having had her on his show and say, "Okay, Susan says this movie is real good so we have to see this movie!'"

"I convinced him to go see *Kiss of the Spider Woman,* and he initially resisted," says Stark.

"Neither one of us was really sure that we got what that movie was all about," laughs Judy McCarthy, who remembers seeing the film.

"J.P. talked about it for weeks after," Stark insists. "He wouldn't admit it on the radio, but I think he secretly liked it and found it intriguing."

Many times, Stark would get calls from the McCarthys on weekend nights as they searched for advice on movie selections. "Joe would always pick the movies," says Judy. "I'd say 'It's my turn to pick,' and he'd say, 'Nah, we'll go to your movie next week.'"

Judy and J.P. would have movie marathon weeks in which they would go to the cinema every single afternoon. And their favorite all-time movie? "We liked to watch *Singing in the Rain* every year," Judy smiles. "We both loved it, and Joe imagined himself a Gene Kelley type dancer. He'd say, 'I bet I look a lot like that when I'm dancing!' It was a joke between us because we both knew dancing was not one of his longer suits."

♣

Sometimes, great movies were made of real life characters . . . characters that sometimes appeared on J.P.'s show, as in the case of Ensign George Gaye, whose story was recreated in the film *Midway*:

Ensign George Gaye with J.P. McCarthy, June 4, 1985

"We thought it would be significant to talk to you today. Fill us in. What exactly was going on in your life forty-three years ago today?"

"Oh boy. Well, it was a lot wetter than it is where I am right now. I was right in the middle of the Japanese Navy in about six thousand feet of water."

"How did that come about, George?"

"I was attached to a torpedo unit off the carrier *Hornet*, and we were trying to prevent the Japanese from taking the island of Midway just six months after Pearl Harbor. The United States was in dire circumstances. We were so outnumbered."

"Now you were in your torpedo plane and were shot down. By whom?"

"By the Japanese zero combat unit over the Japanese fleet. When we finally found them, they had three aircraft carriers in that group who had launched an attack on the island of Midway. That was one of the hardest things we had to do was to sit back and let them hit Midway and kill Americans because there wasn't anything we could do about it the way they had us outnumbered. We were trying to hit them when their force had come back to their carriers out of gas and ammunition, and if we could hit them right at that moment, that was our only fighting chance and it just turned out the timing was perfect.

"Okay, you get shot down, crash land your plane and ditch in the water. You've got your life jacket on and it turned out you had the best seat in the house for the biggest battle of the war in the Pacific."

"Winston Churchill called it a 'fish-eye view,' and this turns out to be the most decisive naval battle in history and I just turned out to be sitting right on the target. My twenty-nine friends, the rest of the squadron, were annihilated. Everybody was killed except me."

"Were you the only one left from the 'Hornet' squadron?"

"That's affirmative."

"Were you floating in the Pacific, as the movie depicted, for two days?"

"Actually it turned out to be thirty hours. It was enough to lose thirty pounds. I was right in the middle of those three carriers when our dive bombers found them and started bombing them, and that's not a very comfortable place to be when all those bombs started going off. Then when they began to blow up and burn, lose headway, and die in the water, those carriers were sitting around me all afternoon and night. I saw them sink during the night The closest one to me, that was burning so fiercely, went down just before daylight the next morning."

Chuck Yeager with J.P. McCarthy, October 14, 1992

"It was forty-five years ago today, on October 14, 1947, that United States Air Force Captain Charles E. 'Chuck' Yeager became the first person to fly faster than the speed of sound, something they said could never be done. The guy about which 'The Right Stuff' was written. Happy anniversary, General!"

"Thank you very much, J.P.! It's nice to talk to you again, man. We've had a lot of fun on the radio, haven't we?"

"What do you remember about that day? We've all seen it depicted in 'The Right Stuff.'"

"We had a great feeling of accomplishment."

"You didn't see any mystique about going through the sound barrier, did you? Or did you?"

"We really had no idea that we were going to break the sound barrier that day. In fact, we had no idea that we could. Duty entered into it. Looking back, I think we were relieved that nothing flew apart. We made the first sonic boom there at Edwards Air Force Base, and a lot of people didn't know what it was. It was quite an explosion."

"I know that you weren't totally satisfied with The Right Stuff, *though you were memorialized forever in it. It was really about you more than the astronauts. What didn't you like about it?"*

"Well, you've got to look at the movie *The Right Stuff* as entertainment. It's not a documentary. You don't recruit guys to fly the X-1 out of Poncho's Bar at ten o'clock one night and have them go fly the airplane the next morning."

"Yeah, but there was a Poncho's Bar."

"Yeah, and we had a good time there, too, but you didn't recruit astronauts out of there. The movie was nice. It was excellent entertainment."

"For those of you who have seen the movie and may not be aware of it, Chuck Yeager did most of the flying scenes in the movie, and actually played a role. He was the bartender at Poncho's!"

"You've got a good memory, J.P.!"

♣

J.P. McCarthy interviewed countless genuine Hollywood types, too: Alfred Hitchcock, Otto Preminger, Charlton Heston, Steve McQueen, Dustin Hoffman, Jane Seymour, Mary Tyler Moore, Candace Bergen, Jessica Tandy, Pat O'Brien, Jerry Lewis, Bob Hope, Joan Rivers, Jane Fonda, Gregory Peck, Fred Astaire, George C. Scott, Elliott Gould, Racquel Welch, Clint Eastwood, Tim Allen, and the list goes on and on.

While McCarthy was making "Oscar bets" with Susan Stark on the outcome of the Academy Awards, he may, in fact, have been daydreaming of Emmy Awards, because despite the fact that he was one of the finest broadcasters in the history of radio, J.P. always wanted to be successful in television. Many of his television attempts were made on WJBK TV 2 in Detroit. There was a weekly talk show called "J.P." from 1983 until 1986. He tried a "Nightline" type TV format called "In Person with J.P. McCarthy" in 1991, and hosted "J.P. and the Lions" in the seventies. J.P. hosted live television specials from the floor of the North American International Auto Shows at Cobo Hall in Detroit, and he anchored the live coverage of Archbishop Adam Maida's elevation to Cardinal by Pope John Paul II.

While these were all fine quality programs, they never came close to equaling the kind of impact McCarthy had on the radio. This surely frustrated him.

"Well, frustrations and disappointments are just a part of life," McCarthy once said. "Probably my biggest disappointment was not getting the 'Good Morning America' show on ABC. When it opened up, I was told that I was a genuine candidate, and went to New York a couple of times and discussed it," he explained.

"I was told that I'd have an opportunity to host it twice live on the air as a live audition. They were doing that for a few guys, and then I never got the opportunity to do that. That was disappointing. It wasn't the end of the world because that would have changed my life considerably, but I'd be lying to you if I said that I didn't want that job. I did, and I was disappointed that I never got the opportunity, at least, to get there and do a couple of them on the air. That would have been fun," McCarthy admitted.

According to the *Detroit Free Press* headline and Bob Talbert's story, the three finalists to replace the outgoing David Hartman as host of "Good Morning America" were J.P. McCarthy, Regis Philbin, and Charles Gibson. All three photos were pictured in the newspaper account.

"The opportunity came up," says Judy McCarthy, "and Dan Burke let Joe know that the opportunity existed and he should try." Once again, the old friend and former WJR manager, who was now president of ABC, was in McCarthy's corner with another opportunity for career advancement. Would the man who brought J.P. McCarthy back home from San Francisco now take him to New York, and therefore to all of America?

"I remembered that when I was in Detroit his primary goal was to get on television," says Burke. "I wanted to do what he wanted because he was awfully good for us and a real pal."

At this point, another name from McCarthy's past resurfaced. Jim Quello, the man who had convinced Burke to bring McCarthy back from San Francisco, had by now made it all the way to FCC Commissioner. "As FCC Commissioner, I had people's attention," says Quello, "so I called ABC Chairman of the Board Tom Murphy and said 'It's none of my business, but he'd be great on TV. I can't tell you how to run your business, and I probably shouldn't be making this call, but I hope you'll give him a chance.'"

"Joe was very excited about it," says Judy, "and they were talking every day."

Free Press columnist Bob Talbert remembers going to Vic Tanny with McCarthy, who was trying to get in shape for television. "We worked out," says Talbert, "lost some weight, and spent time in the Jacuzzi talking."

Close friends and coworkers could sense how seriously J.P. was considering the chance to go national. Some noticed the heightened awareness and extra attention to detail put into his shows.

About that time, Quello received a call from Phil Buth, who oversaw several programs for ABC, including "Good Morning America."

"Jim, I'm considering Joe McCarthy for this job," he told Quello. "He hasn't had any television experience, and his voice is very good for radio."

Quello listened to Buth's questions.

"Does he realize that he has to get up at 4 in the morning here? Right now he's making a lot of money, he's got the whole town there loving him, and he can play golf at Bloomfield Hills Country Club every day at 2 p.m. if he wants to. Why does he want this job?"

"The fellow in charge of the search called," says Judy McCarthy, "and broke the news that Charlie Gibson had been given the job."

"They liked Joe," says Quello, "but I don't think they wanted to lose their number one attraction in Detroit. I think he could have made it."

"Of course he was disappointed," says Judy, "but Joe never let anything last long. 'Okay, I tried, and that's it,' was his attitude."

Judy reveals that J.P. had received television and radio offers in Los Angeles, but turned the offers down because she did not want to move to LA. "It would have been a great job, but I did not want to raise kids in LA," she explains. "WJR made it more lucrative for him to stay, though. I wasn't eager to go to New York either, but since it was important to Joe, I would have done it," Judy says.

♣

Even though J.P. didn't get the seat next to Joan Lunden, he pressed on with his television efforts.

"J.P. and I had a television show for a while," recalls former Governor James Blanchard. "It was our own 'J.P. and the Governor' show on WKBD TV 50. We finally got it down to where it was pretty good, but people were always putting out the notion that J.P. was no good on TV and only good on radio. I watched him, and I thought he was damned good," exclaims Blanchard, who has his own theories about why J.P. didn't make it big on television. "I think radio is a much more intimate medium, and more real and authentic," Blanchard explains. "In television, you're looking at someone through a tube. Immediately, the technology adds a lot of weight to their face and body. They have makeup on. It could be good or bad makeup. There's an incredible amount of artificial lighting, which changes how they look. There are cameras at different angles, which change how they look. Television does not depict real life. People get stiffer and are not normal because they're worried about how they look. It is not a real conversation. Teleprompters are phony. It's not natural. Television makes big people look smaller and small people look bigger," the former Governor insists, concluding that J.P. McCarthy was too real to succeed in television.

"Joe just wasn't an actor," says public relations consultant Anthony Franco, "and even TV news anchorman Bill Bonds will tell you that you have to be an actor."

Another participant in McCarthy's television endeavors, albeit reluctantly, was his close friend John Schaefer. "He would really tick me off when he would get one of these TV things going because he would say, 'I've got to do a pilot for this TV thing. Would you come and be a guest for the pilot? If it's any good, we'll use it!'

"'Yeah,' I'd tell him, 'I'm going to spend my whole evening and you might not even use it. If you get the show, you're not going to have me on. You're going to have Lee Iacocca!'"

"We did a show together once," recalls *Detroit News* columnist Pete Waldmeier. "We were sitting on the set together and the lights were all on and the cameras were ready to go and it was seconds before air time. I whispered to ask Joe if he was nervous.

"He told me sharply, 'I never get nervous for scale!'"

Maybe not nervous, but surely intense, as Holy Trinity pastor Russ Kohler can attest. "On one occasion we gathered to watch one of J.P.'s television debuts that had been taped earlier. It was the only time J.P. was repeatedly insistent that we shut up and let him concentrate on how he was coming across on TV," remembers Kohler. "He met each barb with a higher pitched call for quiet, eventually asking some of us to leave the room!"

♣

"I think Joe loved TV," says Crain Communications Chairman Keith Crain. "He had no idea that he was so powerful in radio that he didn't need TV, but I think he enjoyed trying TV. It just happened to be that the personality of J.P. and radio were so perfectly married that when he stepped out into TV it didn't work as well."

Sportscaster Dave Diles says he and J.P. talked about television often. "I told him that there are people in TV who would burn their money to have your numbers" said Diles—"your numbers in your paycheck and in your rating book!"

Ed Oldani remembers Larry King, who was on a tour promoting his book, guesting on the "Focus" show. "J.P. interviewed him and it was great! J.P. just ate him up and totally seduced him into the interview," Oldani observes. "Larry went to the Recess Club with J.P. after the show, and I just watched. I tell you, Larry King looked to me like he had a case of hero worship. McCarthy was so cool, and you could see Larry just sort of fell into him. He thought it was neat to be with J.P."

Several weeks later, when Larry King finished his book tour and returned to host his nighttime radio show, Oldani tuned in. "Somebody called into the show and asked, 'Larry, you've been on a book tour being interviewed all over the country. Usually you do the interviewing. While you were out there, did you run into anybody any good?'

"'Absolutely the best interviewer that I've been interviewed by any place, any time,' answered King, 'was a great guy in Detroit named J.P. McCarthy.'"

Oldani went with McCarthy to tape a television show with General Chuck Yeager, whom they met with at the Golden Mushroom Restaurant before the taping just around the corner at WXYZ TV. "Chuck always drove," Oldani insists. "When he got into town, we sent a driver to pick him up from the airport, but Yeager would never let anyone drive for him. He had the driver sit in the passenger seat while he drove."

When Oldani, McCarthy, and Yeager piled into the car for the ride to WXYZ, the female driver was pleading with Yeager to let her do her job and drive.

"Yeager was refusing," continues Oldani, "and so J.P. pipes up, 'Ah, c'mon Chuck. Tell you what, she doesn't have to drive. Let me drive.'

"Yeager takes a peek, turns around and says 'The young lady will be behind the wheel before you will, J.P.!'"

McCarthy also loved talking television on his radio show. Similar to his arrangement with Susan Stark, J.P. spoke each week with *Free Press* television writer, author, and television industry analyst Marc Gunther. They discussed everything from the latest sitcoms to the performance of the network TV anchors. Gunther always seemed to have some juicy information, and McCarthy seemed to enjoy hearing the latest television ratings, although he never liked to discuss radio ratings.

J.P. had a warm and friendly on-the-air relationship with Barbara Walters, and loved to tease onetime WJR News director Bill Sheehan for his infamous pairing of Barabara Walters and Harry Reasoner once Sheehan left WJR and reached the network news level.

"One of the most memorable topics of discussion between J.P. and myself was the NBC made-for-TV movie called *Holocaust,* remembers noted psychiatrist and frequent guest Dr. Emmanuel Tanay. "It was a five-part miniseries, and it was a kind of turning point in the whole approach to the Holocaust worldwide," Tanay continues. "Every night this was shown, J.P. would call me on his morning show and we'd talk for fifteen minutes or so about the night before, and we did a whole hour discussion the morning after the conclusion."

Tanay, himself a holocaust survivor who lost both parents to the Nazi terror, says that he received letters from all over the Midwest following the interviews. "That was really a contribution that J.P. made to the subject at the time, and I remember getting very emotional with him," says Tanay.

♣

While an Emmy award does not sit on the shelf behind the bar in J.P.'s den, the National Association of Broadcasters nominated him four times for "Major Market Personality of the Year" and then awarded him the "Marconi Award" in 1994. McCarthy was named "National Radio Personality of the Year" by Billboard Magazine in 1965, 1966, 1970, and 1981.

Then, on an autumn day in 1992, the McCarthy family and friends gathered in a ballroom in downtown Chicago. Sprinkled around the room were some of the elite names in broadcasting, including Paul Harvey and Casey Kasem. "It was his proudest moment," says McCarthy's daughter Kathleen, "I felt like I was with a star. I was thinking, 'God, he's so big. I never realized how big he was. They talk about legends, and he's my father!'"

"This was the cat's meow for him," says McCarthy's oldest son, John. "There were a lot of big names in that place, and that made him feel real good. He was happy about that, and he had a lot of friends there too."

J.P. pal Nino Ciaravino remembers his table of McCarthy friends trying to be sure J.P. got the biggest cheer of the night when called to accept the award. The suspense was building.

"That was the first time I ever saw my dad nervous," says Kevin McCarthy, one of J.P.'s sons. "Because of all of his peers and greats who came to pay homage, he was fidgety. He really accomplished quite a feat in his professional field."

As a waiter refilled the water glass, the tuxedoed McCarthy with the suddenly dry throat rasped, "Thank you." Here in the sprawling, buzzing ballroom, one of his friends seated at the next table recognized his nervousness and implored in a whisper, "C'mon Joe, why don't you have a scotch?"

"I can do a lot of things," McCarthy begged off, "but I can't talk and drink at the same time."

As McCarthy looked around the ballroom over the top of his water glass, he could see many "recognizable" voices, including Chicago's longtime radio star Wally Phillips, who was about to be called to the podium.

The occasion was the Museum of Broadcast History's Radio Hall of Fame induction ceremony, and as Paul Harvey stepped up to the microphone, J.P. McCarthy cleared his throat and winked at his wife Judy, who looked as excited as anyone in the room, which included the McCarthy children. They knew their father was special, but now an entire industry would say so, and generations beyond would learn so. Their father would be enshrined next to the likes of Edward R. Murrow, Arthur Godfrey, The Grand Ol' Opry, and the medium's inventor himself, Guglielmo Marconi. All of the drama and significance was not lost on McCarthy. J.P. was excited, and the family knew that if something excited dad, it was worth getting excited about.

Here was a man who had reached the pinnacle and had a great view from the mountain along the way up. He'd seen it all, and as the crystal voice of Harvey began to command the attention of the room, J.P. McCarthy's attention was racing through the memories of a radio career and life that had surpassed his wildest boyhood dreams.

He'd learned to dream big by consorting with successful dreamers. J.P.'s education came from the 50,000-watt university known as his WJR morning show.

Who else could have learned business strategy from the presidents of Ford, Chrysler, and General Motors? How many people study psychology with Dr. Joyce Brothers, politics with Henry Kissinger, acting with Charlton Heston, and law with F. Lee Bailey?

He got golf lessons from Arnold Palmer, travel tips from George Pierot, talked baseball with Mickey Mantle, sailed with Dennis Connor, and even managed a recipe or two from Julia Child.

He'd traveled to a Moscow Summit, opened a restaurant, flown on Air Force I, sung on stage, hosted television shows, piloted an airplane, owned a racehorse, raced speedboats, been governor for a day, dined with royalty, drunk with characters, and shared it all with his listeners.

These memories surely flooded McCarthy's mind, filled his spirit, and in reality made J.P. McCarthy an icon.

" . . . And now in the category of local or regional personality, here is WGN's Wally Phillips:"

"One score and seven years ago, our fathers, who owned a piece of WJR in Detroit, scoured the country to find a young, brilliant, educated, intelligent, innovative, imaginative, erudite, sophisticated, mature, articulate, devoted, sincere, perspicacious, astute, extremely good-looking talent for their morning drive time. Unfortunately, I was signed with WGN at that time so I wasn't available.

"'So,' they thought, 'let's try a different tack. What if we were to get something so really innovative? The most ignorant, insulting, smarmy, scuzzy, scurrilous, revolting, repulsive, biased, bigoted, angry, tasteless, obnoxious, and obscene broadcaster in America?' But at that time, 'Howard' was only eight years old, and under supervision for a misguided lewd conduct report at a confessional at St. Patrick's Cathedral!

"So they picked J.P. McCarthy, a man who had been turned down twice by the Barbara Walters School of Speech. Nevertheless, he's been waking up Detroit for over twenty-seven years, been rated number one for each of these years, has a knack for getting people to talk to him when they refuse interviews everywhere else. He sends his rejects to Larry King. The only person who ever refused an interview with J.P . . . I don't know where Mr. Hoffa is today, but I'm sure he learned to regret it!

"J.P. is a self-made man, and we'll show you in a minute what unskilled labor can do. The National Association of Broadcasters has nominated J.P. for 'Broadcaster of the Year' four years of the award's existence, and *Billboard* magazine has given J.P. its 'National Radio Personality of the Year' award four times.

"Ladies and gentlemen, the Radio Hall of Fame is proud and I'm proud to be a participant in the opportunity to indict—I mean, induct—Mr. J.P. McCarthy:"

"Thank you, Wally. Gosh, I've missed you, Wally. Those warm and wonderful introductions and moments we used to have. It took me weeks to get over them after we'd talk.

"I do feel like Admiral Stockdale, though. 'Who am I? What am I doing here?' But I love it. Part of the reason I love it is because I grew up around the corner from the old WXYZ studios in Detroit. Remember, Mr. Goldenson, where they used to produce 'The Lone Ranger?' As a boy, I would watch those actors come in and out of the studio. Brace Beemer, the man who played Tonto, John Todd, the great Fred Foy. They always looked like they were having so much fun. I wanted to grow up to be them.

"Well, I missed that, but this is as close as I'm ever going to get, and I am most grateful tonight. It is humbling to be in such august company. Think of it: Leonard Goldenson, for whom I used to work, Paul Harvey, with whom I share my morning time, Casey Kasem, another Detroiter, that great American institution the Grand Ol' Opry . . . I am awed. It is a major, major honor.

"There are lots of people I'd like to thank here. Too many, of course, to mention . . . but I'll try. FCC Commissioner Jim Quello, who took a chance on me a long time ago. Thank you, Commissioner, very much. To the Cap Cities guys and Dan Burke, who brought me to Detroit from San Francisco. I didn't

think it was such a good favor at the time. Thank you, Dan. My good friend and mentor Bill James, and all of my friends, many of whom are here tonight. My wife Judy is here. I've got five of six kids here, and sixty or seventy great Detroiters.

"I have been in radio all of my adult life, which means I have never, ever had a real job, 'cause it's been just wonderful fun and I want to thank all of you for that. From the bottom of my heart, this Detroit boy will cherish this night forever!"

Never a Best Man, But Always a Best Friend

"Good family, close family. Good friends, close friends. Quality time with the people I love. That's what really counts."

— J.P. McCarthy

On the first day of spring in the year 1933, Martha Mary Barber McCarthy, who'd begun feeling labor pains at midnight the evening before, delivered her first baby, Joseph Priestley McCarthy, at 2 p.m. at Doctors Hospital in New York City. "He was like a little lobster, so red and beautiful . . . my first child," beams Martha McCarthy, who would from then on be called "Mother" by the man many would call "J.P."

Martha was born in Nova Scotia, and J.P.'s father, John Priestley McCarthy, was a direct descendant of Joseph Priestley, the discoverer of oxygen. John and Martha took their first

49

son home to their apartment on 57th Street, and eventually moved to Elizabeth, New Jersey, before settling in Detroit in 1943.

Martha gave birth to two more children, but they never lived to meet their big brother. "I had a boy who was born alive but lived only four hours. He was jaundiced," Martha explains. "There are a lot of mysteries attached to having a baby, so they never told me exactly what happened. The little girl I had was pretty much the same way, except she lived overnight. She was a little blue-eyed, blond beauty," Martha sighs, as she explains how six-year-old Joe McCarthy went bravely to help pick out a coffin for his infant sister. "Sad," is all she can say.

J.P. was named for his grandfather, and the tradition continued with his own children, when J.P.'s first son John was named for J.P.'s father, John Priestley McCarthy, and John's first son was named, in turn, for J.P.

"My grandfather was a very intelligent guy who really didn't have a lot of luck in life," says John McCarthy of J.P.'s father. "He never really made a lot of money or was successful, but he was a super guy. Very smart. He used to sit there and do a crossword puzzle in about five minutes, and all of it would be correct!" exclaims John.

J.P.'s father, John Priestley McCarthy, lived a long life, passing on March 8, 1984.

♣

J.P. McCarthy, an only child himself, went on to become the father of six. John, Susan, Diane, and twins Kevin and Kathleen were bouncing products of J.P.'s first marriage to Sally Thompson, and his youngest son Jamie was born during his lifelong, thirty-year marriage to Judy Buttorf.

"The night Jamie was born, Joe had to emcee the 'Red Feather' charity event in Flint," Judy Ann Buttorf McCarthy remembers, "so he called Fred Yaffe, who lived right around the corner from us.

"'Look, Fred, Judy's getting close, and I've got to do this 'Red Feather Drive' in Flint. I'm going to go up, do what I have to do, and come right back, but it's a bad snowy night. Just in case, can you be around if I get detained and Judy needs to go to the hospital?'

"After that, Fred called every five minutes," Judy laughs.

"'Are you okay, Judy? Joe will kill me if I don't get you to the hospital!'

"'I'm fine, don't worry,' I told him, until finally, Joe got home. He was so relieved to be back," says Judy. We got into bed, and one hour later I went into labor. I tapped him on the shoulder and whispered 'I think this is it!'

"Joe jumps out of bed, helps me downstairs, and gets me to the hospital. Even though he's had five kids already, he's so nervous that he's forgotten his wallet, and he has to borrow money from the nurses to call WJR and tell them he's not coming in to work. It was so funny!"

Jamie McCarthy was born at 10 a.m. the next morning, and was named for J.P.'s uncle, who was named James but always called Jamie, and William, which was Judy's father's name. "Joe's uncle Jamie was a handsome, nifty guy who captured an entire town in Germany single-handedly during World War II," says Judy.

♣

Judy Buttorf, born in Detroit, attended Cooley High School and the University of Detroit, and found herself working at General Motors in the personnel department when she was given the task of overseeing the Men's Club and Girls' Clubs.

"Tom Harmon was supposed to come in and emcee the Men's Club night, but he got snowed in in Vermont," explains Judy, who then was sent across the street to ask WJR's J.P. McCarthy if he would fill in in a pinch. "I walked into the offices of WJR and I thought, 'Oh my gosh, this is terrible, because I've never even listened to J.P.,' although two weeks earlier I had modeled in a fashion show for the General Motors Girls' Club and J.P. was the emcee. I walked in, smiled, and told him it was nice to see him again, and we went over the format for emceeing the Men's Club night," Judy recalls.

Three days later, Judy received a call from J.P.

"He asked me if I wanted to have lunch," says Judy, "but I knew that Joe was married and had children, so I was very irate with him. He knew I wasn't married and was just out of college.

"'You know what, Joe? I'm sorry, but I thought you were a nice guy. I'm really offended,' I told him, 'and I can't believe that you'd call me. I don't date married men!'

"'Judy, my divorce is almost final.'

"'Oh sure, I've heard that line before.'

"I was really mad, and I hung up," Judy insists.

"About ten minutes later, Joe's lawyer, Bob Fenton, calls me.

"'Judy, I know that you and Joe have talked. He really thinks you're a nifty person, and I just want to tell you that I'm his lawyer, I'm representing him, and his divorce is going to be final any day. I know this sounds like a crock,' Fenton continued, 'but honest to God it's not.'

"I was still mad," says Judy. "I thought he set the whole thing up. He's got some jerk calling me. He thinks I'm that naive!

"'I'll tell you what,' Fenton said, 'I'm going to give you my telephone number, and then you hang up and call me back and you'll see.'

"I thought, 'Well, hell, he could have anybody answering the phone, but I called Fenton back anyway," Judy explains.

"'Honestly, Judy, it's true,' Fenton said, and then he went into a big speech about how nice Joe was and how he would never do anything like that and he was really a fine man and he'd never be asking anyone out if he were married. So I told Fenton I believed him and we hung up.

"Five minutes later, the phone rings again. I'm at work, trying to do work!

"'Well, Judy, it's Joe. Now will you go to lunch with me?'

"I thought, 'I'm not going to lunch alone with this guy,' so I invited a girlfriend from work to go with me, and the three of us went to lunch," Judy admits. "Joe was so much fun and so cute and I had the nicest time. When I got back to my office, the phone rang:

"'Judy, it's Joe. Will you have dinner with me tonight?'

"'I can't. I have a class. I'm finishing school.'

"'I'll meet you for coffee after school,' Joe offered.

"'I can't. It'll be late and I'll have to get home.'

"'How about dinner tomorrow night?'

"'... Okay!'"

From that moment on, Joe McCarthy and Judy Buttorf saw each other every single day until they were married ten months later, on July 1, 1965. "He called me every single day, two and three times a day," Judy beams, "and he was the most ardent, perfect gentleman and suitor that any girl could ever ask for. So polite, so thoughtful, so sweet to me, and he just treated me perfectly. He was wonderful."

Judy says she didn't "fawn all over" J.P. when she first met him. In fact, she didn't even listen to him on the radio! "I was very casual about the whole thing, and it drove him crazy. He was a real romantic, and always trying to think of fun things to do."

One of their first dates was to the grand opening of Windsor Raceway, a tense experience for both J.P. and Judy, because it was his first date after having been married for nine years. "He was nervous about going out in public with a new person because I don't think a lot of people knew his divorce was final yet," Judy recalls. "We walked in, dressed in formal and black tie, and Joe was so good with names, and he's talking to all these people and shaking hands and getting his picture taken, and at this point I am only beginning to know this 'celebrity' side of Joe, because I had never listened to him on the radio.

"While talking to someone, he turned around to introduce someone to me and he told them, 'I'd like you to meet ...' and he couldn't remember my name! He went totally blank! He was so embarrassed! I was like, 'Thanks a lot!' and I turned around without realizing that there were some stairs right behind me, and I fell down the stairs. Everybody went silent!

"I was so mad at myself I wanted to go home. My face was red as a beet. I was so embarrassed I wanted to die. I thought I was going to pass out, and I thought, 'Why am I doing this to myself?'"

Judy says she picked herself up in her most ladylike fashion, and they ended up having a fine time.

After the night at the Windsor Raceway opening and the hoopla that went with it, Judy began listening to this guy on the radio who called himself "J.P." "I thought I'd better know a little more about this person, and at that time he was hosting the morning show and the afternoon show, so he'd race to his apartment in the Lafayette Towers and take a nap in between shows before picking me up after work to go to dinner or a movie. He treated me like I was a queen," she insists.

Judy remembers being overwhelmed the first time J.P. told her he loved her. "I didn't say anything."

"Aren't you going to say anything?" Joe asked her.

"I have to think about this. It's a little overwhelming."

"He had five children from his first marriage, and I had never been married before," Judy explains, "but what really made me fall in love with Joe was his zest for life. He really loved life more than anybody I've ever known. He was so curious. It didn't make any difference who you were—the plumber, the garbage man, the carpenter—if you did something well, he wanted to know how you did it. He was curious about everything. He was so bright and unbelievably smart, and he had a great sense of humor. I thought he was so funny."

It didn't take long for J.P. to calm Judy's fears.

"We hinted each day and finally one day he took me to dinner at the London Chophouse, got down on his knee very romantically, gave me a ring, and asked me to marry him, and I said 'Yes.'"

While Judy's father was fond of J.P., her mother was a bit more reserved: "My mother liked him, but, typical of all mothers, she thought, 'Oh my God, Judy's going to marry this guy and he's got five kids and she's just a little girl!' As a mother, I would have reacted the same way, but when you're in love, you think you can do anything. Joe had been through a failed marriage once, and he didn't want to go through that again, so he really understood about being married much more than I did, and he really gave a lot in the beginning when I was trying to figure it all out."

Joe and Judy were married in a small ceremony with a reception at Detroit Golf Club. "I teased him that one of the reasons I married him was that it's much easier to say 'McCarthy' than 'Buttorf,'" Judy laughs. When J.P. and Judy returned from their honeymoon, Judy was faced with a seemingly daunting task. "We got to the apartment and all of Joe's children are sitting in a row on the couch. The twins were only two years old and they were all sitting there like perfect little kids. Joe said to them, 'I want you to know that I love you with all my heart. No matter what happens through life, I will always be there for you, but now I'm married to Judy, and she's going to be the boss in our house forever. So if any of us ever want to do anything, we have to ask Judy's permission first.'

"You know he stuck by that through thirty years of marriage," Judy insists. "It would always be, 'Ask Judy . . . It's up to Judy,' and I could hear the kids whispering in the background, 'Judy says . . . whatever Judy says.' Joe knew I'd never been married or raised children, so he put me in a very good position with the children. It set the whole tone for my relationship with them."

♣

J.P.'s relationship with his children is evidenced by the profound impact he had on their psyche. "My dad was quite a mental disciplinarian," says Kevin McCarthy. "He never had to raise his voice because he was so gifted in the art of communication and how to present something in a manner in which you knew you were in trouble. He didn't have to say much to make you feel very small, very quickly."

Kevin recalls an incident that shows a side of McCarthy's brand of parenting: "As kids, a contractor accused us of breaking some windows with rocks. My dad covered for us, but he said, 'I don't know if you did this or not, but don't ever get yourself in a predicament like this again!' I knew underneath he knew we did it, and I very clearly knew his point.

"My father became very impatient waiting in line at a restaurant once," recalls Kathleen McCarthy. "I kidded him, 'Dad, you have to wait in line like everyone else. You are in Florida; no one knows who you are here!' The look I got was deadly. He gave me a 'how dare you' type of look, and he never said a word."

J.P. McCarthy

"He commanded respect," says John McCarthy, "and he was pretty much the same way he is on the radio: very warm and intelligent. He used to say that his father was the smartest man he ever knew. Well, I can say without a heartbeat that he was the smartest man I ever knew."

"Being really young, I always was kind of scared of him because he had a big voice," says J.P.'s youngest son, Jamie, "but the older I got, the more he became my friend."

Jamie describes some mischievous behavior as a young child: "For some reason, they tell me I used to wash things in the toilet. Yeah, I used to put the remote controls in the toilet! I was flushing things down the toilet all the time. My mom would call my dad at work and say, 'He's done it again!' Then she'd call the plumber," says Jamie.

The hijinks apparently made a comeback in later life. "When I came back from college at age 23, my mom wanted to throw both me and my dad out of the house because we were like two young boys in a fraternity house having fun! When I was young, it was all about learning, but when I got older, he let me figure things out on my own. I still hear his voice in my head giving fatherly advice."

♣

John McCarthy remembers a supreme but subtle piece of fatherly advice: "When I was sixteen years old, I had a pretty tough year in high school. I was struggling, and my hair was long and I was sort of a rebel—not sure what to do with my life. My dad offered to take me to Florida with Tim Johnson and some of his other buddies. I went, and we took a boat from Ft. Lauderdale to the island of Bimini. For a couple of days we were over there partying, and I'm only 16 years old. The drinking age was probably 18 at the time. I just had a riot with these guys, just running up and down the street and going to bars. In the meantime, they were helping me along, not talking about anything concrete. Most of these guys were successful, and this was probably my dad's way of showing me how good life can be. I remember this trip as a turning point in my life, because he got me to open my eyes. I knew I couldn't be doing what I was doing at the time for much longer.

"We were there for a couple of days and had a good time diving and eating fresh lobster until it was time to go back to Ft. Lauderdale. To get to Ft. Lauderdale, we had to pass through the 'Bermuda Triangle.' It was a beautiful, crystal clear morning when we started making our way back to Ft. Lauderdale by boat. All of a sudden, it got real nasty. We were out in the ocean, with pounding ten-foot waves coming over the bow. It was getting real bad and I looked around and saw these grown men scared shitless! The owner of the boat didn't know how to use the radio, so we couldn't make a distress call!

"They finally decided that the waves were pounding so bad that we'd better turn back. We had water coming in the back of the boat! We all wondered if we were ever going to make it back because all we could see was the deep, dark, green Atlantic.

"When we finally got back to within five miles of the island, it was like nothing was going on. The sun was shining and the weather was beautiful! The first thing we did when we got on the island was go to a bar. We all sat down and had a shot. We never rode the boat again, and the owner sold it after we all flew back to Ft. Lauderdale.

"On the flight back, I told my dad that I had such a good time and good rapport with the guys. He knew. It was his subtle way of showing me that these guys all made a good living. It was a turning point in my life, because I decided to do something good with my life and work," says John, who went on to climb the automotive retail ladder, eventually owning his own Dodge dealership in Clarkston, Michigan. John's first-born son, in the family tradition, was named for his grandfather, Joseph Priestley McCarthy.

♣

"He would take these special 'kid trips,'" says Kathleen McCarthy, "from the oldest down to the youngest. I think every one of us was able to take a personal trip with dad. John, Susan, Diane, everyone took their trip with him."

57

Kevin McCarthy remembers traveling to Islamorada when he was 14 years old. "We went with Tim Johnson and his son, Tom. We had a great time. My dad let me sip a little beer at the bar, and that was a big deal for a kid like me. We went deep sea fishing and marlin fishing on the four-day trip. When my dad was away from work he relaxed and was a lot of fun!"

"He took Susan and Diane and me up to Boyne to ski with Barry McGuire and his kids," John McCarthy recalls. "We had never been skiing, so he made us take lessons. We didn't want to take the lessons, but we all turned out to be pretty good skiers. When it was time to go home, we'd always try to convince him that it was snowing too bad to drive because we didn't want to go back to school!"

The ski trips didn't go so well for Kevin McCarthy. "I was five years old when I first skied with my dad at Boyne Mountain. My dad and I got off the chairlift together and I skied between his legs, and he would hold me back and control my speed. He let me go, and I fell and the bindings didn't release and I broke my leg. The ski patrol came to get me and I went down in a buggy. I remember how bad he felt because he let me get ahead of him and I fell," Kevin says.

♣

The McCarthy children remember their trips, which eventually turned into a giant gathering at McCarthy's Florida oceanfront home on Jupiter Island. Each year for Christmas, McCarthy would bring his children and their families to Florida for a Christmas week filled with golf, beach volleyball, and the evening cocktail party circuit. "The best gift he gave us was our yearly trip to Florida," Kathleen McCarthy beams. "He paid for the whole family, including grandchildren."

"Before he gave Florida trips as gifts, we'd get up in the morning and each have six boxes to open," laughs Diane McCarthy. "With six kids, the boxes filled the entire room. It was astonishing!"

"Fat Bob Taylor would always play Santa, although I didn't learn that until years later," says Jamie McCarthy, who remembers the Florida trips as exhausting. "Since I was the youngest, my dad made me do all of the household chores while my other brothers laughed at me!"

"We always had a great time on the Florida trip," says Kevin McCarthy. "It was always the highlight of the year. It was rare that all of us could be together and not have any outside influences and really just spend some quality time."

J.P. even tried to pitch in with some of the household duties. "Judy was cooking a roast for dinner and asked my father to slide the lever on the oven over into the 'cook' position at a certain time," Kathleen McCarthy explains. "Judy had everything all prepared, but wanted my dad to do this one little thing so she could get dressed before the guests arrived. When it was time for my dad to throw the lever, he slid the lever into the 'cleaning' position and started to 'clean' the roast! He then tried to push the lever into the 'cook' position and it wouldn't budge. He started to panic and didn't want Judy to know this . . . she'd kill him! My dad started asking all of us how to fix this and starts looking for the manual.

"The doorbell rings, the guests arrive, and the roast is 'cleaning.' I opened the door and said to the guests, 'Hello, thanks for coming. Merry Christmas. Why don't you come in and have some shrimp while the dinner is cleaning?'"

While cooking may have proved a touch too domestic for J.P., the yard and grounds were certainly his domain. "He designed all of our landscaping," says Judy. "He didn't plant flowers or anything like that, but he liked to design the big picture."

"My dad was real happy with his landscaping," Kevin McCarthy recalls. "He planted these palm trees and it was his big thing to have indirect lighting on these as a silhouette to the ocean."

"As soon as I arrived at the house, he'd rush me right over to show off his landscaping," says Diane McCarthy, "especially those palm trees."

"My father loved the beach and the ocean. He always just jumped right in," recalls Kathleen McCarthy. "The rest of us were spoiled by the warm pool, and the ocean could be pretty cold at times, but that didn't matter to him," says Kathleen.

J.P. McCarthy

♣

Jupiter Island, Florida is loaded with celebrities. "Everybody who lives on Jupiter Island has a sign with their name in front of their home," John Schaefer, another Jupiter Island winter resident, explains. "It's just a wooden sign; for instance, mine says 'J.F. Schaefer.' When Joe bought there, I asked him if he was going to get a sign.

" 'I don't think so, John. I don't want people to know where I am.'

" 'Bullshit, Joe. Nobody down here gives a damn who you are. Do you think Bill Ford doesn't have a sign in front of his house?'

" 'I guess he does.'

" 'Yeah, he does, and he lives two hundred yards down the street!'

"He got a sign," Schaefer continues. "It says McCarthy, but it doesn't say J.P."

With all the celebrities and notables in the area, Kathleen McCarthy claims there was never a dull moment on Jupiter Island, whether the family was attending swank cocktail parties or just staying home playing Trivial Pursuit. "He kicked our butts at that game," she says. "He knew every answer!"

It wasn't the only game McCarthy was competitive at. "Believe it or not, he used to love video games like Sega Genesis," Kevin McCarthy laughs. "He'd get right in there with my nephews and and his grandchildren and play golf, hockey, or football. He'd get frustrated because they would kick his ass, but he'd be in there trying to learn."

"He liked games, whether it was backgammon, video games, whatever," says John McCarthy. "I even remember him playing one of those old football games where you set up the little men. One year, I bought him a gift of little cars that you raced around on a track, and he thought that was the greatest thing since sliced bread!"

Of course, the early morning competition was on the golf course. "Oh yes, he'd get up early to play golf, and I'm sure Judy was up, too," says Kathleen. "I know I wasn't awake until I'd hear him click his Gucci shoes so loud on the floor and routinely slam the door. I think sometimes he did this on purpose," she groans.

The competitive highlight of each winter's Florida trip was a volleyball game between the McCarthy family and the neighboring Bosart family. "One day at the country club, the Bosart family folded up a paper airplane out of a napkin and threw it over to our table. It had a message in it challenging us to a volleyball game," Kathleen explains.

"The series went on every Christmas Day for ten years," says Trip Bosart. "His kids vs. my kids. We'd put the volleyball net on the beach and bring a keg of beer and hotdogs. Joe would be the referee."

The McCarthys never lost the match.

"The entire Bosart family is anywhere from 6'2" and up," says Kevin McCarthy, "gargantuan people!"

"We had all these tall people on our side, and my daughter is 6'1" and 'All-State' in high school volleyball," Bosart laments, "and they'd have all these McCarthys on the other side scooting around in the sand like water beetles. We had great games, but we never won!"

Trip Bosart and his wife Sue lived with their children next door to the McCarthys in Bloomfield Hills. "Our homes were separated by trees and heavy bushes, so you couldn't get from one lot to the other," Bosart explains, "so we had a guy come out and cut a path through the woods and called it a 'Friendship Walk' and decorated it with stones and flowers."

The "Friendship Walk," while not exactly akin to the Berlin Wall opening, made for some fun and funny situations. "The McCarthys' dog 'Bing,' a big golden retriever, used to come over and eat our dog," Bosart exclaims. "We went through five dogs because McCarthys' dog would always eat them!

"We were having a cookout, and we had hors d'oeuvres set out, and 'Bing' came over and ate an entire 3-pound brie cheese wheel right off of the table! That dog ate the whole thing! Two weeks later, honest to God, the dog died of a heart attack!"

♣

"My father was fascinated with wildlife and animals," Kathleen McCarthy reveals. "He even brought home a hermit crab and kept it in a tank of some sort. He thought it was kind of humorous and interesting," she remembers. Jamie McCarthy remembers how excited J.P. would get when it came time to feed his piranha tank with live goldfish every afternoon! Kathleen was very young at the time, but she swears J.P.'s most exotic pet was an unlikely one for city dwellers: "When Judy and my father were first married and living in a apartment, he even bought an alligator and kept it in the apartment bathtub. Can you imagine that?"

"We brought 'Madelyn' the Cayman alligator home with us from Florida," Judy McCarthy explains. "Madelyn could fit in your hand when we got her back to the Lafayette Towers, so we kept her in a fish tank. We had to feed her gross things . . . live, gross things, and so we constantly had to clean that tank, because live, gross things smell when they die!"

"It wasn't long until Madelyn outgrew the tank. "That alligator grew while we slept, until finally we had a cage for it in our bedroom. We'd go to bed and I'd hear that thing thrashing around and I'd say, 'Joe, turn on the light and make sure it's still in the cage!'

"By now, Madelyn was as long as your arm, and had become so ferocious that Joe had to wear steel gloves to play with it. He loved playing with this thing!"

One day, Judy McCarthy got a frantic call at work. "It was the maid at the apartment and she was hysterical. The gator had gotten out of the cage. I left work and rushed to the apartment to find the maid up on the counter with the alligator on the kitchen floor hissing at her!

"I got my steel gloves on and couldn't get Madelyn back in the cage, so I got her into the bathtub and called Joe," Judy laughs.

The McCarthy's gave Madelyn to the Detroit Zoo, where she has lived happily for 29 years. Joe and Judy did visit her, and needless to say were amazed at the size she had grown to.

♣

Never a Best Man, But Always a Best Friend

These types of amazing adventures and experiences were commonplace in the family of J.P. McCarthy. Aside from their father's unique personality, did McCarthy's children realize what a significant media star he was while they were growing up?

"I'd get dragged out of bed for school, sit down at the breakfast table for a bowl of cereal, and there was my dad talking to me on the radio, but I didn't realize how big he was until I was out of high school," Jamie McCarthy admits. "I grew up thinking that a radio guy was like a plumber or a carpenter or a car salesman, or a president. It was just a job."

"He'd have radio and TV guys like Bill Bonds and Mort Crim on the porch and I would listen to their conversations, and it was interesting seeing the voices I'd listen to on radio or see on TV all in the same room," recalls Kevin McCarthy.

"People like Paul Carey and Bruce Martyn and Ernie Harwell would visit the house," says Jamie, "but they were never presented as 'stars.' My dad presented them to me as great guys. He never cared that they were the voice of the Tigers or Red Wings." Tiger announcer Paul Carey even serves as Kevin's godfather.

"There were advantages to being his son. You might get certain privileges as far as going to an event or meeting people," says John McCarthy. "When I was younger, it used to bother me to hear people say, 'Oh, there's J.P.'s son.' It bothered me, but the pros always outweighed the cons."

Jamie remembers getting a hard time from his classmates in middle school, and Kevin learned of his father's reach as an adult, too:

"I was fired once by Ross Roy Advertising," says Kevin McCarthy. "I thought I was the only one who knew about it, but my dad had been playing golf with the CEO that day! He already knew!" "You'll notice over the years he never talked about his family on the air," says WJR personality Mike Whorf. "Every once in while he would mention that it was Susan's birthday or Diane's anniversary, but he never mentioned Judy or what he liked to do around the house."

"Joe was very private," Judy admits. "He didn't talk about us a lot, which is good. I was very happy with that because everybody should have their own private life. He was proud of the children and me, but he kept us protected."

"Joe was protective of his family on and off the air," says Tom King.

As his producer, I once asked J.P. why he didn't include more personal references in his show. His answer was very simple: "That's bush," he stated.

"Joe never talked about a lot of the things that many radio hosts drop, saying 'You know who I saw?,' or 'You know who I had dinner with?' Listeners never heard any of that. J.P. was kind of private and probably the kind of man who enjoyed his solitude and his private time," says Mike Whorf. There's no doubt that the lifestyle and career that J.P. enjoyed didn't happen without effort, planning, and complications. The business of being a star is not as easy as it may appear.

♣

"For all his accomplishments, he was a normal person," Kevin McCarthy insists. "When you're looking into a family like that, he's normal just like anyone else's father. For the level he's achieved, it took a lot of sacrifices to get to that level, like time away from his family. I look back at that and think 'I wish I had more time with him.'

"My dad only made it to one of the sporting events I played in," Kevin continues. "I was in junior high. In the only football game he ever attended, I ended up fumbling the ball, and it was a disaster. The one game he came to, and I wanted so hard to impress him. It upset me that we lost the game, but he told me that I played great and made a lot of great plays besides the fumble. The fact that he gave me support meant a lot," says Kevin, who couldn't have been prouder than when his own father really showed his support by giving the commencement address at both Kevin's high school and college graduation.

"If you were his friend, he made you feel like you were part of his family," says McCarthy pal Barry McGuire. "No matter what was on his mind, he always had time for his friends. If a friend had a problem, he took it upon himself as his problem."

Never a Best Man, But Always a Best Friend

♣

McCarthy's friendships and his devotion to his family could not be measured. He was a son, a husband, a father, a grandfather, a friend, a leader, and so many things to so many people. His friendships were countless, from all walks of life, all ages, all economic and ethnic backgrounds. The responsibilities he faced daily were daunting, and the support he offered and received from friends and family was immense.

From the daily radio listener to the charity recipient to the old pal trying to get his boat started, J.P. was there for them all.

Tom King learned something about his old friend while on the *Sea Goddess* Caribbean cruise. "I saw Joe more relaxed than I had ever seen him. We met a couple from Toledo in the bar. They were fans of his and they were getting married on the cruise at St. Barts.

"'Would you mind being our best man? they asked Joe.

"He said, 'Why not?' and we all drove up to this scenic area. The bride and groom were in their tux and gown, and Joe was in his bathing suit.

"During the ceremony, he looked at me and said, 'You know, I have never been a best man.' That was the only time he was ever a best man," King reveals.

♣ Tales from Studio D

"I enjoy coming to work every morning. It's a part of my life. The moment I stop enjoying it, looking forward to it, being surprised by it, I'll probably stop doing it."
—J.P. McCarthy

They actually put him in charge once. It was the early '70s, and J.P. McCarthy was in an official management position: J.P. McCarthy, Program Director, WJR-AM.

"It was generally thought that nothing could be done without his imprimatur anyway," says producer Hal Youngblood, "so WJR management figured 'Let's make him Program Director.'"

Youngblood called it "one of the great bad ideas of all time." "As Program Director, Joe had a rule about meetings: 'Any meeting that lasts more than 15 minutes in length is inappropriate and inefficient in the number of ways it exceeds 15 minutes.'"

"As a boss, he was a riot," says "Kaleidoscope" host Mike Whorf. "There was a restaurant across from the Fisher Building called the 'Steering Wheel,' and he hosted the 'Focus' show from there sometimes. One day, he chose to meet with me there after 'Focus:'

"'I guess I'm supposed to give you a raise and a pep talk,' McCarthy shrugged. 'Mike, I don't care where you write your show or how you write it. I don't care if you do it on the john. Taped, live—it doesn't matter. You can stay home for all I care, as long as you have a new show and your best shot every day. Five out of five is impossible, but if you could do three out of five I would be very happy. Now, there's $2,000 in this raise. Are you happy?'

"I told him I was happy, and really got a kick out of the meeting," laughs Whorf.

The spin as Program Director was short-lived, and far too taxing for a man hosting two shows on the radio station. "He figured out that he could run the station without being the Program Director," Youngblood chuckles.

♣

During McCarthy's long run as WJR morning show host, he was "managed by"—and outlasted—16 different Program Directors. "They always brought various new ideas, and Joe and I would just look at each other and sarcastically say, 'Mmmm, yeah. That'll happen. Sure,'" says Youngblood. "Program Directors want every air personality to say the same thing and the call letters and the logo line every 45 seconds. All programmers believe that a formula is the radio station, and the station is the formula, and the announcers are all replaceable body parts," Youngblood theorizes.

"I think the way you approached Joe was important," says Whorf. "Joe responded well to, 'You know what you could try? . . . You know what might be interesting? . . . Have you ever thought of . . . ?' rather than, 'I want you to get in there and do this, and don't give me any lip about it!' If a Program Director challenged Joe on that basis, they'd hit his hot buttons. Some tried that, but he'd tell them to mind their own business."

Sometimes in order to avoid confrontation with McCarthy, Program Directors would try to work through the Producer, as Hal Youngblood explains: "Management would ask me, 'Why does Joe keep going on so long in the morning?'

" 'Because he's interested in who he's talking to,' I answered.

" 'But not everyone else is,' management responded.

" 'Everyone is interested in what J.P. McCarthy is interested in because he makes them interested in it,'" was Youngblood's answer to the management. To illustrate his point, Hal recalls this example:

♣

"It was April 12, some time in the early '80s. Joe read his 'show starter' to get us going. He told the listeners whose birthday it was and what happened on that day in history. That date was the anniversary of the sinking of the *Titanic*, so Joe read some facts and figures about how long it took the *Titanic* to sink after it brushed the iceberg, the number of total passengers, the number of steerage passengers vs. the numbers of first and second class passengers, etc. While he was doing this, the phone rang.

"A very soft-spoken woman said, 'Would you tell Mr. McCarthy that it's nice to hear that someone does still remember "The Night to Remember"?'

"I said, 'You were on the *Titanic*, weren't you?'

" 'Yes, I was, but I don't want to talk about it.'

" 'You must talk about it,' I implored. 'You have a responsibility to talk about it! You just said that people should remember the day. You owe it to those people and to Joe to talk about it.'

"She said, 'I don't know . . . ' and as she was saying that, I hit the speaker and told Joe that we had a survivor on the line.

" '*We have someone on the line who has a very good reason to remember that night 65 years ago. You were on board that ship?*' McCarthy asked her on the air. She said 'Yes,' and that was at about 6:20 a.m. Joe went straight through until 7:00 and didn't stop the flow of conversation once! I turned to the engineer and said, 'We'll drop all commercials as long as this is going well.' News Director Dave White came running into the room yelling, 'We should be doing the news at this time!'

"'Bullshit,' I said, and then I figured that my ass was really going to be grass because we dumped all of the guaranteed commercials. I didn't care—Joe was rolling, and in the last five minutes of the interview, the survivor even switched from past tense to present tense:

"'I'm watching it now. The stern is completely out of the water . . . Now the lights just went out . . . '

At this point, one of the salespeople came into the room.

"'Go ahead. Do your complaining,' I moaned.

"'No, no! You should have been on the expressway,' he told me. 'People were sitting in their cars, and sometimes there would be ten and twelve car lengths developing because people would be listening so intently, they didn't even realize the line had moved on without them!'

"During the 7:00 a.m. news, I got another phone call," Youngblood continues.

"'When he comes back on the air, the little darlin', I want to talk to him,' she said in an Irish brogue.

"'Don't tell me you were on the *Titanic* too?!'

"'No,' she answered, 'but I might have been, and I can tell him why.'

"Of course, she got on the air and she was a hoot. She and her father were scheduled for 3rd class on the ship.

"'But I don't have to tell you, we stopped at every pub between Dublin and South Hampton on the way to the docks,' she explained. 'When we got there, the British done took the gangway up in steerage. They wouldn't let us board! They told us that maybe we could get on if we tried to go up the first class gangway. We had tickets paid for!' she continued. 'At the first class gangway, they wouldn't let us on.

"'I can still see, as the great ship sailed out of the harbor, my father shaking his fist and calling a curse down on it, and the next day, on his knees thanking the Virgin Mary for saving our very souls!'

"This call went on for 17 minutes," says Youngblood, "and again I dumped all of the commercials. Then Joe talked to five Bulgarian brothers who were scheduled to go on the ship, but one of them had a premonition—a bad dream. They didn't know whether to take the trip or not, so they decided to take a 'wote.' The Bulgarians 'woted' not to get on the *Titanic*. They all would have been on the bottom of the sea," Youngblood insists, and one can still hear the excitement in his voice as he describes this morning of McCarthy magic.

Sometimes—in fact, most times—commercials were a necessity. "Sometimes I'd hold the phone up with a pair of shears to indicate that I was about to terminate an interview if he didn't let me get some commercials in," laughs Youngblood. "That always amused him."

♣

As McCarthy's Producer, I can remember him bemoaning the fact that he'd have to "break in a new PD," every time a new Program Director came on staff. I remember hearing of a classic McCarthy/Program Director confrontation. Firstly, understand that the "Focus" show was not part of J.P.'s contract. McCarthy did the show at will, and was not compensated additionally for it. In the summertime, or whenever he had another commitment, he would duck out and allow a guest host to host the show.

In the case I speak of, ancient comedian George Burns was coming into Studio D for the "Focus" show because a theatre bearing his namesake was opening in the Detroit area. J.P. decided during his "Morning Show" that he'd rather not stick around for "Focus" that day, so he alerted the "Focus" producer—at the time Cliff Coleman—to arrange for a substitute host. Coleman called down to Program Director Phil Boyce's office, and told Boyce the news. Boyce decided to head off McCarthy in Studio D just after his morning show before J.P. could make his fast exit at 10 a.m.

"J.P., have a minute?"

McCarthy, who obviously knew what Boyce had on his mind, impatiently sat back down in his chair and stared at Boyce.

"J.P., we really need you to stay for "Focus." You know that George Burns is the guest, and we think it would be best for you to talk with him, and the people from the theatre will be disappointed if it isn't you," Boyce reportedly pleaded, finally turning stern, "and you know, we really need you to take your "Focus" responsibility more seriously. So I need you to stay today and interview George Burns."

"Are you finished?" McCarthy asked curtly.

"Well, yes."

"Good-bye, then," J.P. said as he rose and headed for the elevator.

♣

"I remember one of the old Program Directors trying to give J.P. a command," says board operator Russ White. "When we asked him if we should follow the directive, McCarthy said 'No, you don't think he runs *this* show, do you? Don't ever make that mistake!'"

"Joe was blessed with terrific judgment and taste," says former WJR General Manager Dan Burke, who went on to become Chairman of Capital Cities/ABC. "He might have overdone the sports a little from some people's viewpoint, but not very much. He was extremely bright and very curious and had a very wide-ranging mind. That's one reason why people reacted to him."

In truth, J.P. was easy to work with, but despite the fact that WJR made him Vice President, he did have a mischievous side. When longtime WJR "Night Flight" host Jay Roberts was faced with the prospect of hosting his last simulated, overnight airline flight-themed show after being fired suddenly, McCarthy advised "Captain" Roberts to crash the "plane" that had for years safely landed listeners in their fictional early morning destinations. Roberts crashed the plane in his final moments of a long WJR career.

McCarthy had an unconventional way of doing his show. He did it his way, guided by an inner sense of what was right for him and his listeners. He did not rely on research, or focus groups, or trends, and therefore, there were many unexplainable quirks that the listeners came to depend on and that made his show unique—features like "What's Bothering You," which invited listeners to call in and complain about everything from a specific car dealer or restaurant to U.S. foreign policy. J.P. would also ask for "Winners and Losers" every day, eventually naming his "Winner of the Day" after hearing his listeners' opinions. Another phone feature was "The Answer Man," in which he would adapt a comical voice and answer questions his listeners had about any subject.

These calls were rarely "screened," because their spontaneous, unpredictable nature and the manner in which J.P. would deal with them made them more entertaining:

"We've got time for one last quick call here. Yes sir, do you have a winner or a loser?"

"Uh, yeah, I have a loser for you."

"Okay, who is it?"

"It's you, bitch!"

"Oh! Heh, heh, thank you very much sir! I needed that this morning!"

What happened when a caller was obviously too incoherent or pushy to put on the air? "I'd put them on hold," says Hal Youngblood. "When the board operator would turn to me and say, 'This gentleman's been on hold for more than one hour!' I'd say, 'Let me show you something. See the number eight, well turn that sideways and it stands for "infinity," and that's how long they're going to stay on hold!' You just had to sweat them out and wear them down," explains Youngblood, who says he would eventually jump back on the line with the caller and say something like, "Geez, I thought we were going to have time for you there, but it just didn't work out. Call us next Thursday, okay? Call us between 7:22 and 7:25, okay? It would just go on forever," Youngblood grins.

♣

J.P. McCarthy

Sometimes even a scheduled guest could go awry, as the late Gene "Santa" Reeves proved:

"Gene has played Santa Claus on a number of occasions, going all the way back to the 1930s and the old J.L. Hudson's Christmas Parade. Fitting and proper that we speak to him as we approach the Christmas season. Merry Christmas, Gene!"

"Uh, . . . 760, I can't get ya."

"Are you there, Gene?"

"Uh,"

"I think maybe Gene fell asleep. Heh, heh. You got me yet, Gene? Are you dialing us in? I wonder what he's doing? Are you okay, Gene? Hey, Gene!"

"Hello?"

"Gene?"

"Yeah."

"Are you okay?"

"Yeah, but I'm trying to get your station. What is it, 760?"

"Where are you?"

"I'm in Westland."

"Well, if you're in Westland and you can't get us . . . you haven't been drinking, have you?"

"Heh, heh, no! Old Santa don't drink when he talks to the kids, you know!"

"Well, I would certainly hope not!"

"Well, hell no!"

"Well, if you can't get us in Westland, you've got a problem!"

"What's on now? Is this Mike?"

"No, this is J.P. McCarthy!"

"Oh J.P.! Hey, how's the Missus?"

"Well, she's fine."

"J.P., how ya doin'?"

"Well, I'm doing better than you are, I think!"

"I can't find ya on the dial, here! Ha ha!"

"Don't even worry about it, Gene."

"Hey, J.P.! My friend, J.P.! Am I glad to hear from you!"

"Congratulations on being named the outstanding Senior Citizen of the Year!"

"Would you say that again real loud again, I'm having a lot of trouble here this morning."

"HOW'S THIS? IS THIS BETTER, GENE?"

" . . . .What?"

"Ha ha ha!"

"You would think this is the day after New Year's! Ha ha ha ha ha!"

"Heh heh, Well Gene, you have a Merry Christmas. It's been 'swell' talking to you!"

Another guest that wasn't "on the other end of J.P.'s line" for long was Domino's Pizza chairman and founder Tom Monaghan. Monaghan was a curious and some would say eccentric public figure at the time J.P. interviewed him in October of 1991. Rumors were swirling that Monaghan—a very religious yet wealthy and sometimes extravagant man—had actually overextended himself and would very soon be forced to sell the Detroit Tigers, one of his prized emotional properties. Some said that J.P. and a group of investors had even poked around at the idea of buying the Tigers from the Ann Arbor–based pizza magnate.

Monaghan, aside from winning a world championship, had done some strange things with the Detroit Tigers. Baseball purists were aghast when, on St. Patrick's Day in spring training, he dressed the team in special green-trimmed uniforms and had every player wearing the number 30 in order to promote Domino's Pizza's thirty-minute delivery policy.

Monaghan was also shying away from media interviews because of the heat and embarrassment he took for a print interview with *Detroit News* religion writer Kate DeSmet in which he related that he had carnal thoughts about Debbie Reynolds, and would not feel comfortable allowing himself to be interviewed alone in his office with the female DeSmet.

Naturally, I had been trying to book an interview for J.P. with Tom Monaghan for some time. In most cases, the request would be smothered in the hands of some corporate media relations assistant who would always find a reason why he was unavailable. One day, I called Tom Monaghan's office directly, in an attempt to bypass the media relations department and go directly to Betsy, his secretary. I dialed Betsy's number, and a man answered the line.

"Is Betsy in?" I asked.

"No, she's at lunch right now," the voice answered.

"I see. Well, this is Michael Shiels calling from the J.P. McCarthy Show at WJR, and I'm trying to reach Betsy to see if she'll ask Mr. Monaghan to do a radio interview with J.P. tomorrow morning," I explained.

"Okay, I'll tell her that you called when she gets back from lunch, okay?"

"Do you think Mr. Monaghan is likely to do that?" I asked.

"I don't know, but I'll give her the message," the voice quickly answered.

Something about the voice was nagging at me, and before we hung up I impulsively questioned:

"Mr. Monaghan, is that you?"

I heard a deep sigh, and then I knew I had caught him.

"You know, I probably only pick up this line two times in one year, and just my luck, it has to be you," he whined.

We laughed, and I asked him if he would grant the interview. He seemed pained, and told me that he just wasn't able to grant interviews and just didn't feel like talking at that time. We hung up, and at that point, I figured that at least I had got a "No" right from the horse's mouth, and gave up the idea of scheduling an interview.

Not long after that incident, a curious press release came across my desk. It was promoting a charity event that Tom Monaghan was throwing to raise funds for his pet project to build a missionary chapel in Managua. It listed a public relations person as a contact at the top and a phone number to call to arrange interviews. I didn't really believe Monaghan would be available, but I called the PR contact and just like that a telephone interview was arranged with Tom Monaghan for the next morning. The PR contact stressed that Mr. Monaghan wanted to talk about the chapel project and its merits. I was vague, but assured the contact that McCarthy would mention the project.

The next morning, I called Monaghan's office from the control room, and Betsy put me through to him. I thanked him for agreeing to do the interview, told him to stand by for J.P., and put him on hold. I then walked into Studio D, informed J.P. that Monaghan was on the line, and handed him the press release and information about the Managuan chapel. J.P. took one glance at it and said, "You don't think I'm going to ask him about this do you? I'm going to talk about the Tigers!" and playfully flung the information up over his head. It flapped in the air, hit the ceiling and floated down into the corner of the studio behind a plant.

I returned to my seat in the control room, where a group of sales executives and station management had assembled, excited to watch J.P. conduct the conversation with Monaghan. The interview began cordially, and as J.P. quickly turned the conversation to the Detroit Tigers, Monaghan went audibly stiff.

"Tom, you once said you'd never sell the Tigers. Can you tell us if you've talked to anyone about selling the team?"

Monaghan declined to answer.

J.P. gently persisted: "But Tom, rumors are circulating that you are in a major cash crunch and the Tigers are on the block. Don't you want to clear up that rumor?"

Monaghan, now getting irritated, declined to answer again.

"Tom, we've got an audio clip here with you joking that 'everything is for sale except Mrs. Monaghan.' Was that statement meant to include the Tigers?"

"Joe, I'm hanging up," Monaghan warned, and as J.P. continued, we heard the phone slam down with a loud "click." Everyone in the room gasped and looked at McCarthy to see what he would do.

Still on the air, J.P., without missing a beat, looked up and grinned, "Gee, he hung up and I didn't even get a chance to ask him about the Managuan Chapel!"

I laughed hard as I looked at the chapel information on the floor behind the plants.

Public Relations executive Tony Franco heard the interview from his car. "I had known Tom—done some work with him—so I called him right away," Franco says. "I told him, 'Tom, that's not a smart thing to do. That's J.P.'s job to ask you questions.'" Franco convinced Monaghan to call McCarthy back.

"I lost my head Joe. I'm sorry. I shouldn't have done that," Monaghan sheepishly said on the air. J.P. then asked him all about the chapel project, in great detail, and when the conversation finally did turn back to the Tigers, Monaghan was much more relaxed and forthcoming, and even promised to keep J.P. abreast of any developments in the Tiger sale situation.

Tom Monaghan wasn't the only sports owner and "pizza baron" to sit across from J.P.'s microphone:

Mike Ilitch with J.P. McCarthy, 1988

"My first guest in 'Focus' today is a native Detroiter, owner of the Red Wings, and Little Caesar's Pizza, Mike Ilitch, who was also once a player in the Detroit Tiger organization. Mike, welcome. You look well and prosperous."

"Thank you, J.P., it's nice to be here."

"Apparently, America can't get enough pizza!"

"That's right. It's a real popular item. I remember when I started, people said, 'Mike, do you think this is a fad?' A couple years later, people said, 'Do you think it's a snack?' It's part of the American household, there's no question about it."

"'Fast food' in America is a way of life these days, and apparently the 'fast food' cycle is not nearing its end either. Pizza fits into that beautifully."

"We noticed a big difference in our business in 1970 when the woman became very dominant in the workforce. With two working and the kitchen shrinking, we started to get very busy."

"1959 was the year you started with a little pizza shop . . . where?"

"Garden City. Cherry Hill and Venoy."

"This is a great American success story. You started with very little money, and one pizza shop. What is the son of a Macedonian immigrant doing making pizza?"

"I came home from baseball one year with a broken leg and my dad told me that was it. He said, 'Mike, you've got to go out and get a job. You're going to become a bum playing baseball.' I went out and looked for a job because he told me he was not going to welcome me back in the home until I got a job. In those days, it wasn't too honorable to get thrown out of the house, so I went and got a job at a pizza place. There were only four or five in Detroit at the time. I worked for free and I learned the business a little bit."

"They were all Italian restaurants. In the '50s we all went to pizza places, and it was sort of new then, but it was good stuff—but who would have ever dreamed! Even Mike Ilitch never dreamed—did he?—that pizza would be that big?"

"No, not really. It was just timing. Kind of fluky and kind of lucky."

"What was your initial investment? Do you remember?"

"I think the initial investment was somewhere around $20,000."

"That's a lot of money for a youngster in 1959. Where'd you get it?"

"I went door to door and sold pots and pans and awnings and things like that, because I couldn't get a job after baseball. I went to school for a year and a half, but we started to have babies, so I had to go out and find some work, and all of a sudden I realized I wasn't qualified for anything. It was a real growing up experience. Anyhow, it turned out, in that business, that I saved about $25,000, believe it or not, and I got my investment back in about 6 to 8 months."

"One store became two stores, and two became four, and four became eight. By 1965, how many stores did Little Caesar's have?"

"We were real conservative in those days. Of course, I was very raw. I had no background, no depth as far as administration, no formal training, so my site selection process was just following the growth of Detroit. As Warren popped up and Livonia popped up, if a shopping center went in there, I put a store in there. We put in about 8 stores a year. In the '70s we became more aggressive."

"How many states is Little Caesar's located in now?"

"Right now, we're in about 42 states, and by the end of the year, we'll be in all the states."

♣

Aside from the big "movers and shakers" that gravitated to J.P.'s show, there was plenty of room for humor and humorous characters. "Miss Wonderful" was a caller who called in occasionally and was very up and lively. "Joe just told her she sounded so 'cutesy-pantsy,'" says Youngblood. "He just pulled that out of thin air. I told him to remember the law . . . nobody's face matches their voice!"

While Fat Bob Taylor would perform the daft characters of "Mrs. Pennyfeather," "Luigi at the car wash," and others, "Grosse Pointe Charles" was a real-life, stereotypical character.

"Charles was a well-to-do Grosse Pointer," Youngblood explains. "Joe knew him well, and he came from a popular family. Joe used to tease him at functions about his 'Grosse Pointe lockjaw,' which Charles actually had a little of, but he exaggerated it on the air:

"How are you this morning, Charles?"

"I'm feeling so spitzy I just can't stand it! 'Hamilton' has just gotten back from doing my three-mile run for me!"

"Hamilton?"

"Yes, Hamilton is my butler. Hamilton is out packing the car now for my trip to Florida."

"You mean you're driving to Florida?"

"Driving? Oh no, Joe, the *railroad* car!"

One of the yearly real-life characters that called was a little girl named "Amy." "Amy's mother called on her birthday when she was a little tyke and put her on the phone with Joe, and it was kind of cute," Youngblood recalls. "Joe wished her a 'happy birthday' and we didn't have another thought about it until she called again one year later, and she did that every year."

In fact, J.P. played "Once in Love with Amy" for her every year that she called. J.P. and his listeners heard "Amy" grow up, from age 3, until she called to tell J.P. that she was getting married.

J.P. had other yearly activities, like getting Mal Sillars or John McMurray to predict when the first snowfall of the winter would occur, and pretending, sound effects and all, to lead listeners in "putting their snow shovels in cosmoline" because it was safe to store them for the summer. McCarthy loved to herald the coming of spring by playing a song called "When the Buzzards Come Back to Hinckley" (Ohio) as a parody of the swallows returning to Capistrano.

On April Fool's Day, J.P. turned the show over to "punchlines only," and invited callers to phone him, one after another, and tell him and his listeners only the punchlines to their favorite jokes! Many of the punchlines were immediately recognizable, and the set-up never could have been told on family radio:

"Rectum? Damn near killed 'im!"
"Shhh, I've got him right where I want him."
"Stand back, I'm not sure how big this thing gets!"

Every once in a while, J.P. would play a comic novelty record like "Gunga Din," or Stan Freeberg's "Green Christmas," or even Hudson & Landry's "Prospectors."

Beginning in the '80s, each year on Thanksgiving, J.P. would anchor WJR's live coverage of the Thanksgiving Day Parade. McCarthy and Paul Carey would sit in a broadcast booth right along the parade route on Woodward Avenue, and describe the floats, tell the listeners who was there, and introduce the bands and acts that passed by the stand. Announcer Paul W. Smith remembers being impressed by seeing the waiting limo behind the booth, ready to spirit J.P. through the crowds to the annual Lions Thanksgiving football game the very second the parade was over. In such a hurry to get to the game, McCarthy would even prerecord the wrap up of the parade broadcast so that he could save five minutes in his effort to make it to the Silverdome in time for the kickoff!

While the idea of a parade on radio may seem odd, McCarthy and Carey did their best to make it entertaining, sometimes struggling to do so, and perhaps producing the funniest blooper in WJR history as a local singing pom-pom squad trouped by:

Carey: "Joe, I had no idea that pom-pom girls could be so delightful orally!"

McCarthy: "Heh, heh, ha! Yes, they certainly are attractive and they sound good too!"

Carey: "Er, yes, yes!"

♣

As yearly events went, McCarthy was very good about recognizing what happened on a given date in history. Perhaps it was his own experience in the service, maybe it was a form of patriotism, or maybe just a curiosity, but J.P. seemed especially interested in the historical significance of military occurrences:

Commander Albert Alvarez Jr., the first American shot down in Vietnam:

"It was an interesting episode because, primarily, we didn't know what to expect, and when I was shot down I was hit by some ground fire, right on the coast. I landed in the water right off the shore, and they captured me almost immediately . . ."

"Yeah."

"They carted me from one local cell to another until I wound up in that old French-built fortress later known as the 'Hanoi Hilton,' and I was the first resident of that."

"How were you treated?"

"Well, initially I was not physically treated badly, but food was somewhat of an experiment with me. They didn't quite know how to deal with me."

"What kind of food? Describe the food for us."

"The food made me very sick. I would find a bird, a cold, black bird floating in grease that I had to tear open and eat the meat."

"Oh, good grief."

"I would find hooves of a hog, or a snout of a hog. I would find something like a big shrimp, a complete shrimp, thrown in there. It was really very greasy food and I was constantly sick, so I lost quite a bit of weight."

"No physical harm, no corporal punishment, no torture?"

"Not for the first year. After the first year, as more Americans joined me, they began to start that kind of treatment, and that treatment lasted quite a few years. At first, they didn't know what to do with us, but that treatment went on until 1970, when the war started to wind down, and the League of Family movement at home led to an increase in the quality of our treatment, until we came home in 1973."

♣

Aside from newsmaking guests, celebrities, authors, politicians, sports figures, and entertainers, McCarthy developed a stable of regular guests that he could call upon to cover almost any issue. Some of his "regulars" were friends of his, and some became friends of his.

Nationally respected forensic psychiatrist Emmanuel Tanay, a Detroiter, probably did more guest turns with J.P. than anyone else. "So much of the news had to do with what goes on inside people's heads," says McCarthy engineer Cliff Coleman. "It made sense!"

"I had written him a critical letter after hearing one of his "Focus" guests speak against gun control," says Tanay, "and the next thing I knew I got invited by J.P. to appear on his show. It became an important show, because as we talked, J.P. told me that his wife Judy had bought him a gun for Christmas, and he was supposed to pick it up at the sporting goods store. By the end of the show, he told me that after listening to me, he decided not to pick it up."

Tanay and McCarthy would often take opposite sides of an issue and engage in very spirited on-air debate. "I was always amazed that he never had any type of 'pre-interview,'" Tanay explains, "not even for a few seconds, and I think that created a certain sense of spontaneity."

♣

Another regular, Birmingham stockbroker Eugene "Trip" Bosart, often referred to as "our man in the market," thought that McCarthy carried this spontaneity to nerve-wracking degrees:

"We met each other through Orchard Lake Country Club around 1979, and Joe called me and asked me if I'd like to come down to the radio station and be a guest on 'Focus' and talk about tax strategies, the end of the year, and what the economy might offer us for 1980," Bosart explains. "That was when Jimmy Carter was in power and the prime rate was 20% and everything was going nuts but the stock market. It was just sort of muddling along.

"I agreed to do the 'Focus' show," Bosart continues, "and I asked Joe when he wanted to get together and go over the questions he was going to ask.

"'No, just show up at noon and we'll just do it,' Joe told me.

"My God, I studied for a week," Bosart exclaims. "I read everything I could get my hands on, and I was awake the whole night before the interview. That morning, I called and asked, 'Do you want me to come down a few hours early?'

"'Nah, just come about fifteen minutes early and we'll make our way over to the broadcast booth,' he insisted.

"I got there thirty minutes early, and we're in his office just joking around when I looked down at my watch and saw that it was only five minutes until air time!

"'Joe, don't you think we ought to get over to the broadcast booth?'

"'Yeah, I guess so,' he said casually, then he pulls open his middle drawer and takes out his advance copy of *Money* magazine, which I hadn't yet read, and it's got all these little yellow tabs in it marking where he's read it and studied it! As we walk to the studio, I'm trying frantically to look over his shoulder and read what the magazine says, but there are only about 20 seconds until we're on the air. We sit down just in time, Joe does his live introduction, and he looks over at me and says:

"*Trip, during 1979 gold prices have risen 1,800%. Rare furniture is up 3,200%, real estate is up 2,100%, art works of old masters are up 1,900%, and the stock market is up only one-half of one percent. Why would anybody buy stocks?*'

"I was dumbfounded. I looked at him with an expression that said, 'I thought you were my friend!' I was totally taken aback. He was thoroughly prepared, and he wanted to catch me off guard to produce a better 'off the cuff' interview. If it had been staged, he knew it wouldn't come off as well on the air," an exasperated Bosart explains.

In fact, the "Focus" interview went so well that McCarthy began to call on Bosart's expertise when market-related news issues popped up during his morning show. "I had five newspapers delivered to me by 6 a.m., and by 7 a.m., I would have them all read," says Bosart, "That way I knew there was nothing he could ask that I wouldn't have read. I would never have done that if I hadn't lived every morning in fear of his surprise telephone call!"

McCarthy did, however, catch his "man in the market" off guard on one occasion:

"I don't know what he read or why he had to know what it was, but he called and asked me on the air: *'Now Trip, what is the mathematical formula for figuring out the Dow Jones Industrial Average?'*

"We were live, and I had no clue," Bosart groans. "I said, 'Joe, I have no idea, but I'd like to be able to get back to you.' He agreed and I quickly called our head of research at McDonald & Company in Cleveland, and he got our economist on the line also, and I asked if either of them knew the mathematical formula for figuring out the Dow Jones Industrial Average.

"'*Who* in the hell is asking that question?,' they wondered.

"We put twenty people to work on it and came back to Joe with an answer. To this day I can't remember it, but those were the kind of curious things Joe would come up with," Bosart exclaims, "and whatever we said had to be good, solid, accurate information, because people view their money as being as important as their health, and I think that if Joe had told his listeners to go up and jump off of the Ambassador Bridge, three or four people probably would have done it!"

♣

McCarthy's close friend John Schaefer, one of the nation's lead-ing divorce attorneys, had similar experiences with J.P.:

"I had never been on the radio before when I agreed to be a guest on his "Focus" show," says Schaefer. "I thought it was ex-citing and I thought it was fun, but I didn't know what to do, so I got to the studio early.

"'What are you doing here so early,' he asked me?

"'Well, I thought we'd go over what you are going to talk about,' I answered.

"'Oh, God no,' he told me. 'We can't do that. We'll leave it all right here. You don't do that with an interview.'

"He gave me a tour of the station and we walked over and visited with station manager Bill James, and the whole time I'm nervous as a cat and kept looking at my watch because we were supposed to go on the air," Schaefer exclaims.

"We finally went up and did the stupid show and, oh my lord, was I nervous! Of course, his voice on the radio sounded so good and mine sounded so bad compared to it.

"He asked, 'What do you call it when you're representing the wife and he's having an affair? Do you call that 'having a cookie in the condo?'"

He's got this grin on his face and he says, 'I'll bet that's called 'plucking the chicken?'"

Schaefer laughs when he remembers that first interview, but as a divorce attorney, he became a McCarthy show regular, even though off the air J.P. referred to him fondly as "PFD"—"Prince of F—ing Darkness."

♣

Hollywood's latest darling, author Elmore "Dutch" Leonard, a Detroit area resident since 1961, also enjoyed the status of a McCarthy regular, and appreciated the spontaneous and friendly interviews he came in for every time he had written a new book. "He was very familiar with my work, but I never got the feeling that he had read the new book. He was very 'off the cuff.' I knew he read them in time, though, because often he would refer to my previous books."

Leonard, whose books often contained dubious characters and mob-related storylines, says McCarthy was delighted to hear that Leonard had once signed one of his books for John Gotti. "I was signing in Boca Raton and there was an individual there who collected books for Gotti," Leonard explains. I signed *Get Shorty* for him, and I wrote 'See what you think' in the flap. Gotti never contacted me with his critique, though."

Another local author who visited McCarthy at least once per year was Bill Kinzle, the former priest who had written *The Rosary Murders* and other titles in the "Father Kessler" series of books. When *The Rosary Murders* was made into a film, parts were filmed in Detroit, and McCarthy interviewed Charles Durning and anyone else involved with the film. "J.P. didn't ask the standard 'showbiz' questions," *Free Press* columnist Bob Talbert remembers. "He asked questions that showed his guest that he'd taken the time to learn a little something about them, and his reputation grew among the celebrities and booking agents in New York and Los Angeles.

Talbert remembers that his first meeting with J.P. McCarthy was as a guest on a "Focus" show that included Frankie Avalon. "Frankie Avalon was a sarcastic, awful little guy that everyone still thought of as Annette Funicello's boyfriend," Talbert groans. "He had a bitterness to him, and during his interview, J.P. looked over at me and raised his eyebrows. We made instant contact that way and became friends ever since."

Talbert, as the *Detroit Free Press'* most popular columnist, has observed McCarthy's work since 1968. "Sometimes I'd go and hang around his studio just to interview people he had on. Sometimes I'd be thirty minutes late for a lunch appointment because I couldn't leave the car during his 'Focus' show."

♣

One gentleman who sat through many lunchtime "Focus" shows was German immigrant and highly successful area businessman Wilhelm Kast, the chairman and founder of DPCS. Kast worked in the General Motors Building early in his career, and, a struggling newcomer to the corporate game, did not have money to go to lunch every day like his officemates. To keep busy, he smuggled a brown bag lunch into Studio D across the street in the Fisher Building, where "Focus" was broadcast live each day during the noon hour in front of a studio audience. To this day, Kast credits some of his phenomenal success in the business world to those lonely lunches, when he very closely observed J.P. McCarthy and his guests, and learned how to communicate, relate to people, be conversational, and carry himself.

♣

The noontime "Focus" shows, marking the end of McCarthy's workday, often led to afternoon socializing with coworkers, pals, and sometimes guests who had appeared on the show. The "Recess Club" in the Fisher Building was many times the afternoon clubhouse. "It was too easy to 'fall down the elevator shaft' to the 11th floor and a place called the Recess Club," producer Hal Youngblood recalls. "All the executives would be in the back room. Sometimes we'd go down to the Chophouse or the Caucus Club, and sometimes even make it as far down Jefferson as Pinky's or Little Harry's. I'd go home after a while," says Youngblood. "After all, someone had to sign us on in the morning."

It was in the Recess Club and during these afternoon sojourns that many inside stories and behind-the-scenes admissions were made to McCarthy, giving him the necessary background and insight to fully understand the issues facing many of his guests. "Network news anchor Chet Huntley came to do the "Focus" show a number of times," says Youngblood, "and Joe became quite friendly with him. We were at the Recess Club when Huntley said, 'I want to tell you something, and it's not for publication.'

"'Remember, Chet, I have resigned from the news media,' McCarthy kidded.

"'They tell me I have terminal cancer,' Huntley confided, 'Could be as little as five months.'"

♣

While that was a somber moment, the afternoons sometimes served as McCarthy's nightlife because he was up so early each

89

day. "I quit drinking a number of years ago," says Mike Whorf. "Until that time, I'd go drinking with Joe once in a while and we'd sit around getting boisterous and boring. Once I quit drinking, I lost touch with that scene, but every once in a while, Joe would come up to me in the hall and ask, 'Are you still on the wagon?'

"I'd say 'Yes,' and he'd say, 'If you ever go back to drinking, will you let me know? We had some good times!'"

"I worked for the McCord Corporation in the Curtis Building, right down the street from WJR," says McCarthy pal Tom King. "The New Center area was the hub of Detroit area culture at one time. Joe was well known around the 'Normandie' and the 'Steering Wheel.' After work, we'd meet for a drink and maybe listen to Chuck Robinett play the piano in a lounge in the basement of the Fisher Building."

King remembers the kind of tales those afternoons could occasionally produce:

"Joe's pal Tim Johnson was getting married for the second time, and Joe and I were hosting a stag party for him in the basement of a place called 'The Kansas City Steakhouse,' which was at 14 Mile road and John R road," King explains. "We invited a lot of nice, prominent people, and Joe decided that there needed to be some entertainment for this party, and the only place we knew we could find entertainment that the fellas would enjoy was in Windsor.

"We went to Windsor and did a little recruiting, and with a little conversation, we found out that that, yes, there was entertainment available. At the time, U.S. customs was giving dancers a hard time trying to cross the border, so Joe gave them a letter on his stationary saying that they were coming over the border to do a radio interview. That gave clearance for the dancers and their drivers and escorts to be on their way to the party.

"On our way back from the 'recruiting mission' to the party, Joe and I were in separate cars, and got tied up in traffic. Traffic on the Lodge Freeway was very bad. He called me on the car phone:

"*'I didn't expect this kind of traffic! I'm in a virtual parking lot here, and I've really gotta go to the bathroom, but I can't get off the freeway!'*"

90

"We hung up, and I felt sorry for him until my car phone rang again:

" *'I'm okay now. Problem solved. I don't have to go anymore.'*

" 'What do you mean you don't have to go anymore?'

" *'You know that plastic bag in your glove box that holds all of the owner's manuals? I took all the manuals out and filled it up three times!'* "

♣

Tim Johnson's wedding proved to be an eventful affair, with King and McCarthy's attendance, as well as another McCarthy pal and show regular, Dr. Gary Knapp, the family physician sometimes called "Dr. Feelgood." "After the wedding we all ended up at the London Chophouse," says King, "and that's where the 'Irish curse' hit. Gary went to the bathroom and didn't come back for half an hour. His wife asked, 'Where the hell is Gary?' We didn't really notice he was gone because he hadn't spoken for an hour, anyway. I go in the john, and the attendant says 'Your friend is there in the stall and I don't think he's doing so good. This ain't right for the place, to have a doctor in there feeling so bad.' Gary was sleeping in the bathroom!" King laughs.

The London Chophouse featured caricatures of famous people on the walls. That was the night J.P. decided he didn't like the way his looked and took it off the wall. "That's not me. It doesn't look like me. It makes me look fat and I don't have enough hair. It's bullshit," McCarthy said.

"We went back there one day and they informed Joe that his caricature had been stolen," says King, "but they offered to have the artist do another for him. Joe sat down in the little studio under the stairway and scolded the artist not to make him look too fat, and kept asking me how he was doing all through the process."

The London Chophouse for a time was a favorite McCarthy spot. Advertising mogul Fred Yaffe threw J.P.'s surprise 50th birthday lunch there, and as McCarthy walked in, everyone in the restaurant was hiding their face behind specially printed newspapers that read "J.P. Turns 50." When everyone dropped their newspapers, they were wearing the "Dick Purtan style" rubber nose and glasses of McCarthy's chief rival!

"Joe didn't dislike Purtan," says King of McCarthy's rival morning radio host, "but Joe was competitive. He didn't like to hear about Purtan."

"There was never any love between J.P. and Purtan," says Bob Talbert. "It was amazing how that little dance worked over the years. J.P. was always #1 in overall listeners, while Purtan did well in the ratings with certain demographics," Talbert continues. "Purtan used to needle J.P. with jokes on the air, calling him 'P.J. CmMarthy!'"

Very early in my career, I was an intern on Dick Purtan's radio show, and a few months after becoming J.P.'s Producer, I ran into Purtan at a media event in Disneyworld. "J.P.'s always been jealous of me because I make more money than him" Purtan told me. We chatted more, and when I returned to Detroit, I told J.P. that I had run into Purtan. "Purtan's a very jealous man," J.P. said. "It bothers him that I make more money than him."

Aside from seeing each other at very rare social events, McCarthy and Purtan never really knew each other. "I regret that," Purtan told Bob Talbert. "J.P. did his show better than anyone ever could have."

♣

McCarthy's on-air style could be described as casual. He was always a calming voice of reason, seemingly knowledgeable about everything he discussed. How did he pull off hosting one of the nation's most significant morning radio shows each day?

Each weekday morning, newsman Dan Streeter would end his newscast at 6:15 by introducing The J.P. McCarthy Show. "Have a Nice Day," McCarthy's theme music would begin. About 2 minutes later, J.P. would get off the elevator, walk through the lobby and into the studio, toss his sportcoat over a chair, sit down in his chair with the theme music still playing, put on his glasses, take a sip of the black decaffeinated coffee left for him, give a barely noticeable nod to the control booth, turn on his microphone and begin the show by saying, "Good Morning, World!"

After greeting the listeners and introducing himself, he would read from a prepared list of events that happened on that date in history and name celebrity birthdays before stopping for a commercial. During the commercial break, he would look over the day's guest list left on the rack in front of him. On most days, that was his first look at who he would be speaking to during a given show.

McCarthy would also begin paging through the newspapers stacked next to him: *The Detroit News and Free Press, USA Today, New York Times,* and *Wall Street Journal.* Throughout the morning, he would bark out names of people he wanted to talk to in addition to or in place of certain guests on his list. I would track them down if possible, and J.P. needed little advance warning if I got them on the line. He could handle any subject at any time. If we were in a pinch, I could deliver a guest while he was on the air, and without breaking a sweat he could begin talking to them and covering the issue. If I couldn't find a guest, he'd just say, "Keep trying." He never panicked, and most people who visited the studio would be shocked at how relaxed he was.

McCarthy would have a small breakfast every day during the 7:00 news, and tea at 7:45. As he became more interested in his health, he chose a bagel with jelly at 7 a.m. For years it had been a blueberry muffin, and in years earlier, buttered toast.

Sometimes during commercials, he would talk on the telephone to his various friends and sources. In many cases, when I'd reach a newsmaking guest who was resisting speaking on the air, J.P. could jump on the line when necessary and personally talk them into it. His warmth toward guests grew over time the more frequently he spoke to guests on the air, until they eventually became regulars. His listeners came to feel that J.P.'s guests were friends dropping in at their homes, much as the guests felt they were friends dropping in at J.P.'s studio "home" . . . Studio D.

On a Clear Day You Can ♣ See the Fisher Building

The car lurched menacingly toward the end of the driveway, and eagerly cut the corner past the roadside letter box and onto Lone Pine Road. As soon as the aerodynamic nose straightened out, the rear wheels spun and squealed as the needles jumped crazily on all of the instruments. As the two young boys in the back seat tugged at their seatbelts, their screams of thrill—or maybe fear—were barely audible as the engine roared and the force pushed them back against their seats.

Surely the noise and vibration was too loud for them to over-hear their father say, "Let's see what the hell this thing can do," as he steadied the wheel, danced on the pedals, and worked the shifter. These boys weren't around when dad raced Corvettes and Mustangs in the '60s, and scenic and sedate Lone Pine Road surely wasn't used to this kind of test. Road, car, and passengers were all in good hands, and although celebrities are famous for getting breaks from traffic cops, the Bloomfield Hills police probably would have been obliged this day to issue a ticket with the name "Joseph Priestley McCarthy" on it.

He loved cars, and he loved talking about cars. Grandson of one of the founders of General Motors, J.P. McCarthy recognized that the auto barons were royalty in the "Motor City." It wasn't just the fact that five of every seven jobs in the area were somehow related to the automotive industry. It wasn't just the "stone's throw" proximity of the General Motors Building to the Fisher Building where J.P. broadcast from, or the unmistakable "glass house" in Dearborn that housed the Ford Motor Company's world headquarters. It wasn't the fact that the freeways he would report about every day bore the names Chrysler, Fisher, Walter Reuther, and Ford, or that you could drive a car that was named after the Frenchman who founded Detroit, or the Indian Chief who occupied it.

It was the fact that our royalty provided a living, breathing drama of touchable personalities who, by earning their daily bread, were constantly displaying comedy, tragedy, pathos, inspiration, ingenuity, intrigue, and competitive fraternal and international jousting in an arena right smack in the epicenter of the WJR broadcast area.

♣

"Lido," "Hank the Deuce," Delorean, Edsel the II, Cole, Lutz, Smith, Bidwell, J.T. Battenberg, Stempel. The people behind these colorful names—and even more colorful personalities— were not only guests on J.P.'s show; they were faithful listeners to his show, and friends of McCarthy's too.

From the Henry Ford Mansion to the Dodge Mansion and Meadowbrook Hall, from the Edsel Ford Estate in Grosse Pointe to the General Motors Proving Grounds in Milford, J.P. covered the automobile landscape from bumper to bumper, from the showroom to the used car lot.

Advertisers could be absolutely certain that their commercials on "The J.P. McCarthy Show" were heard by the decision makers inside the "Big Three," from the chairman, to the division heads, to the purchasers and designers. Specialty commercials with automotive lingo designed to target as few as six key automotive executives would sometimes air on the show, confusing the average listener, but providing suppliers and component salesmen and manufacturers with the next best thing to a private pitch meeting with high level automotive leadership. Commercials on "The J.P. McCarthy Show" gained an extra measure of credibility, which of course came only at a premium cost.

Automotive executives also spoke to each other through interviews with J.P. The show was like a big audio industry newsletter. Lesser executives knew their superiors were listening. Chieftains knew the rank and file and also the competition could receive hints, bluffs, or gentle tweaking by lending an ear to their appearances with J.P.

Think of the automotive storylines that could make the J.P. show a journalistic soap opera: Henry Ford II's corporate beheading of Lee Iacocca; maverick John Delorean's impossible dream turned cocaine sting; or Doug Frasier and the marathon auto labor talks; the struggle to keep the Japanese from claiming nearly half of the U.S. auto market; the government's bailout of Iacocca's Chrysler Corporation; and left-wing filmmaker Michael Moore's cinematic stalking of GM President Roger Smith.

Then there was the rise and fall of GM President Bob Stempel, and the corporate espionage case of supplier-squeezing GM executive Ignacio Lopez, who ran to Volkswagen with secret documents while a jilted Jack Smith prepared a press conference to announce a significant promotion for his longtime confidant and protégé. There was the short-lived Autoworld theme park in Flint, Michigan, which was the butt of many jokes.

And who could forget McCarthy's outrage when Dateline NBC secretly planted incendiary devices into the side of GM trucks to "prove" their explosive nature as a warning to viewers in a crash testing exposé. The stunning passing-over, upon Iacocca's reluctant and overdue retirement, of dynamic right-hand man Bob Lutz, who owned and piloted military jet fighters out of Willow Run airport for recreation, was made even more incredible by the fact that the top job was given to Bob

Eaton, who had been running the European operation . . . for
General Motors!

♣

"Joe had a real fascination with the auto industry," says regular guest Keith Crain, "and as publisher and editorial director of the *Automotive News* we talked often on his show about this huge industry in Detroit. He always enjoyed gossiping about it whether he was on the air or off. Who was winning and who was losing," Crain relates. "The people were far more interesting to him than the cars."

"In 1985, he interviewed me at the Fairlane Shopping Center," says Ford Vice President David Scott, "and we talked all about the history of Ford, the Ford Estate, and the Ford Mansion, and he was fascinated by all of it."

McCarthy often had the inside story on many automotive events, because he socialized with nearly all of the players involved. A member at the exclusive Bloomfield Hills Country Club and a regular on the cocktail circuit, J.P. spent quality time with the executives who made the industry tick, and it gave him a deep appreciation for the automotive industry and its leaders.

"The automotive executives used his show to his advantage as well as their own," explains Crain. "It was a mutual love affair and people enjoyed his company. He could play golf, spend time with people, and learn about their companies while socializing with them. He did that very effectively," Crain says.

"Joe had discussions that were very private with the Big Three guys," says plastics supplier rep Tom King, "and he would never ever challenge that privacy. He knew so much information two or three days before the rest of the media knew it, but he would never use it for his own gain," King insists.

"He liked to have scoops," says Crain, "but the fact of the matter is, if he knew somebody was going to get fired, and they hadn't gotten fired yet, it was always a little bit ticklish to talk about how Ford, Chrysler, or General Motors would handle the elimination or early retirement of somebody who may have been a friend of ours. That was always tricky and sensitive, but we wouldn't ignore it. We never wanted to report that somebody got fired before he knew he got fired, but sometimes we did," reports Crain.

J.P. and John Delorean, founder of Delorean Motor Cars, "Focus" show, 1981

"I have known John Delorean for twenty years, when he was the youngest-ever Chief Engineer for Pontiac. He went on to become the youngest General Manager ever at Pontiac, then on to become the youngest General Manager at Chevrolet. Then he got kicked upstairs to become Group Vice President in charge of cars and trucks. He was the youngest in that job, and it looked like he was slated for stardom. Something happened. Something went awry. John Delorean, what happened? Something derailed you from that express train to the second biggest office in General Motors. Check one of these boxes for me:
    'I quit of my own volition,'
    'I was coerced to quit,'
    'Dick Gerstenberg fired me.'"

"Running a division is the greatest pleasure I've ever had in my life, and as soon as I got past that into the constant, every single day, committees all day long, I couldn't handle it, and I didn't think that I could do that for eighteen more years that I had left to run in my career, so I elected to leave. I left of my own volition."

♣

"The people in the auto industry would respond to Joe because he never embarrassed them," says King. "He would ask a tough question, but he'd never belittle them. He was their friend. He knew this town, he grew up in this town, and he cared about the auto industry."

"If you wanted to know what was going on in this industry, you listened to J.P. McCarthy," states Delphi Automotive President J.T. Battenberg, who sits on the General Motors President's Council, making him one of the top executives at GM and of the world's third largest industrial employer. "I was very impressed by his interest in the industry."

Former producer Hal Youngblood remembers witnessing the special access afforded McCarthy by automotive executives. "I remember when GM President Roger Smith took Joe inside the GM Design Center. Security was so tight, and everyone inside was shocked to see him. No one from the media ever got in there, and Roger just waved his hand and in we went. Smith wanted to show Joe some of the upcoming products GM was going to try to use to recoup and regroup." Youngblood says, "Journalists would have given their eye teeth to have the access to auto executives Joe had."

At least one automotive journalist, *Detroit Free Press* columnist and former *New York Times* and *Wall Street Journal* Automotive Editor Doron Levin, agrees. "J.P. was important for his ability to get players in the industry to come on the air live and give their first reaction to the important things that were happening in the auto industry," says Levin. "It was important for me to hear what those people were saying, and the fastest way to do that was not to try to get them on the phone yourself, but to listen to what they had to say to J.P."

J.P. and Ben Bidwell, Executive Vice President of the Chrysler Corporation, 1985

"You're a marketing man. You certainly were forever at the Ford Motor Company. You're doing other things now, but marketing is certainly one of your strong suits. You're in a business that has to react to market demand. If they want big cars, you've got to build them, right?"

"To a point, yeah, but I think there are ways to discourage them, including the enforcement of the CAFE standards. We at Chrysler have said for some time, 'Hey, we've got a federal deficit that's going berserk. Let's put a tax on gas now and produce an economic motivation to the manufacturers to build more fuel-efficient vehicles because there will then become an inherent demand for more fuel-efficient vehicles.'"

"Your boss, Lee Iacocca, told me two and a half years ago that there should be a fifty-cent per gallon tax on gas. That will get it up to a price that's more realistic. Since then, the gas price has gone down about fifty cents, but you are still recommending the tax. That falls on deaf ears and they look at you like you're crazy when you say that, don't they?"

"Well, the administration does because the administration goes to its pollster and he says, 'No, don't do it that way, because that reminds people twice a week about the tax. Do it in a different way that only clobbers them once a year and they'll only think about it once a year.' We don't happen to agree with that. [The tax] seems, to us, very logical."

♣

"Probably the most numerous times I was on J.P.'s show was in the year of 1979," says then U.S. Congressman Jim Blanchard, "because I was the author of the 'Chrysler Rescue,' and I was giving him updates every week and sometimes every day. J.P. was really into economics and manufacturing and he took a personal interest in it."

Despite the fact that a "Chrysler Bailout" by the United States government was an unprecedented and popular regional cause, McCarthy wasn't afraid to ask the tough questions, as Blanchard recalls. "He was supportive of the 'Chrysler Rescue,' but he wanted answers. 'Can they really survive?', 'Will they really make it?', 'What kind of precedent does this set?', 'How are you going to get people in other states to support it?,'" lists Blanchard.

"Even when he asked the tough question, he wouldn't get anybody upset," says Crain. "He would say 'I have to apologize for asking this question, but . . .', then he'd go right ahead and ask it," laughs Crain.

Of course, on the historic day when Iacocca completed Chrysler's comeback by paying off the government loan ahead of schedule, McCarthy was the first to make him "Winner of the Day":

J.P. and Lee Iacocca

"I'm J.P. McCarthy, just calling, very early this morning, as he's on his way to the office, the Chairman of the Chrysler Corporation, a day after his proudest moment. Lee Iacocca, good morning!"

"Good morning, J.P. How are you?"

"I'm terrific, and I want you to know how good you looked on everybody's television sets when you went down and surprised a lot of people and wrote them a check for eight-hundred million dollars!"

"It's the first fun day I've had in Washington in four years! I appreciate your calling me, J.P., and it's a nice feeling."

"Congratulations, again!"

"Yeah, thank you."

"Always a pleasure to talk to one of our 'Winners of the Day' in person. That was great fun."

"Thanks again, J.P."

"Lee Iacocca, the still smiling Chairman of the Chrysler Corporation, in one of the most amazing American business stories of our time!"

John Delorean, 1981

One of the not so successful automotive stories that intrigued McCarthy was the John Delorean saga. In 1981, he asked Delorean why his upstart car company, Delorean Motor Cars, failed. Delorean's reply:

"It ultimately turned out that nobody really wanted us. We were too high risk of a project, and the only people that would take us were the people of Belfast, where we built a factory in the middle of what had been a battlefield between Catholic and Protestant settlements in West Belfast. The reason Belfast took us is that nobody else would take them. It was like when two really ugly people get married because no one else will marry either one of them."

"Did that make the British government your partner then?"

"Absolutely. They owned every single piece of equipment right down to the pens and the paper clips. They were our partner, and they also had majority ownership of the company."

"There were people who said you'd never produce a single car, and that no one would make any money on this venture except John Delorean. You did produce the car, though. You produced a lot of them."

"We produced about nine thousand cars, and today we would be one of the profitable companies in the business if we had been allowed and permitted to survive. We were put in by the Labor Party, and when the Conservatives came in they elected not to finance our project. We filed fraud charges against the British government. When Mrs. Thatcher came in, she wouldn't give us the working capital called for under our agreement. She decided to get rid of all state-owned enterprises—British Telecom, British Airways, British Steel, and all the rest.

We had sold cars beyond anybody's wildest expectation, we had two years of orders on the books, we had a trained workforce; everything was perfect except we didn't have any working capital. We didn't have enough money to buy one component, bolt, or screw. We were trying to buy components on credit, [and] get the cars sold quick enough to get a little bit of money to pay the suppliers. Very unstable.

I said, 'Look, you can have all my interest, all my stock, everything. I don't want anything. I just want this company to succeed.' We actually made 27 million dollars in the last six months of 1981. We were the only profitable automobile company in Great Britain. We didn't go bankrupt. We were bankrupted by the British government."

"Was it because of the economic climate that you couldn't get the financing you needed through the more normal areas? Banks and so forth?"

"Well, we had nothing to pledge as collateral because the British government owned everything. Every desk, every lock, every screw. They owned every single thing. Looking back, it's clear that some of their actions were possibly somewhat punitive. For example, a short time ago, when it looked like we were going to put the car back in production again, the British government ordered the body dies—which as you know is the most expensive and long lead time single component, in our case worth 18 to 20 million dollars—they ordered them taken out into the middle of Galway Bay and thrown into the ocean. How would you like to be one of the car owners now [in need of] a fender when the body dies required to produce that fender are in the middle of Galway Bay! Why would they do that?

"That was punitive, clearly. Apparently they did it because they got word you were going to start your company up again, and they weren't going to let you do it!"

"Can anyone think of a rational explanation for it? I guess they thought they were doing it rather secretly, except that the dockworkers who were taking the dies out on the barge to dump them thought it was so amusing that they all had their picture taken with 20 million dollars worth of dies. Everybody had a photograph of themselves next to all this tooling as it's being thrown into the ocean! We're filing a class action on behalf of everyone involved, including the car owners. I think everyone's not only going to get their money back, but make a profit."

♣

In addition to supporting the Big Three on his show, McCarthy was also hired by the auto companies to be the voice talent for many of their national television and radio commercials. "Over the years, he did car commercials for everybody," recalls Judy McCarthy.

"He knew how to sell a product," says Michigan Attorney General Frank Kelley. "Give him copy about the new Chrysler with Corinthian leather and he was right at home reading that copy. You would think that he designed the car, put the leather in himself, and drove the car hundreds of miles," exclaims Kelley.

Mega car dealer Martin "Hoot" McInerney explains how his friend J.P. got "voice work" from the automotive bigwigs. "I used to take him around to all the auto guys," says Hoot. "I used to walk up to the car guys and say 'Goddammit, give him some work,' and they did! Joe said, 'You ought to be my agent!' I told him, though, 'You'll never do a Toyota TV commercial because you could never jump up in the air and click your heels together. You're not coordinated enough,'" McInerney laughs.

♣

Whether he bought the car from Hoot or not, J.P. always drove American cars. "He never drove a foreign car, ever," says J.P.'s son, Jamie McCarthy. "He drove a Cadillac, Corvette, Cordoba, but he was very into supporting the American made car," Jamie insists.

"Joe was committed to driving Detroit cars, domestically produced cars," says Keith Crain. "He liked speed, though. I remember taking him down Long Lake Road in a red Ferrari at breakneck speed. It took his breath away," laughs Crain, "and he talked about it for five years. He thought it was one of the most exciting things!"

On one occasion, McInerney came up with a car and driver for McCarthy when J.P. had to be without his car due to a bout with phlebitis. "WJR paid for the car and my driver to pick him up in the morning and drive him around all day," explains McInerney. "After a week, the driver told me 'I'm going to die. He's got me taking him to every bar in the city after work!' Judy was so mad at the driver that she wouldn't let him in the house when he came to pick Joe up!" laughs McInerney.

McCarthy did drive a sporty deep red convertible Jaguar, but only after Ford Motor Company purchased the British line. He loved to pronounce the car's name the way the British would: "Jahg-you-ahr."

Aside from the "boys with toys" frivolity of examining new car models and "seeing what they've got under the hood," there was a serious "home team" bonding that took place when the Japanese car manufacturers began to threaten the American way of life and the jobs of countless Detroiters and Americans by "dumping" exports onto American roads and capturing as much as forty percent of the United States market share. "Less expensive," "better quality," "more reliable" were descriptions that embarrassed auto executives, engineers, and even line workers who were challenged by the spartan Japanese team work ethic.

"The first time I was on J.P.'s show was when I recommended that Congress create an 'Automobile Industry Task Force' to look at the health and long-term prospects for the auto industry," says Jim Blanchard. "When I went to Congress in the middle to late seventies, the auto industry was sagging seriously, reeling from the Arab oil embargo and the huge demand shift to Japanese cars," recalls Blanchard.

Keith Crain recalls McCarthy's first journalistic endeavor with the Japanese: "A friend of mine named Yamamoto was the Chairman of Mazda, and Mr. Yamamoto was coming to the United States, which he did not visit that frequently, to speak at our 'Automotive News World Congress.' Joe heard about that and he asked me to set up a 'Focus' interview with Yamamoto for him. I said I'd be glad to," recalls Crain.

"So Mr. Yamamoto made his speech, which was aided by lots of audiovisuals, and the next day he went up for an interview with Joe on the 'Focus' show. Joe introduced him as the Chairman of Mazda, and in his first question asked him if he was related to Admiral Yamamoto, who planned the Japanese attack on Pearl Harbor in World War II. Yamamoto was very flustered and insisted, No, no, no, he was not related to him," laughs Crain.

After that "ice breaker," things got worse, Crain continues. "Yamamoto had great, great pride in his ability to speak the

English language, but the fact of the matter was that his English was pretty difficult to understand, if not impossible. I don't think Joe understood one word Yamamoto said through the entire interview.

"Here Joe has to carry on a live interview with the Chairman of the Board of one of the largest auto companies in the world, who was speaking in what he thought was perfect English," Crain chortles, "which nobody in the world could have understood. It was one of the most hilarious interviews that J.P. ever had to do, and we laughed about it for a long time."

"The way Joe evenly and diplomatically handled the very competitive top guys at the Big Three, I think he would have been a wonderful guy to solve the trade disputes between Japan and the U.S.," says supplier rep Tom King. "He had the capability to do that."

Perhaps that's what McCarthy had in mind when he decided to broadcast his morning show live from the Land of the Rising Sun at the 1991 Tokyo Motor Show, a convergence of Detroit's top carmakers with the Japanese executives and a massive display of new product and technology held every two years just outside of Tokyo.

After the thirteen-hour flight to Japan, "The J.P. McCarthy Show" set up camp at the Okura Hotel, a traditional, business-friendly hotel across the street from the U.S. Embassy that was a favorite of Detroit business executives and visiting dignitaries. Publicity photos wired back to Detroit showed McCarthy posing in front of Japanese lettered signs, and listeners in Detroit prepared to hear tough talk from right inside the "enemy camp:"

"I'm joined now by the President of General Motors, Lloyd Reuss. Nice to see you."

"It's good to be here"

"I know you're here for the Tokyo Motor Show. What are your thoughts?"

"Well, we spent two full days literally hitting every floor of the show, and I just left a gathering of all the GM people who are over here, and one of the comments I made to them is that in thirty years, I've been to a lot of auto shows. The Tokyo Motor Show is one that we always have high expectations for, which are generally met and were met again this year.

One of the interesting things that we saw was that we went through all the exhibits the last two days and we compared notes, and there was a lot of new technology, but there wasn't any new technology that we weren't already working on somewhere in General Motors. When you look at the tremendous competition, you can see that no one is backing off one iota, and there are literally, every year, more competitors doing more things. It's an international business, it's a tough business, but on the other hand it's bringing out the best in all the competition."

♣

It was a little odd to be on the other side of the globe, but it was comforting to be surrounded by the familiar faces of Detroit's best and brightest, all dropping in to the small meeting room in the conference center of the Okura Hotel where McCarthy hosted his show each night—that's right, each night!

"In order to be on the air at 6:15 a.m. in Detroit, J.P. had to begin his show at 7:15 in the evening in Japan," recalls Keith Crain. "He was stashed in this meeting room at the Okura, so I would stop by and do a guest shot at the beginning of the show, then go to dinner, and then stop by and do another guest shot toward the end of the show near 11 p.m.," says Crain, who served as McCarthy's erstwhile "color commentator" at J.P.'s auto show remotes. McCarthy often referred to him as his "John Madden" of auto shows.

"After two or three days of these evening remotes at the hotel," laughs Crain, "I suggested to him that it might not be a bad idea if he actually went out to the motor show because he had yet to set foot at the actual Tokyo Motor Show!" Crain, McCarthy, and the rest of the small crew were driven out to the motor show, which was over an hour outside of town because of the oppressive traffic that clogged Tokyo's roadways.

On a Clear Day You Can See the Fisher Building

The show was indeed massive, housed in what appeared to be giant airplane hangars. After a breezy walk-through that included running into Mariel Hemingway, we piled back into our chauffeur-driven Nissans and went to record an interview with Bob McCurry, a former Chrysler Executive and Michigan State alumnus who was Vice Chairman of Toyota Motor Sales in the United States. McCurry, whom McCarthy often referred to by his nickname, "Captain Crunch," was staying at the Disneyland Sheraton Hotel, and after the interview in the hotel lobby, we made a quick stop at Tokyo Disneyland.

J.P. was very blasé about the visit, but he got quite excited when he spotted the thrill ride "Space Mountain." We actually stood in line and climbed aboard the rocket car—J.P., Judy McCarthy, me, and WJR sales assistant Nancy Dyke. Somehow, having only been J.P.'s producer for two months at that time, it all seemed somewhat surreal to be riding Space Mountain in Japan with a radio legend I had grown up listening to.

After Disneyland, it was back onto Tokyo's strangled highways to return to the Okura for the evening radio show:

"The President of the Ford Motor Company, Phil Benton, is with me. Phil, you've heard the arguments in recent days, and over here for years, that the Japanese are difficult to do business with. That they don't play on an even playing surface. You've had Japanese partners here for a long time, [for example] Mazda. How's it working? How has it worked?"

"I think very well, J.P. I don't think they're difficult to do business with. They're different. You have to learn how to do business with them. Our difficulties as an industry are the same as our difficulties as a country. It's the difficulty of our way of running an economy and their government's way of running an economy more than it is differences between the companies."

Following the show each evening, there would be a "show meeting" in the hotel's "Orchid Bar," which basically was cocktails with Detroit executives who mingled in the bar. Ford Vice President David Scott, American Sunroof Company owner Heinz

Prechter, and others would spend more time chatting with McCarthy than they did during their interviews on the show. J.P. would relax and show off his funny impression of the Japanese martial arts pose and groan, "which he perfected with GM Executive J.T. Battenberg," says Judy McCarthy. One evening we ran into PGA Tour golf star Hale Irwin, proving that it is, indeed, a small world.

McCarthy was also very curious about Japanese culture and lifestyle. Speaking with the *U.S. News and World Report* Tokyo Bureau writer, he and his listeners learned that a 1,500 square foot, one-bedroom apartment next to the freeway in Tokyo cost $5,000 per month. Japanese representatives of Ann Arbor–based Domino's Pizza delivered a pizza to McCarthy during his show, and he wondered how Domino's managed to complete its "thirty minutes or free delivery" policy in a traffic-jammed Tokyo where the street addresses are extremely complicated. He was also surprised to find squid and corn are regular items on Japanese pizza, and that the Japanese had never even heard of pepperoni.

Judy McCarthy remembers a more authentic Japanese dining experience on a sightseeing trip she took with her husband to the traditional city of Kyoto during downtime. "We sat on the floor and ate this raw food," groans Judy. "I was not good at that. Joe was much better. They brought us sushi, and then they brought us Kobe beef, almost raw, with a raw egg on top of it! I said 'Joe, I can't handle this!'"

Once in the city, McCarthy took to using the underground subway system. "We decided it was easier to take the underground train because it took forever to get anywhere in a cab," explains Judy McCarthy. "Neither one of us knew how to read the Japanese signs, so both of us were standing down there, and from the looks on our faces, it was obvious we were not having an easy time. Finally, this wonderful Japanese man, dressed so nicely, bowed and said, 'I speak English, and I think you're having a problem,'" Judy smiles. "Once he gave us a little guidance, we took the trains everywhere and never had a problem," she recalls.

On a Clear Day You Can See the Fisher Building

♣

I knew it to be a matter of pride for J.P. to learn the underground subway system in whatever city he was in. I'll never forget an afternoon trip we made alone together from the Okura to the Imperial Palace Hotel. J.P. took me there to "drink where MacArthur drank" and have lunch. He was genuinely proud of his mastery of the Tokyo subway system, even though we made a couple of stops we needn't have.

Traveling in Paris, he also loved to explore and learn his way around "the City of Light," eschewing taxis in favor of the infamous "Metro."

"The J.P. McCarthy Show" originated from the Mondial de l'Automobile Exposition in Paris in October of 1994. This time, the time difference with Detroit worked out perfectly, as McCarthy broadcast right from the Ford Vehicle Stand on the floor at the expo center:

"I'm pleased to be joined by the Chairman of the Ford Motor Company, Alex Trotman. Last night at your press conference, you talked global. That was obviously the keynote of your speech, but you spoke of the burgeoning market in Asia, where eighty percent of the population of the world is, and only eight percent of the vehicles are!"

"That's a grabber, isn't it?"

"It's a grabber and it's an interesting market, but can anybody afford to buy cars?"

"Not nearly as many people can afford to buy cars as they can in Western Europe or America or Japan yet, but one day they will be able to, and even if that day is a long way off, in percentage terms, you're talking a very small percentage of people in those markets to get into the car business and you're talking about very large volume.

In China, the whole car industry is only about 1.3 million, roughly, and there are two hundred manufacturers, by the way, in China."

J.P. McCarthy

"Incredible. Are they tiny cars in China? Would we call them subcompacts?"

"No. Absolutely not. They're all shapes and sizes, from small to large—things like sport utilities and commercial vehicles of one sort or another, but a wide range of vehicles. A lot of trucks, a lot of working vehicles. But that market, there are over a billion people there. In percentage terms, four million units a year, of course, is a very tiny percentage of car ownership."

"But it's a lot of cars."

"Four million is about what the forecast is for the year 2000. So small percentages, but yes, big numbers. India is the same. The market there is tiny right now—fewer than a million, a lot fewer than a million. But again, even if our projections for future growth are wrong, it's still going to be a big business. Indonesia's another one. Thailand's another big market. That part of the world over the next twenty or thirty years . . . well, there's little doubt in my mind that's going to be the big market of the auto business."

Staying at Le Warwick Hotel just off the Champs Élysées at Rue de Berri, McCarthy enjoyed mixing the breathtaking beauty and excitement of Paris with, once again, socializing with the huge contingency of Detroit automotive executives who had made the trip. This time, instead of "drinking where MacArthur drank," our afternoon escapes were to the famous Fouquet's sidewalk cafe right on the same Champs Élysées that General DeGaulle paraded down. Kronenbourg beer replaced Sapporo, and we lunched at La Belle, a restaurant perched high above Paris in the Eiffel Tower. J.P. seemed to enjoy ordering French "cuisine" in his best attempt at the language. He'd carefully tell the waiter something about "pommes frites" and "jambon et fromage" . . . French fries and a ham and cheese sandwich!

Ford executive David Scott sent a car to pick J.P. and Judy up and bring them to meet him for dinner on their first evening in Paris. "I wanted their first experience in France to be not at an American restaurant with Americans," says Scott. "This was not a tourist restaurant. It was in the old city, Montmartre, with many French people."

"Some of my most memorable times were with him in Paris," J.T. Battenberg fondly recalls. "We spent some evenings together, but the one I always laugh about was the night we went to a terrific restaurant with our wives, and after dinner, instead of going back to our hotels, we squeezed into my little European car with a sunroof to tour the Arc de Triomphe. Joe and Judy were in the back seat, and we were singing and Joe would stand up with his head out the sunroof and enjoy the scenery of 'gay Paris,'" laughs Battenberg. "This is Paris! I am in Paris!" Judy says he'd exclaim with his head out the sunroof.

Later in the week, McCarthy got his own car and he and Judy headed for Reims for a winery tour set up by the "Merchant of Vino," Detroiter Eddie Jonah. "Joe never thought he'd make it out of the hectic Champs Élysées traffic roundabout," laughs Judy, "but he made it out, and I helped navigate!"

Guests on J.P.'s Paris Automobile Exposition remote also included French journalists, food and wine experts, and French tourist guides, but the mainstay guests were automotive-related. Executives from Rolls Royce, Porsche, Peugeot, Mercedes Benz, and Fiat were joined by American journalists Paul and Anita Lienert from the *Detroit News,* Jerry Flint from *Forbes* magazine, William Jeanes from *Car & Driver,* the irrepressible David E. Davis from *Automobile* magazine, and of course, Keith Crain from the *Automotive News*—J.P.'s "John Madden."

In a throwback to Tokyo, by coincidence, EuroDisney had just opened outside of Paris, and the Chief Operating Officer was a man named Steve Burke, son of former WJR general manager Dan Burke. Interviewing Steve Burke by telephone, McCarthy asked him, "How's your French?"

"Better than yours," was Burke's kidding response.

♣

Back in Detroit, the North American International Auto Show took place every January, and while it was in his own backyard, McCarthy was certain to give it as much attention as any of his remote auto show trips. This time, he spent the entire week on his morning show talking with everyone involved with the show.

Barry McGuire, head of the Michigan Automobile Dealers Association, was an annual interviewee. "He knew that it was 'Motown,' and Joe and the Big Three were all part of it," says McGuire.

"Those auto show programs were a classic example of his interest in and love for the industry," says Battenberg. "He worked hard at those shows. He worked hard at the obvious stories of the cars, but he worked equally hard at the stories of the people and what was going on in the industry," Battenberg insists.

The North American International Auto Show at Cobo Center in Detroit features a black tie grand opening charity fundraiser that has been called Detroit's prom night. Each year, a local Detroit television station would produce a live television broadcast from the show floor. The TV show featured interviews with auto executives, analysts, and a sneak peek at some of the cars. "The logical choice as host of that show was Joe," says Keith Crain, who was also interviewed on the show. "It didn't matter who they put with him, he carried the show. He was Mr. Detroit," says Crain.

Crain is referring to the fact that a collection of assorted co-hosts would be brought in to work the television broadcast with him, which was syndicated to other television markets. Robert Urich, Marilu Henner, Aretha Franklin, Anita Baker, and Robin Leach all hosted with McCarthy.

"Live television at the best of times is a technical nightmare," said Leach, "but live television when you are running around the size of Cobo Hall can be maddening! My dream while I'm here in Detroit," Leach told McCarthy, "is to persuade one of the American car manufacturers to put a device into the back seat of a car that allows me to get champagne on tap."

♣

After the television show was finished, McCarthy had a chance to "hoist one," as he would say, with many of his friends in the car business, including the always controversial Lee Iacocca.

"Lee was an interesting fellow," says Judy McCarthy. "When he was going to have his very first date, his 'coming out party' after his wife had died, he went to Bloomfield Hills Country Club for dinner with Peggy, and he was uncomfortable. He came to our table and asked Joe, 'Where are you and Judy going to go after you leave here?'"

"'Home,' Joe told him."

"'Good, Peggy and I are coming over too and we'll have an after dinner drink,' Lee said."

"I felt bad for him," says Judy, "so he ended up coming over here and Joe's mother Martha was here, so she came down to our bar and joined right in. She kept looking at Lee and looking at Lee and looking at Lee, and finally she says to Peggy, 'He's rather homely, isn't he?'"

"Peggy says, 'I don't think so!'"

"Martha says, 'I don't mean homely. I mean rough looking,' and Peggy says, 'I don't think so!'"

"Martha says, 'Well . . . big.'"

"Finally Joe jumps in and says, 'Mother, go to bed!'"

"Iacocca was a good sport about it all," Judy shrugs.

Martha McCarthy remembers her night with Iacocca. "Yes, I met Lee at the bar at Joe's house," she says, and then inquires, "Does he ever remember me? He was married to those funny young girls and they cost him some money! He ought to have more sense and get someone that'll stay with him, but that's the way it goes," she sympathizes.

Peggy Johnson with J.P. on "The J.P. McCarthy Show," January 30, 1985

"The front page in this morning's Free Press *says 'Iacocca's Engaged!' and it has a picture of Lee and his fiancée Peggy Johnson, who is at her apartment in New York at this very hour. Forgive the ungodly time, Peggy, but congratulations! We think that's terrific!"*

"So do I."

"When did this all happen?"

"Last week."

"Did he get down on one knee and propose and the whole thing?"

"Well, that's rather personal, J.P."

"You know, Lee is almost a deity in this town. He's probably the best known, most visible businessman in the country, but here in Detroit he is, as I'm sure you know, very special. He's kind of a combination of a movie star, businessman, savior, all of those things, as you're well aware."

"Yes, I am."

"People are very interested in everything that he does. Millions of people have read his book, and it's all work, work, work, work, work. Tell us that he can relax once in awhile!"

"Rarely, but he does."

"What does Lee Iacocca do for fun?"

"I would say one of the things he enjoys for fun is cooking."

"You're kidding?"

"No."

"What kind of things does Lee cook?"

"Italian."

"Stupid question."

"Right."

"Pasta."

"Mostly."

"Is he a tennis player?"

"Not really."

"Does he like to go to the opera?"

"No."

On a Clear Day You Can See the Fisher Building

"What kind of music does he like?"

"Jazz and big band."

"He loves the automobile business. Will he ever leave it, do you think?"

"Uh, no. If he retires he will simply retire and still be involved in some way or another."

"Well, you know there are always rumors about big political things in the offing for Lee, but he always denies that. What do you think?"

"No."

"No cigar."

"Nope."

"Any date set for the wedding?"

"No, we haven't."

"Presumably you will be moving out here?"

"Eventually, yeah."

"Well, we're very happy for you. You're nice to talk to us so early in the morning."

"Thank you, J.P."

"We look forward to welcoming you to the Detroit family."

"Well, thank you very much. Just be sure you welcome me at a later hour."

"I'll never call you this early!"

"That's okay, J.P. I forgive you!"

"Thanks Peggy!"

♣

While it was obvious McCarthy was always interested in the newsmaking automaker, it was only two years later when the news McCarthy was discussing wasn't so cheery.

"In 1987, I was representing Peggy Iacocca in Lee's first divorce case," says attorney John Schaefer, a very close friend of McCarthy. "I did not want to talk about this case on the air, so I told Joe, 'Leave me alone, I'm not going to talk to you about this.'"

"One morning my phone rang early at home and I knew who it was, and I wasn't going to answer the son of a bitch, so I didn't answer the phone, because I told him to quit bugging me," Schaefer laughs. "So at about 7 a.m. I'm in my car and my car phone rang. I picked it up and Joe said, 'Counselor, you're on the air!' I was on the air! He nailed me! I had no choice but to talk to him," gripes Schaefer.

Iacocca married again, and divorced again, and Schaefer again got the call to represent Mrs. Darrien Iacocca. "This time I went on the air with Joe freely," says Schaefer, "and I went through all of the arguments and talked all about the case. Lee Iacocca's attorney, Phil Vestovich, heard the interview and went crazy! This time, though, McCarthy ran like a scared rabbit because he got a letter from Vestovich," laughs Schaefer, "and I called Joe a sniveling little weasel!"

Iacocca was a good sport throughout his association with J.P., attending the McCarthys' 25th wedding anniversary under awkward circumstances, according to Judy McCarthy. "We had a dinner dance at Orchard Lake Country Club right after Lee had been fired at Ford and moved to Chrysler. Iacocca was one table away from the Fords', and it proved that men can be gentlemen when they have to be," laughs Judy. "It was a fabulous night."

"Normally, in Detroit, those hitters wouldn't be seen together," says Tom King, "but there they were for Joe!"

"J.P. and I launched 'Lee Iacocca for President,'" says *Detroit Free Press* columnist Bob Talbert. "One night I got a call at 2 a.m. on my private line.

"A little whiskey voice said, 'Do you know what the public is missing the boat on?'"

"I said, 'No.'"

"The voice said, 'Lee Iacocca ought to be President of the United States and he's willing to run.'"

"I said, 'Who is this?'"

"The voice said, 'Who do you think would be calling you? This is his wife, and if you don't believe I'm telling the truth, call Hoot McInerney in the morning.'"

"I called and asked Hoot if Iacocca's first wife Mary would do something like that."

"He said, 'She already called me and told me she did it, and she wants you to write about it and talk about it with J.P.'"

"I wrote about it, and J.P. interviewed Lee the next morning. After that, it became a national story," says Talbert.

♣

McInerney is a friend to many Detroit media people and national celebrities, but he was closer to no one than J.P., whom he called 'darling,' and kidded constantly. McInerney and McCarthy, giants in their respective businesses, had a playful relationship. "Joe confided in me a lot," says McInerney, "and I in him. I respected him for what he was. Joe was not a phony. What you saw was what you got," McInerney insists.

Sportscaster Dave Diles remembers some of the good-natured ribbing that went along with their friendship:

"J.P. and I were together at a roast for Hoot McInerney's "Man of the Year" award. We ripped Hoot apart, and when you did well, J.P. was the first to congratulate you. He never competed for a laugh. We always kidded each other that when I left the business, I left J.P. in charge of Hoot's publicity. Myself, J.P., and Bob Talbert made Hoot famous!

"So I'm at the podium roasting Hoot. Hoot was building this home, this sixteen-bedroom mansion on Bloomfield Hills Country Club, and it was longer in the making than *War and Peace.* It took three years to build! Why a man his age was going to build a sixteen-bedroom home I don't know, but everybody had heard about it because Hoot told everyone, 'I'm four doors from Roger Smith! I'm four doors from Roger Smith!' 'I don't care if you're next door,' I said in front of the crowd, he's not inviting you over!'

"Then I talked about the new $250,000 organ Hoot donated to St. Hugo Church. He was so proud he used to keep a picture of it in his pocket! I said, 'What he should have bought St. Hugo was what he wore out: a confessional!' J.P. jumped out of his chair," laughs Diles.

J.P. himself was the target of a charity roast at Cobo Hall in 1994. His friendship with the auto industry was summed up by Chrysler executive Ben Bidwell when he stepped to the podium and brought down the house with this:

> "I'm going to do McCarthy in twenty words:
> Big heart,
> beady eyes,
> enormous lungs,
> severely damaged liver,
> medium sized balls,
> tiny schwantz,
> short on hair,
> long on bullshit.
> That's the definitive McCarthy. Anything else said is jabberwocky.
> Plus, six more:
> The best there is.
> My hero."

The Wearin'
♣ of the Green
—and Fairway

J.P. McCarthy was the original radio representative to the game of golf. J.P. had a running dialogue with the touring pros, club professionals, men who made the rules, and the boys who played the game. McCarthy played the game, he loved the game, and he represented the game.

"His grandfather and his dad taught him the game of golf," says McCarthy's mother, Martha McCarthy. "J.P.'s father, Priestley, studied medicine, and he would have been a doctor if his father hadn't kept taking him to all these clubs to play golf! He loved it!"

Naturally, J.P. learned the love of golf from his father. "They even played golf together in our living room!" Martha chuckles.

J.P. would go on to teach the game to his children. "Golf was probably the quality time I knew with my dad," says Kevin Mc-Carthy, "Busy as he was, we could kick back, relax, and play a

121

nice game of golf. He was helpful, but he hurried you along if you were hitting slow that day. He didn't like to impose on others waiting to play."

McCarthy's lifelong friend John Schaefer agrees. "He used to taunt me about slow play, which really annoyed me because I don't play slow. I walk slow because of my bad knee, but I do not play slow. He was taunting me and would not get off my back until we were cursing each other across the table and talking about stepping out to the parking lot to settle it!"

"While he'd be the first to tell you to 'pick it up' if you were taking too long," remembers Kevin McCarthy, "he'd also be the first to compliment us when we were on our game and remind us how much fun it was for him to get out with his sons and play golf."

J.P.'s youngest son, Jamie McCarthy, learned quickly how seriously his father took the game. "We had a big backyard where we grew up on Lone Pine Road, and I'd hit balls in the backyard. I always just chipped around with a pitching wedge, though, because he warned me that if I ever hit one through a window I would die!"

Once out of the informality of the backyard, Jamie remembers his father's respect for the rules and etiquette. "The first time he took me to a real golf course was a very, very big deal. He wanted me to enjoy golf like he did and not take it for granted."

McCarthy friend Trip Bosart remembers one lesson Jamie learned the hard way. "J.P. was a traditionalist when it came to golf and golf etiquette, and he taught Jamie that the game of golf means too much ever to throw a club." "I was very young and I was playing terribly," recalls Jamie, "and Hoot McInerney was in our group and they were laughing at me and making fun of me. I got pissed off like a spoiled kid and threw a club. My dad said, 'Because you've thrown your club you'll now walk back to the first tee and sit there, and you won't move until I finish and come get you.' I went in and sat on a bench and didn't move. When he came in, he told me that one of his friends threw a club twenty years before and he had never played with him again."

♣

The Wearin' of the Green—and Fairway

"J.P. liked to have a good time" explains Bosart, "but he never wanted to do anything to denigrate the game or violate the rules of golf. He was strangely serious that way."

Another McCarthy friend, public relations executive Tony Franco, says J.P. could relax, too. "He didn't always play by the rules. He didn't cheat, but he could make up some rules sometimes. One time we were hitting our tee shots and he hit a ball only about fifteen feet and it rolled under a pine tree right next to the tee. I prodded him that he had to play it from there," Franco laughs. " 'Bullshit!,' came J.P.'s reply."

J.P. McCarthy actually helped many youths learn the game of golf through his reverence for caddie programs. McCarthy himself caddied as a teen at Detroit Golf Club. "J.P. won the Caddie Championship at Detroit Golf Club in his youth," explains former Bloomfield Hills Country Club golf professional Mike Kernicki, "He never forgot that experience and was always prepared to do anything to maintain the caddie program and make sure the caddies were getting something out of the program."

J.P. regularly snuck the caddies extra tips over the club limit. "At Bloomfield Hills Country Club we gave our caddies a higher base rate than any club in the area," explains Kernicki, "but there was a maximum tip of eight dollars printed on the card. J.P. always felt the caddies needed to make more money, so he wrote down whatever tip he wanted to."

A McCarthy caddie worked hard, however, according to Kernicki. "Every time he came out to play, he'd come flying in and buy three to six new golf balls for the round. Every time. He'd never use that many balls in a round, and he'd never take them out, so his bag just got heavier and heavier, until finally someone from our golf staff would have to go into his bag, remove the balls, and put them in his locker because it was so loaded down the caddies couldn't carry it!"

McCarthy even went so far as to use his celebrity influence to make sure a prominent speaker attended the year-end Caddie Banquet. "We had Isaiah Thomas, Joe Dumars, Ernie Harwell, Rick Forzano, Chuck Daly, Dan Petry, Sparky Anderson, George Blaha, Eric Hipple, and even Grant Hill! All of those people came indirectly because of J.P.," Kernicki says, "because he could get to anyone."

J.P. would also use the radio show to make listeners aware of the Evans Scholarship program, which rewarded hard working and studious caddies, by interviewing Brett Marshall, Executive Director of the Golf Association of Michigan, every year.

♣

Michael Kernicki was J.P.'s golf professional at Bloomfield Hills Country Club for thirteen years. What kind of player was J.P.? "He'd always say, 'Pro, I'm trying to get a fix. He had the opportunity to talk to so many professionals—Greg Norman, Jack Nicklaus, Rick Smith, Lee Trevino. Whatever part of his game ailed him at a certain time would always find its way into the interviews he would have with these pros. On tour, they say a player has 'big ears' when he hears every tip talked about on the practice range and tries all the quick fixes, thinking they pertain to him. J.P. had 'big ears.' It didn't matter if he was talking to Tom Kite or Bill James, he was always looking for a 'magic move.'"

"He had lessons with Chi Chi Rodriguez and Jim Colbert," remembers Jamie McCarthy, "and one day he came home and said 'Guess who my new good pal is? Greg Norman!' He'd get a kick out of that. He always rooted for Norman when we'd watch golf."

"He liked to say that he was neighbors with Greg Norman," says John Schaefer. "Greg lived down the street from where our houses were in Hobe Sound, Florida . . . *a couple of miles* down the street! We sort of lived in 'Brooklyn,' while Norman lived in 'Midtown Manhattan.' Neighbors, indeed!"

"Since he was intelligent, he liked athletes who could excel in the more intelligent sports," theorizes Michigan Attorney General Frank Kelley. "That's why he loved golf. That's the toughest solo game there is. There's nothing tougher than taking your clubs out there and you are all alone! He appreciated the challenge of that and the drama of being a golfer."

♣

"He was very fun to play with," says General Motors executive J.T. Battenberg. "It was great fun to walk the four hours with him. He always had great stories and he knew everybody," Battenberg recalls.

Beaumont Hospital surgeon Dr. John Murphy remembers being invited by J.P. to be his partner in tournaments. "In a two-day tournament, we would always do well on Friday, the first day of the tournament. Then we'd get five or six couples together and go out on Friday night, and neither one of us could do anything on Saturday. We'd be destroyed!"

"There were a lot of late Friday nights," adds Ford executive David Scott, "but he was pretty good at getting up for Saturday morning golf, even when we'd had many 'final final' Dewars toasts the night before. He liked to think he was competitive," adds Scott.

I know he was competitive. Sometimes on Monday he'd come in for the show, and even though we didn't play together we'd match scorecards to see who would buy the morning muffins.

According to TEK Sales President and J.P. buddy Tom King, McCarthy took competition very seriously. "One of our opponents hit a shot up into a tree and I just instinctively said, 'Go through!' When we walked off the tee he asked me, 'Why did you say that? You don't mean that!' I told him that I was just being polite and he said, 'Well don't say that. We don't want it to go through, do we?' He meant it!"

"We'd play together at Orchard Lake Country Club," says pro golfer and "Long Drive Champion" Evan "Big Cat" Williams, "and he liked to try to hit it past me. He was always searching for a little more!"

"He was even competitive with me," insists Judy McCarthy. "He would give me incentives. My shoes were wearing out and he'd tell me I couldn't get new golf shoes until I got two pars in one round."

There was one big category that Judy surpassed her competitive husband in. "I had two aces and he only had one!"

J.P.'s hole-in-one came at Detroit Golf Club while playing with sports announcer Bob Reynolds, columnist Judd Arnett, and Jerry Rideout. Judy's first ace came at Orchard Lake Country Club's third hole. "I called him between nines and I said,

'Joe, guess what!?' He said, 'Judy, I'm on the air. I don't have time to talk to you right now!' I said, 'Yes you do. I just got a hole-in-one!' He was so excited. It was so cute!"

♣

The competition sometimes could also stretch off the course. "We used to have a mythical contest between us," Trip Bosart explains. "When one would get a toy, the other would have to get it too and make the other one mad. J.P. would call and say, 'I just got a fifty-two-inch television,' and then I'd have to go out and get one. In the last year of the Cadillac Eldorado convertible, I bought one under the assumption that it would be a good investment. As soon as he found out I bought one he called every car dealer in Detroit until he found one and then went out and bought it! All through the years one would get one thing, and the other would have to get it," he continues.

"So J.P. and I were playing golf with our head pro Mike Kernicki and J.P. told Mike that the new Ping Eye 2 clubs looked great and that he just had to buy a set of them. Kernicki said that although they were brand new on the market and almost impossible to get, he knew a guy at Ping and would give him a call and see if he could get a set for J.P. Well, I overheard that and I approached Kernicki and I whispered, 'Michael, I want a set too. You've got to get me a set.' He said, 'Okay, okay, I'll try to get two sets.' The only reason I did this is because I knew that if J.P. was going to have a set, I was going to get one.

"So they're all ordered, and Kernicki calls and says he's got two sets and they're going to be air-freighted down to Florida where we were, and that we should have them in two days.

"The next day, I'm playing golf with J.P.'s son Jamie, and I say, 'Did you hear your dad and I got two new sets of the new Ping Eye 2's?' Jamie tells me, 'Yeah. Dad's real excited about them and I can't wait to hit them, but I can't understand anybody willing to pay $1600 for a set of irons!' I dropped right to my knees and said, 'What?' I had no idea they cost that much! The clubs came in, and I had to cough up the dough."

The Wearin' of the Green—and Fairway

♣

Publishing magnate Keith Crain remembers McCarthy challenging even the weather. "We were partners together in a member/guest tournament at Ocean Reef in Key Largo in the Florida Keys. We played well in the first two rounds and we wanted to get the third round in, but a hurricane was passing between Key West and Cuba. We stuck it out and spent the whole night watching the Weather Channel trying to find out if we were going to be swept out to sea. Was it going to veer north and just decimate us? If that was going to happen, we'd have to make a run for safety because we were literally on an island connected to the mainland by a causeway which would have been flooded. We stayed up all night laughing and joking, watching the Weather Channel and accumulating candles from bars or wherever we could find them in case the power went out. It was a real adventure! We were ready to move, but after a pretty thorough dousing, the storm went the other way and we went on to win the golf tournament! Most of the other competitors had left for fear of being flooded!"

♣

Tom King remembers playing in a member/guest tournament that was very important to J.P. "We were playing at Detroit Golf Club when he realized on the third hole that he didn't have his wedge," explains King. "He got on his cellular phone and called Mike Kernicki back at Bloomfield Hills Country Club and had him look though the bags of people he'd played with the previous day and check with the caddies. Sure enough, we didn't finish the next hole when a club staffer drove the wedge out on a cart after Kernicki had it found and driven out to Detroit Golf Club."

Further north, in Harbor Springs, Michigan, another member/guest tourney also turned out to be an adventure. This time, Trip Bosart was the partner: "The Birchwood Country Club member/guest is probably the best member/guest in Michigan," explains Bosart. "During the final round, both players' scores count, and it was a very tense round. Joe hooks one deep into the woods, and we take the cart over there to find his ball. He pulls out a club and says, 'I'm gonna take this 4 wood and put it right between these trees and get it to roll right in front of the green.' So he takes a mighty swing and nails the ball. It advances down the tree line of about fifty trees and hits a tree dead center, comes back, hits another tree, and another tree, and another tree, and, honest to goodness, rolls right back into the divot mark he made when he originally hit it! It had gone 150 yards out and 150 back. It was incredible!"

"We played poorly, but we played," says former ABC Chairman Dan Burke," and I used to have him come to Sailfish Point in Stuart with Chrysler executive Ben Bidwell. He had a period of three or four years when he was long but very wild and discouraged," remembers Burke, "and I think that was when he was spending too much time with his boat."

"He had a bet with some cronies one year," relates golf professional Mike Kernicki. "At the time he was a 17 handicap and he made a bet he'd get it down to 10 by the end of the season." Where did the pressure go? "Not on him," explains Kernicki, "but on me! He came to me for lessons and said, 'Pro, you've got to get me to 10 by the end of the year!'" Kernicki says J.P. had some flashes of brilliance but teetered between 11 and 12 and never made it to 10.

Despite the occasional "rub of the green," attorney John Schaefer knew how much J.P. loved the game, because he says they played together at least twice a week. "If he called me to play and I tried to beg off because I had clients or other matters to handle," exclaims Schaefer, "he'd berate me and say, 'If you can't get your work done by noon, you ought to work with your hands!'"

Car dealer Hoot McInerney and J.P. always made time for golf, too. "He'd call me up and only say, 'Balls in the air at 1 p.m.!' We could play eighteen holes in two hours," says McInerney, "and if we bet and he was hurt or playing bad he'd come up to me in the middle of the round and say, 'Here's your money. The bet's off.' If he was winning, though, he'd come up and say, 'Give me my goddammed dough right now!'"

The Wearin' of the Green—and Fairway

McInerney and McCarthy had some great golf experiences. "We played in the Tucson Open, Hawaii, Bob Hope Desert Classic, the Crosby, and Burning Tree Country Club in Washington." Jamie McCarthy says playing these courses always pleased his father. "I think he was a big kid realizing he got to play all these great courses," says McCarthy. "He got to play places like Pebble Beach and Seminole Country Club."

Aside from great courses, Hoot says he and J.P. also partnered with some great company. "We played with a lot of different people in Cy Laughter's Bogey Buster golf tournament in Dayton, Ohio," he remembers. "We met with Billy Graham, Neil Armstrong, Curly Neal, Tom Harmon, Ernie Banks, Andy Williams, Ray Bolger, Eddie Arcaro, Dan Rostenkowski, Forest Evashewski, and Fred MacMurray," says Hoot.

One of J.P.'s more infamous golf partners was O.J. Simpson, just one year before he would be charged with murdering his wife. They played together in an event in Dearborn at the Tournament Players Club of Michigan, and their conversation during the round would prove ominous. John Schaefer remembers J.P. calling him from the car following the round. "He couldn't wait to tell me about his round with O.J.," recalls Schaefer.

"He said, 'Wait till you hear this: I'm with this guy for five minutes, and he tells me that the best lay of his whole life is his former wife Nicole. I don't know who he was trying to impress." Simpson also told J.P. that he had to find a way to get back together with her."

♣

John Schaefer remembers a more lighthearted round in Florida with J.P. and Senior PGA Tour player Tom Shaw. "Joe and I and Tom Shaw are playing a threesome. I think Shaw hit a titanic second shot over the green on the par 5 first hole. He made an 8 on the hole and then went on to shoot 69 from the back tees. On the sixth hole, Tom found his ball in the frog hair just off the edge of the green. He had just a little chip shot, and Joe and I are sitting in the cart. We watched him take five clubs out of his bag and carry them to his ball.

"I said, 'Joey, look at that. He's got five clubs with him!'

"Joe said, 'Can a guy hit that many different kinds of shots from that little lie?'

"I said, 'I don't know. Let's see which one he uses.'

"So he goes over to his ball, looks at the ball, looks at the clubs, picks out a wedge, hits the ball up and taps in for par. Walking back to the cart, Joe says, 'Tom, we were amazed when we saw you take those five clubs out there for that little chip shot. You've got that many different types of shots for that little shot?'

"Shaw says, 'No, actually what happens is if I only take one or two clubs out there I end up leaving them on the green, but if I take five I can never forget them.'"

Another golf partner, former Michigan governor Jim Blanchard, remembers playing with McCarthy at the Shanty Creek Resort in Mancelona. "He was a better golfer than I, but that's not saying much," jokes Blanchard, "I'm sure he would have loved to devote even more time to his game." McCarthy happened to be one of the original investors in the Shanty Creek Resort, and helped Arnold Palmer open his "Legend" course there.

J.P. with Arnold Palmer at the opening of the "Legend" Course—1985

"Michigan has always been lucky for Arnold Palmer, and I think he enjoys coming back here. It was in this state where Arnold won his very first major championship: the United States Amateur, at the Country Club of Detroit."

"I love it. I only wish there were more golf tournaments for me to come here and play. I won the Amateur, I won the Senior Open at Oakland Hills. I think the whole thing started many years ago with a guy named Bob Thompson, and James George, and we came here to play in the Grosse Ile Invitational, and I had a ball. That was right after I had come to play in the Hearst Newspapers National Junior Golf Tournament in 1946."

"Don't give the years away!"

"You're right!"

"You and the late President Eisenhower were great friends. You and he are generally given the credit for giving golf that tremendous spurt in popularity it enjoyed in the 1950s. I suspect you were more responsible for it than he, but he did have a good deal to do with it, didn't he?"

"Oh, people related to him. They liked him. He was an American hero with a great personality. The fact that when he became President of the United States, everyone knew he loved golf—I think Eisenhower and television had a great deal to do with golf's popularity."

"People loved watching television and seeing Arnold Palmer coming down the 18th hole, hitching up his pants, and grabbing a heroic victory!"

"I've been fortunate to come up in golf during that growth period. I don't think there's ever been a better game in the world. I know you like it, and I'm happy that people like you and Bob Hope have contributed to the growth of the game."

♣

The "Legend" opening wasn't his first association with "The King."

Arnold Palmer never missed talking with J.P. when he came to town. In what would be their last interview together, Palmer asked, "J.P., have we really been doing this together for thirty years?"

J.P.'s connection to the PGA Tour did indeed run over thirty years. His voice can be heard narrating the highlight film for the 1964 Buick Open won by Tony Lema. He broadcast radio shows from the Buick Open at Warwick Hills throughout his career. In 1993, he won the Buick Open Celebrity Skins Game with playing partner Brad Faxon. At 6:30 the following morning, Faxon walked to the WJR mobile studio just off the 18th green to be interviewed by J.P. and revel in their $10,000 charity win. They had captured all nine skins.

McCarthy partnered with Greg Norman one August day in 1991 at the Country Club of Jackson in Roger Penske's Charity Pro Am that featured PGA Tour players and professional race car drivers. J.P. hosted a radio show from just behind the first green that morning, and his guest list ranged from Bruce Lietzke to Bobby Rahal. Following the show, McCarthy had to rush to the 1st tee to begin his round with Norman.

J.P.'s admiration for Greg Norman is well documented. Listeners to the radio show knew that J.P. was a Norman fan and Norman was friendly with him. "My dad always rooted for Greg Norman when we'd watch golf on TV," says Jamie McCarthy. Unfortunately for J.P., his debut as Norman's partner began with a nervous worm-burner just off the first tee box.

PGA Tour players loved to play in Penske's tournament because they were given the opportunity to drive race cars at the nearby Michigan International Speedway during the event. Many PGA Tour players have an affinity for fast cars. Word is that, after J.P.'s 1993 rain-shortened Police Athletic League Tournament, Fred Couples test drove his Ford Mustang courtesy car on the way to the airport by doing "donuts" in a slick, empty Kmart parking lot with a terrified Mike Hulbert buckled into the back seat.

♣

The J.P. McCarthy Pro Am to benefit the Police Athletic League was indeed one of the finest Pro-Am tournaments in golf. The formula for putting it together was a testament to McCarthy's influence and the automotive industry's respect for him. Amateurs paid up to $1,200 to play in the tournament. Each foursome had a professional golfer captain their group in a scramble format. There were players from the PGA Tour, the Senior PGA Tour, the LPGA and the Nike Tour.

Many of the professional golfers were under contract to automotive companies in endorsement deals. The same automotive executives that were guests on McCarthy's show or played golf with him on Saturdays signed the lucrative paychecks that have become a staple of any professional golfer's income. So while Cadillac would send Fred Couples, Dave Stockton, and

Lee Trevino, Toyota would be sure that Chi Chi Rodriguez played, too. If Chrysler sent Tom Kite, then Buick would have Ben Crenshaw on hand.

"Joe got a lot of players for PAL through Bob McCurry at Chrysler, and me," says Hoot McInerney. "Chrysler sponsored a lot of tournaments, and at that time if you gave a golfer a car to use, he'd do anything for you."

Players without endorsement contracts were offered $2,000, transportation, and accommodations in return for their participation. While $2,000 was a welcome paycheck to some of the younger Nike Tour players, some pros declined to accept payment.

J.P.'s PAL Tournament began in 1973 at Wabeek Country Club in West Bloomfield, Michigan. "The PAL Tournament had a bigger crowd at Wabeek than they did at Oakland Hills for the PGA Championship," exclaims McInerney. "J.P. had the winner of every tournament, plus Ben Crenshaw, Johnny Miller, Jerry Heard, Nicklaus, and Palmer."

"The Detroit area had not had a regular tour event for many years, and a lot of people didn't get a chance to see these pros," remembers Trip Bosart. "There would be 12,000 spectators and a major name pro in every foursome."

Jamie McCarthy remembers the year his older brother Kevin caddied for J.P., and President Gerald Ford joined his foursome. "I remember my brother caddied and I remember thinking that my dad was being really nice to this guy," recalls Jamie. "Turns out I was carrying coffee for the President of the United States."

"They were very complimentary of each other," remembers Kevin McCarthy. "My dad was really excited and the attention they got from the gallery was really cool."

Judy McCarthy was excited too. "We went to a party after that PAL Tournament and Betty Ford asked me to go to the restroom with her," says Judy. "I remember thinking 'Oh, my God, I'm in the restroom with the First Lady!' I was so nervous I couldn't even go!"

"I was in the locker room with Johnny Miller," Trip Bosart recalls, "and I think Miller thought he was going to play a quiet best ball with four businessmen. He had no conception of what this event was about."

"Outside the locker room was the practice putting green," continues Bosart, "and the crowd ringing the putting green was three deep. I walk out of the locker room with Miller, and he takes one look at this scene and says, 'Holy Mackerel, this is the real deal! You guys aren't kidding!' He went back into the locker room and changed his shoes and put on a different shirt. He was totally floored at the crowds and J.P.'s drawing power."

> *"At 12:13, McCarthy eased into Studio D and was informed that President Clinton, speaking to J.P. from the White House, was running ten minutes behind schedule. 'Tell him to make it snappy,' said McCarthy. 'I've got a golf game.'"*
>
> — Detroit Free Press

The round with Gerald Ford wouldn't be the last time J.P. encountered a President on the golf course. J.P.'s friend Tom King remembers the occasion at the Jupiter Hills Club in Florida. "President Bush was visiting his mother on Jupiter Island. They had the course blocked for certain hours," King says, "but Joe and I got off early before the President started playing. As we headed toward the tenth tee, we stopped the cart at the seventh tee to watch as Bush dubbed two tee shots into the palmettos. The secret service agent said, 'Did you notice the great drive of the President?'

"We said, 'We sure did, sir!' Joe played right along with it! We later watched him try to hit out of a sand trap with dust flying everywhere."

♣

Tom King played in many PAL Tournaments, and I remember him approaching J.P. before the round, saying "Joe, I was at the driving range next to Fred Couples and he was hitting his wedge farther than I was hitting my driver."

J.P. calmed King with a comparison. "Big deal. Can he sell $100 million in plastics?"

The Wearin' of the Green—and Fairway

The PAL Tournament "blind draw" that determined which professional would play with which amateur group was the subject of some speculation. "I'd get a kick out of how he'd put certain people with certain pros," says Tony Franco. "You could tell who was on his list and who wasn't. If you were at the top of the list and important, you were okay. Otherwise you could end up playing with Barney Oldfield, who once played in one tournament and hadn't made a cut in thirty tries. Joe was loyal in returning favors, though. If you did something for him he never forgot it."

"I knew the fix was on in the blind draw," whispers longtime J.P. friend Barry McGuire, "because I'd always end up with Lee Trevino or Freddy Couples and I played with Chi Chi Rodriguez. That just doesn't happen by luck!"

In later years, the pairings were actually carefully selected in McCarthy's office, where tournament organizers would gather in a scene that looked like old party bosses brokering a political deal in the back room of a convention hall. J.P. always made sure that the pairings were fair and that the good players rotated through a field of yearly regular amateurs.

In 1992, Ford marketing executives and PAL officials Bob Rewey and Tom Wagner, along with tournament administrator Frank Guglielmi, revived the tournament after five or six of the quiet, private versions and moved it to the Tournament Players Club of Michigan in Dearborn. The event still raises over $150,000 annually for the Police Athletic League, and Rewey and Wagner have served as PAL Chairmen. Under the direction of the Ford Motor Company, other sponsors, including Northwest Airlines, Jacobsons, Comerica, and Hoechst Celanese, have pushed total tournament funds raised to over $1,000,000.

J.P. made sure the event made money, even in the quiet years when the event was a private, quiet function held at Bloomfield Hills Country Club in early autumn. Bloomfield Hills had never opened its doors for a charity outing until J.P. put the arm on then club president John Schaefer.

"Those were some of the most fun tournaments," says Mike Kernicki, who as BHCC golf professional helped organize the event. "Eighteen foursomes of Joe's buddies, and they'd still raise about $28,000."

J.P. McCarthy

"Lee Trevino, the top money winner on the Senior Tour, just walked in. It was 19 years ago this week that we had our first PAL Tournament out at old Wabeek. 1973. There were 12 pros that came in and you said to me that night at the dinner party, 'This is a great idea!' Remember, this kind of a charity pro-am was not nearly as popular as it is now. There were only a few of them then. You said, 'This is going to happen, and what you can do is get a whole field of pros in here. You'll have 15,000 people out there watching!' You were right, and you never missed any of our tournaments. You were there every single year!"

"Hey, I had to be there, J.P. I was working for Dodge at the time and McCurry would have cut my neck off if I wouldn't have been there. But you had something that no one else had. You had the avenue of getting the best players in the world in here! Johnny Miller was with Ford, Tom Watson, Lanny Wadkins, Tom Kite at the time was with Dodge. You had Nicklaus, who at the time was with Cadillac, Palmer, who was with Lincoln-Mercury, there were tournaments that we had around the country for $500,000 that didn't have nearly the field you had for the PAL Tournament!"

♣

Michigan pros loved McCarthy. J.P. understood that while he could talk to the Gary Players and the Fuzzy Zoellers of the golf world, there were many fine local players right here in the state, and the winner of the Michigan Open or the Michigan Match Play Championship was just as important to him as any other professional golfer. He also had a tremendous respect for his good friend Tom Chisholm, who served on the USGA Executive Committee and the Golf Association of Michigan.

"J.P. spearheaded local golf coverage with interviews from any local tournament, state open, state amateur, or any tournament of consequence," said Evan "Big Cat" Williams. "One of the reasons Michigan is such a big golf state is because J.P. was so proactive. I've never seen a media celebrity get involved in a local level as much as J.P."

The Wearin' of the Green—and Fairway

Ken Devine, Executive Director of the Michigan PGA, confirms McCarthy's impact with this illustration. "One guy told me that he never watched golf on television and dreaded all of J.P.'s golf talk on the morning show. I asked him why he didn't just turn it off, and he told me that he couldn't bring himself to turn off J.P. He couldn't change the channel, and so finally he just decided to take up golf!" exclaims Devine.

The Michigan golf pros were happy to help out J.P. in the leaner years of the PAL Tournament at BHCC. Having the outing at BHCC also gave it some prestige, but outings were a new concept at Bloomfield Hills, recalls Kernicki. "One year on the 5th green or 6th tee, which is very near some homes, somebody hooked a ball out of bounds and uttered a profanity. A neighbor heard it and mentioned it to Joe, and the following year everybody got a funny little slip on their scorecard telling them to watch their mouths! You wouldn't expect to see that at BHCC, but Joe felt a reverence for the grounds. He embraced the traditions of the game, and that's what that club is founded on. Right or wrong, it's a real conservative club, and I think Joe respected it," insists Kernicki.

♣

I can remember talking golf with J.P. one day, and he mentioned that he was a member of the ultra exclusive Double Eagle Golf Club in Galena, Ohio. I said, "Wait a minute. How many clubs are you a member of?" He gave me a puzzled look, and after a few seconds of thinking, said, "I don't know!" I remember thinking how outrageous that would be to not even know how many country clubs you might belong to.

"Joe was a club guy," says Tom King. "If there was a club, he wanted to belong."

Near as I can tell, J.P. McCarthy at one time or another belonged to Orchard Lake Country Club, Double Eagle Country Club, Jupiter Hills Country Club, Loblolly Pines Country Club, and Bloomfield Hills Country Club. Ford Chairman Red Poling had asked him to join TPC Michigan. John Schaefer says, "We were about to join the Everglades Club when he passed away." Schaefer and McCarthy would sometimes "put the top down, drive three hours to Double Eagle, play eighteen holes, and drive back in the same afternoon just to play there," says Schaefer.

Membership in no club pleased him as much as his membership at Bloomfield Hills Country Club. "I think he was surprised when he got in there," says Schaefer. "Historically, Bloomfield Hills had been a real private enclave for the business elite of Detroit, and they forbade any kind of media attention, so he thought it was pretty special to belong."

After serving as Caddie Chairman, Golf Chairman, and Board Member, McCarthy went on to serve the one-year term as President of Bloomfield Hills Country Club. "He was a good President," says Kernicki. "He came to every event, he utilized the club a lot, and if he walked through the dining room he'd make people feel good by stopping at all the tables to say 'Hi.'"

John Schaefer says J.P. took the job of President very seriously. "When I was President, I used to tell him everything that was going on there," Schaefer says. "When he was President, he used to treat me like a caddie! I'd say, 'Who the hell do you think you're talking to?'"

"Some days one of my staffers would come running to the course, saying, 'Mr. McCarthy needs to talk to you on the phone right away,'" recalls Kernicki. "I'd drop everything, come over and jump on the phone, out of breath, figuring it was some club issue, and I'd be right on the air, with him asking me, 'What happens when you pull up the flagstick and the cup comes with it and your putt hits the cup? This listener wants to know if that's a penalty.' He'd catch me off guard, and I'd have to say, 'Joe, I'll have to get back to you on that one!'"

Kernicki says Joe's legacy to the club was the new men's locker room. "Joe was a guy's guy and a man's man, and the locker room was one of the shabbiest things in the world. The members that resisted change were the same ones who wore the same pair of pants that were their 'golfing pants,' even though they had holes in them," Kernicki laughs. "These were guys that wore $700 suits but wore frayed golf shirts and you'd want to give them a shirt just to see them look better."

Even with the additional cost involved, members were proud of the remodeling. "That bar in there is special," says Kernicki. "They liked the fact that they could go in there and no women would be in there. In this day and age with gender equity, women were forcing their way into the men's grill at Oakland Hills. That was not going to happen at Bloomfield."

♣

While gender equality was never a problem at Bloomfield, an unpleasant and much misunderstood situation did develop under J.P.'s watch as club President. J.P.'s photo was splashed across the front page in stories that speculated that General Motors Vice President Roy Roberts may have been turned down for membership because he was black. *Detroit Free Press* columnist Doron Levin explains his understanding of how the situation developed:

"For some time, Bloomfield Hills Country Club had been an all white club. Ben Bidwell from Chrysler and Bill Hoglund from General Motors, after the controversy at Shoal Creek Country Club, decided that they didn't ever want to be in a position, as the members of Shoal Creek were, to explain why they didn't have a single black member. It was time to get serious about integrating the club, because it was unthinkable in this day and age that these people who were officers in public corporations and public figures—spokesmen not only for their companies but for entire industries and American capitalism—could be asked, 'Why is it that you belong to a club that doesn't have any blacks?'

"So Bidwell and Hoglund worked to nominate Roy Richie, who is General Counsel at Chrysler and a neighbor and a golfer, and they got him in."

Richie is also a member of the USGA Executive Committee.

"Then Roy Roberts was promoted to Vice President and head of the Pontiac division," Levin continues, "and was proposed for membership. It was done in a highhanded way according to some at the club. Some people at the club didn't presume he should just come sailing in as a member. Normally, there are a series of dinners and social events for member candidates to meet other people and then afterward the people at the club can give an informal yea or nay.

"In the case of Roberts, people didn't feel they knew him well enough, and he hadn't really been introduced to a lot of people there, so when it came to an informal straw poll, the feeling was negative, and that was reflected to the people on the board, who went back to his sponsors, Bill Hoglund and General Motors CFO Mike Losh, and said it probably wouldn't be a good idea to put Roberts up for membership right now because a lot of people didn't know him and therefore weren't inclined to vote for him.

"That caused a lot of misunderstanding and outrage, and there was some feeling that now he was being rejected on the basis of his race. At that point, GM President Jack Smith resigned from the club, Mike Losh resigned from the club, and Bill Hoglund resigned from the club."

"It was a shame because Joe liked Jack Smith," says Judy McCarthy. "It divided and separated what was once a nice friendship."

The rift became apparent at the Paris Auto Show, when Jack Smith refused to be interviewed by McCarthy. Smith's aide, Bruce MacDonald, helped Smith avoid the interview, even though he was only steps away from McCarthy's broadcast site.

"Joe's position was never because of a black or white issue," says Tom King, "because Joe was not prejudiced in any way. Roberts was not well known enough to qualify for membership, and Joe defended the membership."

"Joe knew, being the personality that he was, that it was bound to come back on him," says Wayne County Executive Ed McNamara. "I think it took a helluva lot of courage to make that kind of expression. To be so non-racist . . . I think the racist individual would have never taken that stand for fear of being labeled a racist. J.P. was extremely honest and not politically correct," concedes McNamara.

"J.P. was reasonably courageous insofar as he was willing to risk people mistakenly thinking he was racist in order to make a certain point about clubs and private associations and how they ought to work," says Levin.

Word is that two years before Roberts' application, even GM members panned the idea of nominating him for membership. Still, there was McCarthy's picture in the paper, and his phone ringing off the hook.

"It caused him a lot of sleepless nights," remembers Judy McCarthy. "He was in the worst position as President of the club. They [those suggesting Roberts for membership] hadn't followed the rules and they tried to avoid the membership process. That wasn't fair."

"J.P. was in the middle because everyone knew he was club President and many of the people he had on his show were members," explains Levin, who wrote some columns on the incident, "but while as club President he may have run meetings and done some administrative work, he didn't have the power to let people in the club or keep people out."

"That power belonged to the secret membership committee," says Kernicki.

"Still, it pained J.P. that they were being painted as a bunch of racists," continues Levin, "when in fact it had more to do with the influence of General Motors and the nomination process."

♣

J.P. McCarthy covered golf on the radio from many different golf locations, and right from Studio D. Former McCarthy producer Hal Youngblood remembers one morning when McCarthy came in and inspected the guest list Youngblood had booked for him.

"I'm not interested in any of them," McCarthy snapped petulantly. "I want Arnold Palmer."

"I said, 'Okay,'" remembers Youngblood, "So I called, woke up Palmer, and said, 'Okay, Joe, Arnold Palmer is on the line.'

"He said, 'What? It's 6:40 in the morning! You must have woke him up!'

"'You said to get Arnold Palmer, and I did,' was my retort. So Joe put Palmer on the air and apologized by telling Palmer that his producer must be smoking funny cigarettes."

"Arnold Palmer, the best known of them all, is on the other end of my line right now. The two holes-in-one on the same hole, with the same club two days in a row—Arnold Palmer has done everything there is to do in golf, but you hadn't done that before!"

141

"Thank you, J.P.! It's been a fun week so far. It's certainly a different experience and something I never thought would happen in golf, or that I would have anything to do with!"

♣

Anyone who worked for McCarthy had to understand his intense interest in golf. I left a position with the PGA Tour when J.P. asked me to be his producer. It was a big benefit to understand the sport and have connections in the golf industry.

A few weeks after I left the Tour and began working with J.P., a friend of mine named Art Wahl telephoned me in the studio during the show. Art Wahl was a schoolteacher from Allen Park, and J.P. picked up the phone first, and passed it to me, saying, "Art Wahl is on the line for you."

I took the call, and after I hung up J.P. said, "What did he want?" I couldn't understand J.P.'s question because I knew he didn't even know who Art Wahl was. I looked at him with a puzzled look until I finally realized that he thought I had been talking to *Art Wall, former Masters Champion.*

I paused for a moment, because I thought it was kind of neat to let him think that. "Oh, we worked together on a few projects at the Tour earlier this summer," I fibbed. He seemed impressed, and when I told Art Wahl the story later that day, he howled with laughter, and he agreed to use a different Tour player's name every time he called the studio to talk to me.

Weeks went by, and one afternoon, Art Wahl called me in my office. He sounded nervous.

"I called you in the studio this morning," Wahl said. I told him I hadn't got any message. "I know," he continued, "because J.P. answered the phone, and when he asked to take a message because you weren't there, I told him to tell you that Bob Tway called."

"Yeah? So what," I prodded.

"Well, when I said I was Bob Tway," Wahl explained, "J.P. said 'Bobby, how are you doing? I haven't seen you since we played last year.'"

"I realized he knew Tway and I didn't know what to do at that point," a breathless Wahl explained, "so I panicked and answered him."

"What do you mean, you answered him?" I implored.

"Well, I told him that I was doing fine and he wanted to know how I'd been playing. I had no idea how Tway has been playing but I told him that I had been not playing so well because I was nursing an injury and had some pressing family matters to take care of," Wahl answered.

I asked him how J.P. responded to that.

"He wanted to know all about it and asked me where I was and a few more personal questions," Wahl said, "and by that point I was in so deep I had to bullshit my way through it all."

From that point on, Art Wahl and I always nervously watched the weekly leaderboards and hoped that Bob Tway never won a tournament or showed up at a PAL Tournament, for fear of our little ruse being discovered. Art Wahl also stopped calling me in the studio, and if he did he disguised his voice and called himself the generic name "John Smith."

♣

In May of 1994, J.P. broadcast live from the Cadillac NFL Senior Tour Classic in Upper Montclair, New Jersey. The tournament was unique because NFL players were partnered with Senior Tour golfers, and during the first round of the Pro-Am, J.P. played with New York Giant Lawrence Taylor and Senior Tour player Bob Murphy. The next morning, he hosted his morning show from under a tent just off the driving range.

Remote broadcasts can always be a little nerve-wracking because you don't telephone guests for live interviews, you talk to them face to face. It was pouring rain that day, so many of the scheduled guests didn't come to the driving range location. As producer, I was frantically searching the area for golfers or NFL players to escort over to J.P. for interviews. At last I spotted Washington Redskins kicker Chip Lohmiller, who happened to be leading the tournament after the first round. "A coup!" I thought.

I went over and introduced myself to Lohmiller, and he agreed to come and do the interview. We chitchatted on the way over about the rain and the course conditions and how well he was playing. When we finally got to the tent, he ducked in out of the rain and sat down at the microphone. J.P. was in the middle of reading the last live commercial, so I had gotten Lohmiller there just in time so that J.P. wouldn't be stuck with time to fill without an interview.

With no chance to speak to McCarthy, I circled Chip Lohmiller's name on the roster sheet and put it in front of J.P. He gracefully finished the commercial, glanced down at the circled name, and launched right into his on-air greeting to the first round tournament leader and successful Washington Redskins kicker, reading his credentials and finishing his introduction with a hearty "Congratulations, Chip. How are you doing?"

There was an uncomfortable pause, and then Lohmiller said, "I'm Jim Arnold."

I had the wrong guy!

McCarthy's jaw dropped, and my stomach flipped as I realized that I had mistaken our own hometown Detroit Lion punter Jim Arnold for Chip Lohmiller. I was mortified. Aside from feeling sorry and embarrassed for Arnold, I had strung J.P. out so far on a limb, that after he did the best he could to save face and save the interview, I went over to him and offered my resignation. Thankfully, he would have no part of it. He must have understood the depth of my embarrassment, and he let me off the hook with very little discussion.

As it rained harder and harder, the whole broadcast site turned into a mud pit, and another case of mistaken information hit. As Cleveland Brown and University of Michigan alumnus Leroy Hoard came over for an interview, McCarthy scanned the press information provided about Leroy Hoard. Someone in the tournament public relations department had mistakenly typed Bengals instead of Browns next to Hoard's name, and McCarthy's first question was, "I didn't realize until this morning that you had been traded from the Browns to the Bengals. How do you feel about that?"

Hoard nearly fell out of his chair, figuring the Browns had just not yet reached him to break the news! After all, it was early in the morning and he was probably hard to reach at the golf course. To the relief of everyone, a tournament official stepped in and claimed responsibility for the misprint.

♣

J.P.'s coverage of golf on the radio was sometimes criticized by those who didn't understand the game or the high interest level in Michigan, as *Free Press* columnist Bob Talbert remembers:

"The Senior PGA Tour was in town for the Senior U.S. Open at Oakland Hills. There was enormous golf coverage going on and lots of national attention, and everyone was doing some kind of golf coverage. Well, *Detroit News* columnist Nicki McWhirter wrote a column bashing J.P. and the golf coverage.

"So I called J.P. about something else I wanted to talk about and when he answered the phone I thought we were off the air. He asked, 'Bob, what do you think of Nicki McWhirter's column today knocking all of the sports guys, particularly golfers?'

"I said, 'J.P., Nicki just needs to get laid.'

"He says, 'Bob, we're on the air! We're live!'

"I said, 'Not for very long. I've got to call someone and apologize!'

"I called Nicki immediately and apologized, but she was pretty pissed and never forgave me. J.P. thought it was a hoot!"

♣

J.P. got a surprise of his own while broadcasting live from the Ford Senior Players Championship at the Tournament Players Club of Michigan. Senior Tour player Larry Ziegler came into the WJR mobile studio RV parked next to the first tee for an interview with his old pal, J.P. Ziegler pulled a marking pen out of his pocket and asked J.P. for his autograph on a tournament program book. J.P. at first seemed embarassed, but then agreed to sign the book for Ziegler. When he pulled the cap of the pen off, a little explosive "bang" went off and nearly scared McCarthy through the roof. Ziegler had given him a trick firecracker pen, and when the interview began, McCarthy had still not caught his breath.

J.P. could return the favor to some of his Senior Tour buddies, according to Barry McGuire. "I was with Joe and J.C. Snead and he egged Snead on until Snead said, 'J.P., those are the worst goddamned greens I've ever played on. We've got better greens on the Carolina cowpatches than that!' J.P. knew some players Snead didn't like, so he'd mention them and get him all fired up."

"The Senior Tour players still tell me how much they miss him," says Judy McCarthy. "I go to tournaments and they always approach me and take a minute to remember him."

♣

The spirit of J.P. McCarthy and the spirit of golf live on at Bloomfield Hills Country Club during every J.P. McCarthy Memorial PAL Tournament, and at the Boyne Monument Golf course in Boyne Falls, Michigan, where you'll find the "McCarthy Hole"—the par 3 ninth hole selected by the McCarthy family and dedicated by his old friend, Boyne COO Art Tebo, to J.P. with a giant boulder naming McCarthy Michigan's true Ambassador of Golf:

> *J.P. McCarthy was our true ambassador of Michigan. For over 30 years, J.P. promoted Michigan travel, tourism, and the sport he loved on WJR radio in Detroit. A low handicap golfer himself, J.P. supported the golf industry with informative and entertaining interviews with golfing greats and duffers alike. He continually promoted golf events, examined equipment, and played golf courses around the world. J.P. dedicated personal and professional time to the benefit of others through golf fundraisers, such as his tournament for the Police Athletic League of Detroit. His passion for the game was recognized by the golf world and evidenced by the joy golf brought to him and so many others.*

Even through his fatal illness, McCarthy played on in humor, albeit grim, besting his son Jamie in what would be their final match. After the rare victory over his talented son, J.P. told him, "You may never beat me again."

♣ Radio's Box Seats

J.P. McCarthy may have been the only morning radio host in the country to broadcast his own sports report every morning. Instead of tossing to some deep-voiced, macho, sneaker-wearing statistics geek, J.P. would scan the sports pages and run down the important items himself. Out of town NBA scores? Well, maybe. Second-round results of the Bay Hill Classic? Definitely. Fight stuff? Absolutely. Tiger game details? Without fail. Little League World Series? Why not? NASCAR results? Hmmm, if there's time.

In fact, J.P.'s sportscasts were a living entity. In most cases, he covered the big stories not by reading a report, but rather by having a conversation with someone involved. From Bo Schembechler to Bo Jackson, Bill Laimbeer to Billy Martin to Bill Ford, from Wayne Fontes to D. Wayne Lucas, he had the players from on the field and off on the other end of his line.

J.P. may have been criticized for doing too much sports on his show, but it was definitely the personalities he talked to that attracted him and made the sports stories come to life!

"Joe Namath, how is your relationship with Howard Cosell after working with him in the 'Monday Night Football' broadcast booth?"

"We don't get along at all right now, J.P. I do respect him for his professional talents, though, but that's about it."

"He took a lot of shots at a lot of people when he left the booth."

"Yeah, you know, a lot of people that helped him along the years, too. People that were friends and bailed him out in a lot of ways over the years. He turned around and treated them rather poorly in his book, and I can't appreciate someone like that."

"Have you spoken to him recently?"

"Oh yeah, I saw him around a year ago and I was about to give him a good smack. We were having dinner with Mr. and Mrs. Werbling, actually. He started talking about some people in a very derogatory way—the coach of the New York Jets, for an example. He kept referring to him as a 'moronic idiot.'

"After about the third time I said, 'Excuse me, Howard. If Joe Walton were sitting here would you say that to his face?'

"He said, 'Yeah, I'd say it to his face.'

"I said, 'No you wouldn't. You're a coward that way! You wouldn't do that.'

"Howard said, 'Well, if I called you that, what would you do? Would you slap me?'

"I said, 'No, sir.' What I said, though, I wouldn't say on the air here. Unfortunately, I didn't behave like a gentleman at the time. We don't get along."

"What did you do? Did you grab him?"

"No, I didn't grab him. I'm not physical. I just told him I'd spit in his face, is the first thing I would do, and let him make the move."

"Well, it's clear how you feel about Howard Cosell."

"The feeling is probably mutual."

"J.P. Morgan had been interviewed by J.P. near the time she was dating Joe Namath," says producer Hal Youngblood:

" 'Are you still dating Joe Namath?'

" 'No, J.P., I called it off.'

" 'Well, Joe tells us that he called it quits?'

" 'Are you kidding?' she asked. 'Why would I want to date a man with weak knees and a quick release?' "

♣

"Joe was a bigger star in the sports world than he realized," says Hoot McInerney. "We'd run into Howard Cosell and he'd say, 'J.P. McCarthy, why did you ever stay in that small town? You belong in the big city!' "

While sportscaster Dave Diles and Frank Beckmann both had short turns as McCarthy's sportscaster, McCarthy's knowledge and interest in sports, along with his access to the players and coaches, made it impossible for him to let anyone else handle the sports duties on his show.

"At first, Joe loved the idea of having Dave Diles do his sports," says Hal Youngblood, who was producer during the time that the Diles experiment occurred in the early '70s, "but in the long run the chemistry wasn't there. Diles was a moody guy who was becoming disenchanted with the world of sports, calling it the 'toy department.' I just think the fact that he had only this short shot with Joe in the morning didn't really befit him," Youngblood theorizes.

"After a few months, station manager Bill James came to me and said, 'You know, this thing in the morning is not working out. It's pretty much run its course,' " Dave Diles recounts. " 'In other words, I am fired?' I asked."

" 'Well, I don't like to use those terms,' James answered, 'It's been a nice little run, and we've enjoyed having you here, and

149

that's it.' Rumors began to circulate that there wasn't enough room in the studio between J.P. and me when it came to sports," says Diles, "but J.P. called me and we had a nice talk about it all, and we had a relationship the rest of his life without any problem."

Dave Diles with J.P. McCarthy, "Focus" 1993

"Do you miss the sports scene or did you outgrow it?"

"I don't think I ever 'outgrew it.' I was never a 'figure-Filbert.' I couldn't tell you who played second base for the St. Louis Browns in 1923 because I could look that up in a book. I was never a devotee. I stopped getting up in the morning and wondering what game I could watch some people play that day. I miss the people, I miss the fans, I miss whoever might have liked me, and I miss the town. The athletes and the front offices I really don't miss that much. I don't miss interviewing athletes. There are very few of them that I'd want to interview today."

"Why is that? Because, frankly, you made your career, you made your reputation—both good, by the way—by dealing with sports. And without athletes, you have no sports. Why do they no longer interest you? Or did they ever?"

"They interested me, but I think that over the years the whole thing has changed. They're not as much fun. I think early on, general managers, and presidents of clubs, when they ceased to be sports people, when they became lumbermen and other business people, the 'play' was no longer the thing, it was the bottom line. Then the advent of agents and managers became an unwitting conspiracy to take the fun out of sports. When it quit being fun, I quit doing it."

♣

In the '70s, when McCarthy's popularity and influence as a morning talk show host and sportscaster began to grow, the local professional and college coaches and players listened to his show and were always in touch with him to do telephone interviews about the game the night before or the game coming up. "Instead of playing the music he was supposed to play, he'd get his sports buddies on the phone," Youngblood groans.

In later years, J.P. would start an industry trend by ensuring the coaches would call by having WJR pay them to check in.

Former Detroit Lions head football coach Rick Forzano laughs when he remembers receiving a box of WJR pens at the end of the season as payment!

"Today, these coaches are paid fifty or sixty thousand bucks to do interviews on Monday mornings," exclaims NFL Hall of Fame linebacker and onetime Lions coach Joe Schmidt. "When I was coaching and did interviews with J.P., WJR sent me a big glow-in-the-dark scuba diving watch at the end of the year as payment," Schmidt laughs. "I told Joe, 'I never get near the water, but I'll take it!'"

Although paid guests could earn a nice check for their interviews, most sports figures were always available for J.P., even if the payoff was a diving watch or a box of WJR pens. "He had a unique ability to ask questions without making you upset. Some reporters can ask you questions and antagonize you," says Schmidt, who does remember being antagonized by McCarthy when he was a player, though:

"We had played the 49ers," Schmidt explains, "and the 49ers introduced the shotgun offense to us that day. We'd never seen a shotgun offense before, and we got beat 49-0.

"The next morning, I'm driving to the stadium and listening to the radio, and I hear this guy named McCarthy say, 'If you're expecting Joe Schmidt for any reason, Joe Schmidt is probably going to be a little late today, because they are still trying to exhume him from the turf at Candlestick Park.'

"That aggravated me, and I didn't know the guy at the time. I had a job in the Fisher building working for a rubber company, because in those days we didn't make enough money in the NFL, so you had to have a second occupation. I get in the elevator, and I hear someone mention J.P. I swing around and see this guy in the corner, and he spots me, and he evidently knew who I was, and now I knew who he was.

" 'So you're J.P.!' I growled. We both laughed, but I thought about choking him."

♣

J.P. grew up playing baseball, but he never played football. "He wanted to play football, but his dad didn't want him to," explains J.P.'s mother, Martha McCarthy. "He was afraid he'd get hurt, so Joe became the student manager, and was always telling everybody what to do," she laughs.

Once Schmidt was coach of the Lions, he tutored McCarthy on the finer points of the game so that J.P. could serve as TV color analyst during the games. "We sat down and went over offensive and defensive formations and terminology, and I'd tell him what to watch for," Schmidt explains. "We drank quite a bit of red wine on the road after bed check. It was always very interesting with Joe because he always had so much to contribute to the conversation on so many subjects. We'd laugh and giggle."

"I was on some of those road trips," says Dr. Bob Nestor, who was the Lions' doctor. "When he'd had too much fun, I'd have to see J.P. in the morning and give him throat lozenges so he could do the TV broadcast!" Nestor laughs.

McCarthy had a similar relationship with Lions coach Rick Forzano, whom he rode to the airport with for travel to and from road games, and he knew coaches Monte Clark and Wayne Fontes socially.

"We'd see Wayne Fontes at Norman's Eton Street Station or the Fox and Hound restaurant," says Tom King. "Joe would subtly get his point across by asking him the right questions about the team's problems."

McCarthy kept Lions season tickets and remained a big fan, eschewing the luxury suite to sit with the crowd in his seats. "WJR had a suite at the Silverdome," says King, who accompanied McCarthy and his kids to many games, "but he'd rarely go there. He'd stay right down in his seats on the 40-yard line, where he would cheer and holler like a true fan."

Sometimes the game came to him. "Charlie Sanders once came over to our house," Jamie McCarthy remembers. "He had on a pair of pants that had holes in them. They were like white denim pants with holes the size of quarters all though them!"

Jamie McCarthy remembers another peculiar event, when Mr. Hockey—Gordie Howe—came to the McCarthy home. "He grabbed me and picked me up, but I threw up on him," Jamie groans. "It's embarrassing for me."

McCarthy watched Red Wing hockey games with equal intensity at Olympia Arena or his season tickets at Joe Louis Arena. "He knew the game and what players were performing and whether or not the back-checking was effective and such," says King.

In fact, J.P. and a small group of investors nearly purchased the Red Wings before Mike Ilitch eventually acquired the NHL franchise.

Gordie Howe with J.P., 1989

"You know, there was a time—and this is hard to believe— when Gordie Howe, the greatest player to ever play the game and certainly the greatest player to ever wear a Red Wing uniform, was not really welcome on the Red Wing ice at Olympia and when they first moved to Joe Louis Arena. Isn't that hard to believe?"

"I don't know if it was jealousy or they didn't want to remind folks that we had a love affair going here between player and fans, but I can understand when Mike Ilitch took over. I can understand his thinking. He wanted to divorce himself from the past."

"Well, the Red Wings had left such a bad taste in everyone's mouth during the 'Dead Wings' period, but why get upset with Gordie Howe? That never made any sense!"

"Well, they made it very easy for the Howes to leave here."

"Do you remember your famous line about what you were doing for the Red Wings?"

"I sure do . . . the 'Mushroom Treatment.'"

"The mushroom treatment."

"Basically, the mushroom treatment was that they keep you in the dark and every now and then open up the door and throw fertilizer on you."

Jamie remembers his father taking him to Tiger Stadium too, where he also had season tickets for baseball games. "He always had me bring my glove to protect myself from foul balls in those seats." Longtime Tiger announcer Paul Carey served as godfather to McCarthy's second son, Kevin.

In fact, Tiger manager Billy Martin was the first "Morning Show" guest to be paid cash to appear with J.P. each morning after a game. "We were at the Lindell AC with Billy Martin and Norm Cash on many occasions," says McCarthy pal Barry McGuire. "Cash would make a big show of throwing the *Free Press* on the floor and saying, 'Why would anybody read this rag?' He'd use lots of language you won't hear in churches, but Joe knew how to handle Billy Martin," McGuire explains. "He knew how to praise him and build up his ego, which had to be built up constantly. Joe knew how to do that so he'd get the best information out of him. Martin liked Joe."

♣

Some years after Billy Martin's tenure as Tiger manager, McCarthy sat down with one of Martin's closest friends, and his former teammate, Mickey Mantle.

Mickey Mantle, 1985

"Mickey Mantle retired from baseball in 1969—actually '68 was his last season. His final game was an emotional catharsis for a packed Yankee Stadium who came to honor the player who had five hundred thirty-six lifetime home runs, three Most Valuable Player awards, winner of the Triple Crown—one of only four players in the history of the game to do that. He was

the very symbol of America's national pastime from almost the moment he joined the Yankees until his last game. He is, in fact, the Babe Ruth of our time. What a pleasure it is to see, in the flesh and looking wonderful—welcome back to baseball and welcome back to Detroit—Mickey Mantle."

"Thanks a lot, J.P. Both of those things is very nice. I haven't been back to Detroit for a long time. I used to love to play here. People are always asking what ball park did you like to play in the best, and I think Tiger Stadium would have been as good a ballpark for me as any."

"You'd have hit nine hundred home runs if you played here."

"Well, I'd have hit more than I did in Yankee Stadium. The left-center and right-center was my power alleys, and in Detroit they're not that far. I hit four balls over the roof here, and Norm cash hit four, too."

"Yeah, but he played here all the time!"

"That's what I told him. He was always telling me, 'I hit as many balls over that roof as you did.'"

"I want to ask you about an incident that I witnessed. I happened to be in the broadcast booth. The year was 1968. It was September, the Tigers had the pennant all wrapped up. Denny McClain was on the mound. He'd already won his thirtieth game; he was pitching. It was late in the game. The Tigers had the game won, it looked like."

"Six to nothing."

"Yeah. Everybody knew it was your last appearance probably ever at Tiger Stadium, so there was a good crowd on hand to say so long the 'The Mick.' McClain called Freehan out for a little discussion, and that seemed very unusual because there wasn't anything going on that called for a discussion. Then Freehan went back, and McClain tossed you a ball and I think you fouled it off.

Then I think he tossed the next one and you knocked it out of the ballpark, and as you went around, I recall, you tipped your hat to McClain. Do I recall that correctly?"

"Well, he winked at me. When I come around third base, I looked. Well, actually, he came up to Freehan. He walked almost all the way to home plate and called him out. I could hear what he was saying. He said, 'Let's let him hit one. This is his last game.' But you know McClain—you don't know if he's really going to let you hit one or hit you in the back. So anyway, the first pitch I took, and he gestured at me like 'What's the matter?'"

"Was it a fat one?"

"Yeah! Right down the middle, and I looked at Freehan and he says, 'Yeah, he wants you to hit one!' Then I fouled one off, and the next one I hit into the upper deck. And like you said, as I was rounding third I looked out at him and he gave me a big wink and a grin and I tipped my hat to him. A lot of people think that was my last home run. That was my five hundred and thirty-fifth home run. When we went on back to New York and finished out the year I had another one, so that wasn't my last one."

"It was the last one at Tiger Stadium."

"That was the last one here and it broke Jimmy Foxx's home run record. I was glad I hit another one, because, I don't know if you remember or not, but there was a lot of controversy and the writers got mad, saying that 'he let Mickey break Jimmy Foxx's home run record' or something like that—instead of just saying that it was a nice gesture on his part, or something."

"It was a nice gesture."

"Oh, it was! I would have probably hit one off of him anyway."

"You could now. He's playing for a prison team and getting hit pretty hard."

"That's a shame."

"Oh, it is a tragedy. We talked to Denny from jail, and talked about his sad plight now, and we also talked about that game and that day, and that was the first time he'd ever admitted that, yeah, he did throw you one because he wanted you to hit one out. You have lots of memories of Tiger Stadium—not all of them pleasant. Tiger fans have never been crazy about the New York Yankees. The reason that a lot of people around this town and a lot of other American League cities grew up resenting those guys in pinstripes is because they won the pennant every year. How many pennant races were you involved in—where the Yankees either won it or were close?"

"The first fifteen years I was with the Yankees we won it thirteen times."

"That's incredible. . . . Billy Martin in his stay here as manager made a lot of friends. He won a Division Championship for the Tigers with a team that was getting a little old. He did a lot of great things and he did some things that probably cost him his job, as he always has. But he never forgot Mickey Mantle, and he never forgot that Mickey Mantle was and maybe is his best friend."

"Actually they called us the Dead End Kids or something. Cartoons of us were like Casey Stengel was a judge and we were all standing in front of him with our hands behind us and I had a BB gun and Billy had a beanie flipper and Whitey Ford had a rock in his hand, and the three of us were more notorious for getting into trouble and everything. Bill and I got all the publicity, but Whitey was just as much of a character. He could drink more than me and Billy both, probably."

"I don't know how you guys won so many pennants, because it sounds like you were stiff all the time."

"We had a lot of good times. Maybe that's the reason we played so good. But I want to tell you, J.P., we never went to the ballpark loaded. When that game started, there wasn't anybody that tried harder than us three."

"You know, salaries in baseball today are really out of whack, particularly with your times. You were the best baseball player of your time—no question about that. What was the most money you ever made in a single year?"

"One of the best. I was no better than Kaline. Kaline was stuck in Detroit. If he had played in New York—I mean, we had more magazine editors and writers and sports columnists following us than we had players."

"That's high praise for Kaline from Mickey Mantle, but that's a moot point. Anyway, people remember Mickey Mantle in every corner of this globe. What was the most money you ever made in a single season?"

"I made one hundred thousand a year. That wasn't bad then. In fact, I always felt like I was overpaid. Whitey and Yogi and guys that were doing just as good as me weren't even making half of what I was getting paid. I didn't realize that the owners made as much as they did until they had to open their books. I always felt sorry for them. They'd call you up there and almost make you cry!"

"No telling what Mickey Mantle would have made with 1985 salaries. Maybe three million, maybe four million—who knows? Only George Steinbrenner and Lee Iacocca maybe. More Billy Martin stuff. Tell me something about Billy Martin that maybe would surprise us."

"I think probably how big a heart he's got. I think people don't realize that he can cry at the drop of a hat. I mean, he knows every one of my kids' birthdays. He knows my birthday. He knows my wife's birthday. I would like to tell you a funny story that happened a few years ago.

Billy was visiting me in Dallas for Christmas. Me and Billy had been out all night. Went 'fishing' or something."

"Heh heh."

"We come home about eight o'clock in the morning and was having a beer. My wife gets up and she comes out into the den where we're sitting in my house and me and Bill are sitting there having a beer and I hear her coming and I said, 'Uh-oh.' She opens the door, and we're just sitting in there sipping on a beer and she says, 'My God, are you two at it already?!' Billy looked up at her and said, 'It's a jungle out there!' He was funny!"

"You were friends with another great Detroit athlete, still revered to this day, Bobby Layne. Tell us a Bobby Layne story."

"Golly, there's a lot of them. One of the only games I ever got kicked out of was here in Tiger Stadium. Bobby Layne took me to the Flame Bar. We went out to eat. I don't know if you've ever been to the Flame Bar or not, but it's not a good place, no, I'm not going to say it's not a good place to go . . . but I was scared! Put it that way. Anyway, we stayed out quite late that night, and I had a terrible hangover the next day. And the first time up, I don't know who was pitching for Detroit, but I barely saw the ball. It went right by. Before the next pitch I said to myself, 'I've got no business in this game.' So the next pitch I yelled at the umpire. You know I hardly ever yelled at the umpires."

"Never!"

"The catcher looks at me like, 'Hey, Mick! That was right down the middle!' I said, 'No it wasn't,' and I could see that I'd have to say something worse. So I called the umpire something. He said, 'If you're trying to get out of this game, you're gone!'"

"And you were!?"

"And he kicked me out of the game! Bobby Layne's sitting in the club box when I come back to the dugout and says, 'Nice going. I'll see you in a few minutes!' I said, 'No, no. That's enough!'

"The great Mickey Mantle—'the Mick,' 'Number Seven.' His autobiography is available, and it is chock-full of Mantle memorabilia. Thanks so much for being with us."

♣

159

A Tiger manager who had a warm rapport with McCarthy was also the highest paid sports guest in the history of the show, reportedly earning $65,000 per season to talk on the phone with J.P. the morning after games. "A lot of times I hadn't woken up yet," Sparky Anderson admits, "and although he knew it by my voice, he never once said, 'You just woke up!' No, he would carry it quick—bang, bang, and that would be it. Sometimes when I went to bed I dreaded the fact that, 'Oh, my lord, tomorrow I have to talk,' especially after losing seven or eight in a row, but J.P. always went to the plus side. I don't even know if Joe knew he was looking after me, but he did."

The daily interviews reportedly made Tiger General Manager Jim Campbell nervous. "I think it scared Mr. Campbell every time I opened my mouth," Anderson allows. "He used to say he was afraid to get up in the morning and listen to me on the radio. He'd get chills worrying about it."

"Sparky sounded like he was half asleep many times," recalls Hall of Fame Tiger announcer Ernie Harwell. "On the road, I would walk with Sparky after he was on with J.P., and we'd discuss what he talked about or didn't talk about. J.P. got about as much out of Sparky as anybody did, and Sparky sort of 'runs around the barn,' you know, and doesn't say anything."

"He was the best interviewer I was ever interviewed by in my whole career," says Sparky Anderson, who sometimes affectionately called J.P. "Giuseppe." "I called him that, and that, to me, meant he was my friend. I worked with him for seventeen years, and he was my friend and I knew that. I could tell him anything off the air and trust him with it," says Anderson.

Harwell remembers McCarthy's trips to Tiger spring training. "He would come to Lakeland and set up his show at either the Holiday Inn or the ballpark and stay for about a week, and I remember going on his Opening Day 'Focus' show from home plate at Tiger Stadium just before the game," says Harwell. "The governor and mayor would be there, along with Sonny Elliott and all the reporters."

Anderson remembers being on that special Opening Day show too, in the middle of the media crunch on the field.

J. P. McCarthy   WJR Studio   9-5-58

"The Kid." A 27-year-old Joe McCarthy selects 45s years before he would Frisbee them at producers.

Not even public outcry could stop McCarthy—
a "touchable Sinatra"—from crooning.

Two world renowned singers . . . Julio Iglesias and J.P.!

Ha-cha-cha! A 1966 visit with Jimmy Durante.

Network radio star Arthur Godfrey during a 1969 visit to J.P.'s show. Years later, both men would enter the Radio Hall of Fame.

J.P., lights, camera, action! On the set of another of his televi-sion endeavors.

J.P., 1966, working on the game he played his entire life and became an ambassador of.

McCarthy partnered with his favorite golfer and Florida neighbor, Greg Norman, at Roger Penske's charity golf invitational.

J.P. laughs with Chi Chi Rodriguez as they co-host a golf clinic at TPC Michigan. Golfer Agim Bardha looks on.

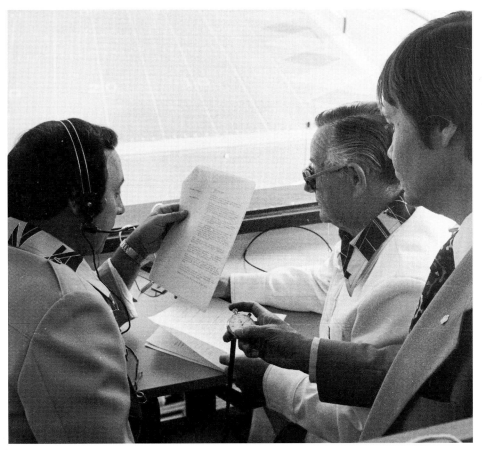

McCarthy showing his versatility in the broadcast booth, serving as color man for the Detroit Lions.

Michigan Attorney General Frank Kelley, J.P., and Jack Mulcahy at the very first St. Patrick's Day party in the WJR lobby.

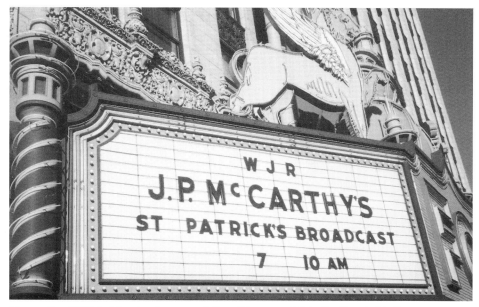

From the WJR lobby to the grand Fox Theatre. J.P.'s St. Patrick's Day party grew to become an annual spectacle.

Oakland County Executive L. Brooks Patterson shares an Irish joke with Michael Shiels and J.P. at McCarthy's St. Patrick's Day party.

Mayor Coleman Young presents J.P. with the Key to the City during McCarthy's final "Focus" show in June of 1994.

McCarthy, at Oakland Hills, celebrating with the bride
. . . his daughter Kathleen.

"Muscle Beach?" J.P., John Schaefer, Trip Bosart, and Dr. John Murphy.

President Jimmy Carter enjoyed this foreign policy discussion with J.P. and returned to the show many times.

"Governor McCarthy" hosted his morning show from Jim Blanchard's desk with the aid of producer Hal Youngblood, and held a cabinent meeting later that day.

McCarthy discussed the auto industry with publishing magnate Keith Crain at auto shows all over the world. This 1994 interview took place at the Paris Automobile Exposition.

McCarthy's long-running involvement in the Buick Open began in 1964. J.P. played in the Pro-Ams and broadcast his show from Warwick Hills Golf Club.

J.P. with partner Brad Faxon at the Buick Open Skins Game . . . they won all nine skins!

President Gerald Ford and his golf partner in the 1978 PAL Tournament at Wabeek Country Club. Large galleries gathered for the event.

J.P. and Judy McCarthy enjoy one of their exotic vacations in a faraway land.

Martha McCarthy beams at her only son, who was no "average Joe."

STATE OF MICHIGAN

Executive Office

John Engler Governor

Certificate of Special Tribute

Governor John Engler Hereby issues
this Special Tribute to honor

J.P. McCARTHY

LET IT BE KNOWN, that Joseph Priestly "J.P." McCarthy is to be recognized for three decades of outstanding service to radio station WJR in Detroit.

WHEREAS, born in New York, but raised in Detroit, J.P. graduated from De La Salle Collegiate High School and studied at the University of Detroit before entering the Army in 1953. There, stationed in Alaska, he discovered his true calling after joining a drama group for Armed Forces Radio. After graduating from the Armed Forces Radio and Television School in Anchorage, he finished his military duty as staff announcer; and

WHEREAS, following stints at station KFAR in Fairbanks, Alaska and WTAC in Flint, J.P. signed on with WJR in 1956 as staff announcer. Seven years later, he went west to station KGO in San Francisco, where he quickly became a popular broadcast personality. Perhaps regretting their profound loss--or realizing his enormous talent--WJR officials enticed J.P. back to Detroit on December 7, 1964; and

WHEREAS, since his return to the airwaves at WJR thirty years ago, J.P. has been, quite simply, the radio voice of Detroit. His warm wit, versatile intellect and easygoing nature, along with his smooth voice, perfect delivery and remarkable staying power, have made him into a local, not to mention a national, radio legend. His morning show has won every ratings battle it has fought over three decades, giving J.P. distinction as the only radio personality in the United States to have been on top of his market for so long; and

WHEREAS, J.P.'s immensely successful career has earned him many industry honors, among them four "National Radio Personality of the Year" awards from Billboard Magazine and six Marconi Award nominations. In 1992, he was inducted into the Radio Hall of Fame; and

WHEREAS, despite the fame and fortune that has found him, J.P. remains a dedicated community servant, giving much of his time and effort to assist local charitable organizations. For the last 17 years, he has chaired a golf tournament to benefit the Detroit Police Athletic League, raising over $1 million to benefit the youth of Detroit. The March of Dimes has named him "Humanitarian of the Year" for his good work, and each year, he shares his personality as host and master of ceremonies for numerous charitable events;

NOW, THEREFORE, I, John Engler, Governor of the State of Michigan, do hereby sign this Special Tribute to honor J.P. McCARTHY on 30 years at WJR and I encourage all citizens to join with me in recognizing this fine man for his many contributions to radio and to benevolent causes in our state.

Given under my hand on this fifth day of December in the year of our Lord one thousand nine hundred and ninety-four and of the Commonwealth one hundred and fifty-eight.

Governor

Certificate of Special Tribute to J.P. McCarthy.

"When they said J.P. wanted me, I went," Sparky insists. "He was the one person that I would never delay, because I knew, over the years, what he had done for me. When his runner told me J.P. would like to have me, I left what I was doing. He's got me."

"J.P. was a good ambassador for baseball," says Harwell, "and the Tiger organization recognized that. I always got a kick out of the way he'd call out of the clear blue to try to answer a listener question like, 'What does the word *fungo* mean?' or 'Why do they call it the *bullpen*?'"

♣

Harwell, a legendary and nationally renowned baseball voice, had broadcast Tiger baseball on WJR for thirty years before stepping to the podium at a press conference in December of 1990 to announce:

> *"The radio station WJR, and the Tiger Baseball Club, have decided that 1991 will be the last year that I will broadcast play-by-play for the Tigers. I've signed a contract for '91. I wanted to go farther. I wanted to work more years, but the station and the ballclub combined told me that they didn't want me to broadcast Tiger baseball after 1991, and that they were going in a new direction."*

Tom King remembers meeting with J.P. and WJR General Manager Jim Long the night before the press conference. "Jim Long called Joe down to the bar in the basement of the Fisher Building to tell us that he'd fired Ernie Harwell and that the story would break the next morning," says King. "Jim Long was concerned about whether he had made the right decision. He needed solace and counsel, and I don't think Jim Long was sure that was the right thing to do, but he felt he should do it."

The stunning decision to end Harwell's Tiger career touched off an explosion of media coverage and public outcry that lit up WJR's listener lines nonstop for days. When asked what kind of reaction the team and club expected after the announcement, the Tiger's own Vice President of Marketing Jeff Odenwald answered the media: "I would imagine it will be negative, certainly."

"Joe was protective of people he cared about," says Judy McCarthy, "and I know he felt Ernie did not get the right deal. He was concerned about it because he had a tremendous amount of respect for Ernie and knew that Ernie was an institution at the station."

"Joe was concerned, but he would never interfere with a decision that had been made," says King. "He was concerned about reaction. Concerned about the station. Joe thought about the station like a businessman," King insists. "Was the timing right? Was it the thing to do? He was worried about it." Tiger General Manager Bo Schembechler, on the other hand, took a very hard line position on the issue which many perceived as insensitive.

Newspaper stories and varied accounts of the decision making process swirled though the national media. Reports began to focus on the question of who had insisted that Harwell be fired. Was it WJR? Was it the Tigers? Was it then Tiger General Manager Bo Schembechler? Whose idea was it? Is it true what we're hearing about Harwell's health and poor eyesight?

In an ultimate and definitive McCarthy version of damage control, he finally quieted the issue by assembling all parties involved on his morning show. The interview was a compelling high-wire act that included Ernie Harwell and Jim Long. Long, who had initially avoided all media inquiries and attention, had taken to claiming that he promoted the firing of Harwell, prompting the *Detroit News* to run a Sunday banner headline reading, "I Fired Ernie Harwell," with a photo of Long. Many in the media speculated that Long was taking the bullet by naming himself the fall guy because of WJR's business arrangement with the Detroit Tigers and the value of carrying the Tigers on the station.

"That interview was a supreme test, I thought, for J.P.," says Harwell, "because he did represent the company."

"Joe just tried to quell the charging bull," King explains, "not to defend, but to understand and quiet."

The interview went as follows:

"Joe, I just don't like for these rumors to be flying around and all the innuendoes about my eyesight. My health is good, and the rumors about my decreasing ability on the air—when I talked to Jim Long and Bo, and Jeff Odenwald at the Tigers, I asked point blank if there had been any dissatisfaction, or negative reaction to my broadcasts, and all of them said, 'No.' When you begin to lose it, people let you know. My mail never reflected it. I think last year was one of my best seasons ever. I know that's a matter of opinion, but I don't understand who started these rumors at WJR. Now could you tell me the answer to that?"

"Well, this is a rumor-filled business. I guess, Ernie, I've got to tell you the truth, that when a guy gets to be 72 or 71, there will be rumors that he ain't as good as he was when he was 60 or 50—but who is?"

"Well, Ronald Reagan and George Burns kept going!"

"And still are. . . . Your plan is to go to Lakeland, go into spring training and . . ."

"Right, I want to give WJR and the Tigers the very best year I can give, because I think we've had a great association, and I don't want it to end on a sour note. I haven't bashed anybody. I've told everybody all along that I have no ill will toward anybody at the Tigers or WJR."

"Do you think at this point it might be possible for you to negotiate another year or two?"

"Well, I think it's something to be considered. I just want to get this all past me and over with."

"Well, Ernie, thank you for coming on with us this morning. My best to you, as always, and to Lulu, too."

"Thank you, Joe."

J.P. McCarthy

"It is the eighth of January, my first day back on the air after the New Year, and I'm glad to be among the gainfully employed, although, hey, that could end at any time, I must tell you! The Ernie Harwell business has been with us for three weeks, since Ernie Harwell held that fateful press conference down at Tiger Stadium. The chain reaction in this town has pushed all of the news off of the front pages.

The sequence of events, as I know them, are as follows: Ernie made that announcement on the 19th of December. Both Jim Long, the president of our station, and Bo Schembechler, the president of the Tigers, said it was a jointly agreed upon decision. That was what I thought had happened, until I read the newspaper this weekend, in which Jim Long admitted that it was his idea. He did it.

I'm talking to my boss now, so you must understand that. I'm going to try to make this as objective an interview as I possibly can, because it's high time we cleared the air on this very painful issue for all of us. The General Manager of WJR Radio, Jim Long, is on the other end of my line right now. Good morning, Jim."

"Good morning, Joe."

"Well, how are you?"

"Well, not too well. I'm a little confused."

"Will you help us clear the air? Tell us the sequence of events?"

"When I heard that Ernie wanted to come in and talk to both Bo and myself about his future, I got together with Bo and we laid out the options. Ernie had just completed a five-year contract, but in my professional judgment, I felt that his broadcast abilities had deteriorated a little bit. I suggested that we call it quits now and look to the future. I suggested that to Bo, and he did not see it that way. He thought it would be proper to offer Ernie one more year to give him a chance to go out in style and class, which he deserved. At that moment, we agreed to offer Ernie one more year—not a multi-year contract—and give him a chance to announce it and go out in style. We all signed the contract."

164

"I saw you the night before Ernie's press conference, when you wondered what Ernie would say in his announcement. Ernie held the press conference, and the explosion began!"

"Maybe it was naive to question why Ernie was holding a press conference, but I knew the contract had been signed. I also knew of his disappointment. I was naive enough to wonder why he was holding a press conference, and figured it was to announce that he had signed a one-year contract and that it would be his last year and that he'd had a lot of fun."

"Yes, it was naive of you to think that."

"Absolutely."

"You've been criticized, God knows, roundly—maybe even crucified—over not saying anything and keeping absolutely quiet, avoiding everyone up until now."

"That is correct."

"You know that I urged you to talk to the press."

"Absolutely."

"I begged you to."

"Absolutely."

"Why didn't you?"

"Whatever I would have to say would be revealing something that happened in a private conversation. I think it's privileged information. I don't even discuss it with my family. I finally came forward because I felt guilty that Bo was taking all of the public abuse."

"Have you had any conversation with Bo or anyone in the Tiger organization, since Ernie's announcement, about reversing your decision?"

"It was discussed. No one expected what happened to happen, but I still feel we made the right decision of a one-year contract."

"Is it a possibility that you could go back and renegotiate something else?"

"That would take two of us. The Tigers and WJR."

"And there's been no indication that the Tigers are interested in that?"

"None that I know of, but I'm available."

"I know how much in pain you are, and I know how you've been beaten up psychologically over the past few weeks. I know also that you would like to reverse that decision you made so many weeks ago. Thanks for talking, I wish you well."

♣

"He was very, very fair," Harwell remembers. "I realize that people in business make decisions, and they don't even have to explain those decisions," Harwell told the media, "and I realize that broadcasters don't go on forever." McCarthy would later say that his friend and boss Jim Long was never the same after the Harwell firing incident.

Tom King remembers the kind of loyalty that McCarthy displayed on many occasions. "When Denny McClain got out of jail, Joe spent some time with him," King explains. "Denny was looking for a way to get back into society. Denny was affable and polite, and Joe liked him, but he turned out to be a crook."

"Joe tried to be nice to Denny McClain," Youngblood agrees. "Joe interviewed McClain on the phone while McClain was in prison, which was unprecedented at the time. I remember telling Joe that when McClain got out of prison, he should keep his distance from him, but Joe had a keen sense for the underdog, and even though McClain was a crook, he liked him."

"Sometimes J.P. would call and ask me what I thought of a particular person," *Free Press* columnist Bob Talbert recalls. "I'd say, 'You want the truth? I can't even understand why you hang out with the guy! You ought to hear what he says about you behind your back!'"

"If he didn't like them, he wouldn't hang around them," McInerney insists. "He loved Joe Schmidt, but he wouldn't hang around Alex Karras." Karras sold used cars for McInerney during the off-season when Karras played for the Detroit Lions from 1958 to 1970.

Alex Karras with J.P. in 1992

"At the time you were in the NFL, player salaries were such that you needed a job in the off-season in order to make ends meet."

"Yes, and I went to work for Hoot. I told Hoot that as soon as I reached a certain 'X' amount of dollars during the week, whether it be in the middle of the week or at the beginning of the week or at the end of the week, I would leave and come back the following week!"

"You told me once that you were burned out of the bigtime sports scene."

"I don't watch sports very much. There's more important things in my life. I never was a real great sportsman. I didn't think it was a big deal that I went down and knocked the shit out of everybody for 42 minutes and got paid $9,000 to do it. When people examine my career, they say, 'Geez, imagine how well you could have done if you'd gotten along with everyone.' Well, I don't think it's possible to always get along with everyone."

♣

"When Joe was around a new athlete or an old respected one, Joe would pay court to them," says Youngblood, "but he'd quickly get bored with them. After a while, the luster had worn off their crown, and the fawning frequently came from the other direction."

Still, it was the varying personalities of sports that caught McCarthy's interest. Take, for instance, the irony of one of the nation's finest football coaches, Bo Schembechler, making a deal with Tom Monaghan on a cocktail napkin to become General Manager of the storied Detroit Tigers, only to eventually be fired by Monaghan . . . by fax!

Bo Schembechler with J.P. McCarthy, 1991

"Bo Schembechler, surely during your football coaching career, you certainly must have had some opportunities to coach in the NFL. Why didn't you do that?"

"Well, I'll give you an explanation. I was pursued heavily by the New York Jets back in 1975. The organization at that time seemed to be in somewhat of a turmoil. I turned the job down and Lou Holtz took it. He didn't even last the whole season!"

"What did he win? Two games?"

"Yeah, he won a couple of games and that was the extent of his professional experience. Then when Hank Stram was fired in Kansas City, Lamar Hunt and his people came to my house in Ann Arbor and we discussed the Kansas City job. At that time, they felt one of the reasons they got rid of Hank is that he was meddling into the trades and drafting and assigning of players."

"He wanted to run the show."

"Right, and they wanted someone to accept whatever was on the field and coach it. I said to them, 'I think you made a mistake in flying out here, because I would never take a job in professional sports where I didn't have control over the draft or the trading or the makeup of the team.' So that interview didn't last long."

"Did the Lions ever offer you a job?"

"No."

"Did they ever romance you at all?"

"No. I never, ever discussed the Lions job while I was at Michigan. Never."

♣

University of Michigan football coach Bo Schembechler had a nice, long relationship with J.P. McCarthy. Aside from the many morning interviews, they would bump into each other often at events, and they even traveled with their young sons Jamie and Shemy to Florida for a boys' getaway. While he was portrayed in the media as a blowhard general, Bo had a great sense of humor that he often allowed J.P. and his listeners to enjoy.

One morning, J.P. asked me to get Schembechler on the phone for an unplanned interview. When I rang Bo's home, Millie Schembechler answered on a cordless telephone, and promised to quickly get the phone to Bo so he could do the interview with J.P. I waited nervously until Millie finally got the phone to Bo. When he came on the line, I apologized for calling unexpectedly, and told him that I hoped I wasn't disturbing him.

"You know what I'm doing right now?" Bo playfully growled.

"No, coach, I don't," I answered.

"I'm sitting on the head!" Schembechler announced with pride.

We both laughed hard.

"Can you talk to J.P. while you do that?" I queried.

"As long as you don't tell anybody," was Bo's answer.

That was one interview where I attempted to close down radio's "theatre of the mind."

♣

Although he supported all of the schools and leaned toward Michigan State in his later years, J.P. made his mark as a Michigan man by really making his Friday morning shows during football season a show that college football fans couldn't miss, especially before the Michigan/Ohio State game each year.

That November Friday, McCarthy would spend the entire show on one subject: Michigan vs. Ohio State. J.P. would play both fight songs, talk with both coaches, and interview players who had participated in the great rivalry. Broadcaster Bob Ufer, and later, Frank Beckmann, would preview the matchups, and OSU alum Daryll Sanders would sing the Buckeye rouser, "Round on the Ends and High in the Middle . . . Ohio." "J.P. would never let me sing 'The Victors' in response," gripes Michigan alum Ron Kramer. "He told me my voice was too bad and he'd rather play the record!" J.P. also played a little-known sultry, sexy version of "The Victors," sung 'Marilyn Monroe style' by singer Pat Suzuki.

Through the years, J.P. interviewed Woody Hayes and Schembechler, and then OSU's Earl Bruce, and Michigan's Gary Moeller and Lloyd Carr. After Ufer passed away, McCarthy played some of the memorable and enthusiastic highlights from the radio announcer who came to symbolize the great Michigan spirit. Other regulars were Wolverine alums Jim Mandich, Jim Brandstetter, Dan Dierdorf, John Gabler, and sportscasters Dave Diles and Beano Cook.

Cook, the chief college football analyst for ESPN, told McCarthy on McCarthy's OSU/Michigan tailgate show that if he had one more day to live, he would want to spend it "attending the Michigan/Ohio State game and then eating chocolate chip cookies and milk while watching *Casablanca* with Morgan Fairchild!" Cook, by once losing a college football bet with McCarthy, promised as payoff to eat dinner with J.P. at the Townsend Hotel in Birmingham while wearing a winged Michigan helmet.

How did this Friday morning tailgate get started? McCarthy's virtual co-host for these shows, Michigan alum and local favorite Ron Kramer, who played at Michigan from 1953 until 1957 before going on to the NFL to play with the Green Bay Packers and the Lions, tells the story:

"Daryll Sanders and I were just out of the NFL, and we were out with McCarthy very late on a Thursday night, and we came right from where we were to the WJR studio at 6 a.m. We started fooling around with the fight songs and calling up pals, and the phone lines lit up. People loved the show, and J.P. loved the competition between the schools, and so the show became a tradition," Kramer explains.

Bo Schembechler and former U-M wingback John Gabler with J.P. McCarthy, 1994

"John Gabler, what do you remember about playing in that classic 1969 Michigan upset over Ohio State?"

"I remember when Bo was hired to be Michigan's coach, Don Canham hired him for one reason and one reason only: to beat Ohio State. We didn't practice against a 6-1 or an 8-1 line in August; we went against a 52-slant, and guess who runs that?"

"You were practicing all year to beat Ohio State, is that it?"

"That's right."

"Bo is with us now on the other end of my line. Coach, is that true?"

"That's exactly right. When we took the job, in our first meeting I said, 'We're not here to beat anybody except Ohio State.' That was because they were so dominant in the Big Ten at that time."

"And see, you weren't here in '68, but Kramer and Gabler and I remember the 1968 game down in Columbus when Woody went for two points and he was leading 48-14 because he wanted to get to 50! A lot of guys remembered that! You remembered that, didn't you Gabler?"

"As I was going off the field that day, one of the 'great' Ohio State fans threw a Coke bottle at me and hit me in the back of the head and put twelve stitches in my head, so I remember that pretty good. We were a pretty mean and angry team when we got done being beaten by Woody that year."

"How'd you get that team fired up for that 1969 game, Bo?"

J.P. McCarthy

"I had our demonstration team that the first string starters practice [against] all wear the #50 on their jerseys! I had the number '50' in front of them all year!"

♣

Sportscaster Dave Diles, a Detroiter who hosted ABC TV's college football coverage at the network level, remembers hearing from McCarthy from his tailgate show. "Many times he would call me in New York while I did 'The Scoreboard Show,' Diles recalls. "He said that I couldn't be impartial in my coverage of Ohio State vs. Michigan because I was born in Ohio. I reminded him that I attended Ohio University, that great citadel of learning nestled snugly in the gently rolling hills of southeastern Ohio. He laughed and told me that the difference between Ohio State and Ohio University was that Ohio U. spikes the ball after a first down!"

♣

Ron Kramer recalls that McCarthy would interview Bob Ufer long before he broadcast Michigan football games for WJR. "Ufer was on WUOM, which was not a very big station. J.P. started having Ufer on his show, and people from everywhere began to learn of the wild enthusiams of Bob Ufer," Kramer explains.

Kramer, a big, brash, but endearing fellow, displayed an enthusiasm all his own, and became a good friend to McCarthy. "J.P. was the most competitive guy in everything he did," Kramer insists. "We'd play pool in the Recess Club, but he really thought that he could run, jump, skip, hop and play with the pros. We went to a formal party with our wives, and we ended up staying out until the sun was coming up and there was dew on the grass. J.P. looked at me and pointed and said, 'Ron, I can beat you in a race to that wall over there.' Even though we'd had a few glasses of champagne, we got in our stances, in our tuxedos, and started running. When he hit that wet grass, he slipped and hit it face first," Kramer laughs.

"Grass stains were all over the front of his tuxedo and he was covered with dew!"

McCarthy and Kramer shared their laughs over the years, even on the air! "J.P. was about to host his "Focus" program, and he asked me to do him a favor," Kramer reveals. "J.P. said, 'When Chloris Leachman gets on the show, I want you to run into the studio as I'm interviewing her and grab her and kiss her and tell her that you still love her!'

"So I broke into the room, grabbed her, kissed her, and said, 'Oh, Chloris, I still love you!'

"She was shocked. 'Who the hell are you?' she yelled. Then she picked up on the gag.

"'Oh, yes. I remember you. I'm just kidding. I still love you too, you big hunk of a thing!' The studio audience was roaring because no one knew it was a put-on!" Kramer bellows.

Hoot McInerney remembers the horseplay between McCarthy and Kramer. "Joe loved Ron Kramer. One time Joe was at a party dressed as Humphrey Bogart in *Casablanca*. Kramer picked him up and threw him into the pool, white tuxedo jacket and all!" laughs McInerney.

♣

The good-natured, locker-room, backslapping mentality of athletes was a big part of McCarthy's morning show, and the sports types J.P. talked with genuinely maintained that image at public gatherings too. "Many times J.P. was emcee of fund-raising stag roasts with many of the Detroit athletes," *Free Press* columnist Bob Talbert explains. "Once we were roasting old Lions quarterback Bobby Layne, and everybody got up and said every dirty word in the world. Sonny Elliott was there, the Butsicaris boys from the Lindell AC, Joe Schmidt, and all the regulars. Well, when it came time for me to get up and speak, I stood up and said, 'Well, everyone here has said every word, every joke, so there's nothing left for me to do but this'—and I mooned the crowd! The crowd roared, and laughed for a long time," Talbert continues.

"The next morning, I've got to call J.P. to talk on the air about what happened at the roast. Toward the end of the interview, I told J.P. that 'I was real happy. The event was so prompt and well run that I made it home by 11 p.m.'"

Well, I didn't know that these guys go out on a night like that, knowing that the event ends early, and then stay out late partying. Their wives heard the show and began giving the guys trouble, saying, 'Bob Talbert made it home by 11. Why couldn't *you!*' J.P.'s friends were pleading with him to go back on the air and say that Bob Talbert was just kidding!" Talbert exclaims.

♣

Another yearly "theme" show J.P. hosted occurred each May on the Friday before the Kentucky Derby, when he would spend every single minute talking about the "Run for the Roses." J.P. actually hosted that Friday show from the backstretch at Churchill Downs one year, but even back in Detroit he would line up the top racing experts, jockeys, and trainers for his show. ABC TV's track announcer Dave Johnson, the President of Churchill Downs Tom Meeker, "Bennie the Bookie," "Mr. Z" the dosage man, ABC's Jim McKay, *Sports Illustrated's* racing writer William Nack, *Free Press* racing writer Bev Eckman, racing authority Andy Beyer, Detroit Race Course spokesman Bob Raymond, and Dale Lawrence from Ladbroke in London would all give their race predictions, and McCarthy would play "Fugue for Tinhorns" from *Guys and Dolls* and "My Old Kentucky Home" to get everyone in the mood. McCarthy even had frequent financial interests in race horses, "He'd complain, though, that while everyone else sleeps, those horses eat," says pal Barry McGuire. "I don't know if it's true, but it was said that Joe's mother taught him to read by showing him the Daily Racing Form," McGuire laughs.

♣

Of course, no sports magazine or program would be complete without a "swimsuit edition," and so McCarthy would follow suit with his own campy version. Svelte models would trot in and out of his purposely chilled studio, showing off the latest and littlest in swimwear fashions while Judy McBride from the

Don Thomas Sporthaus helped McCarthy describe the wares for the viewless listeners who listened to the ogling with tropical music in the background.

♣

McCarthy, aside from being a great fan, observer, and reporter of sports, led a very active lifestyle when it came to athletics and leisure activities. "When he went on vacation, he had to be doing something all of the time," says McCarthy pal Barry McGuire, who has seen McCarthy snow ski and water ski. "His vacations were like marathons to other people."

"J.P. and I went skiing up in the mountains in Colorado with Tim Johnson," McInerney remembers, "and they were used to little places like Pine Knob ski hill. Tim took off first and hit every tree on the way down! So Joe said, 'Forget that,' and took his skis off and went back down the ramp!"

"Joe would try everything," says Tom King. "If he had been born a little earlier, he would have bungee jumped at one time!"

Judy McCarthy, when asked if J.P. would have bungee jumped, says, "Well, Joe did adore roller coasters. I hated them. I'd close my eyes and he'd say, 'Open your eyes! Look and see what's coming!' and I'd yell, 'I can't! I can't!'"

King remembers a ride on the Blue Streak at Cedar Point. "Joe loved it. He said, 'Wow, I had just enough tape to keep this rug on!' He would take on any ride!"

While Judy was pregnant with Jamie, J.P. decided to take flying lessons. "I was huge with child, and he was so proud he wanted to take me for a flight around the city of Detroit. It never occurred to me that he'd just got his flying lessons and it could be dangerous. I had implicit trust in Joe. In everything he ever did, he did it with his whole being, and believe me, when he was done with the flying lessons, he knew everything there was to know about flying that plane. We flew over the Fisher Building, over the Penobscot Building, and it was so exciting and a nice sunny beautiful day."

While he reveled in spectacular days like that one, the flying kick didn't last real long for J.P. "Joe told me that flying up there by himself caused him to whistle and get bored," King reveals. "Joe needed people. Soloing and flying just wasn't his thing."

"Once he wanted to try skydiving," Judy reveals. "I told him, 'Forget it! I'm not doing that!' He almost talked me into doing it, but then we went to watch and Joe asked them all of the important questions and finally decided not to do it, thank God!"

That doesn't mean there was no daredevil in McCarthy, though. "He once came to my place up north to ride snowmobiles. He arrived Friday night, and we were all having some libations, and Joe decides he wants to go for a ride on the machines," recalls King. "It was a bitter night and extremely cold. Joe had purchased brand new boots, gloves, and pants . . . everything you need for snowmobiling. Just like when he took up fishing, he had to buy all the right gear. So out we went!

"As we went along, there was a creek on the property that continued to flow, never freezing. It was just narrow enough, about an umpire's stretch, that we could just catapult over it, kind of glide over it, by just powering the machines. I went over it, and I told Joe, 'Stay on the throttle when you feel the machine dropping! Don't stop, just keep going! It'll drop a little bit, but you'll be fine.'

"Well, Joe did what every guy does and took his hand off the throttle when he felt the snowmobile dropping. Of course, that caused him to slide off the back of the machine into waist-deep water at about twelve below zero!

"I was concerned about him, but I was mostly concerned about my machine," King continues. "He had enough 'antifreeze' in him that it didn't matter! I grabbed the snowmobile, pulled it up, and got it out, and there he stood, in waist-deep water!

"His brand new boots that he bought for a snowmobile weekend went back home by the fire, and at the end of the weekend when it came time for him to drive back to Detroit, they still were not dry. He never wore them again!" laughs King.

♣

J.P. McCarthy. He had broadcast from Wimbledon, America's Cup, countless PGA Tour golf tournaments, Churchill Downs, rinkside at Joe Louis Arena before a Red Wings game, from the tailgate parties at the Michigan vs. Michigan State games, from the broadcast booth of the Detroit Lions, from the owners' suite at the Palace of Auburn Hills for the Pistons Opening Day, from Tigers spring training, and on home plate in Tiger Stadium.

He'd interviewed A.J. Foyt, Billie Jean King, Bruce Jenner, Ted Williams, Bobby Orr, Wilt Chamberlain, Walter Payton, Dorothy Hamill, Pete Rozelle, Earl Anthony, Muhammad Ali, Stein Erickson, Jack Nicklaus, Chip Hanauer, Willie Shoemaker, and just about anyone that ever bounced a ball, put the puck between the pipes, knocked one 'outta here, scored a perfect ten, wore a gold medal, or crossed a goal line or a finish line.

J.P. McCarthy was an American sportsman, and a weekend warrior.

"Drink a ♣ Round to Ireland, Boys"

**The Irish Rovers with J.P. McCarthy on the
"Focus" Show in March 1992**

" . . . If you took our show with Irish jokes and all and tried to
put it on Irish stages, we wouldn't even do it. We would
change our show and make it more traditional."

"Really. Why? Haven't you ever toured Ireland?"

"Never as a touring band."

*"Why? Why couldn't you go to, what's that famous place in
Dublin on the Green, the Abbey Tavern, why couldn't you do
your act there?"*

"Because we probably would make more in one night's concert here in Michigan than we would playing for a whole month at the Abbey Tavern. That's the practical thing of it all."

"That's a good reason, but surely your act would be accepted and appreciated there!"

"As long as we did the right material, because the music we play is as good as any Irish music being played in Ireland. We couldn't do the shillelaghs and shamrocks and leprechaun stuff."

"That's really 'stage Irish' and American Irish, isn't it?"

"Which is not wrong, you know. People put a negative thing on that."

♣

Joseph Priestley McCarthy's paternal grandmother, Anna Mulcahey, was born on the Emerald Isle, and although his father, John Priestley McCarthy, always warned him not to "wear his Irish on his sleeve," J.P. became a symbol of St. Patrick's Day in the Detroit area. His mother Martha remembers that even her husband sometimes didn't follow his own admonition. "On St. Patrick's Day, Joe and his father used to sing all kinds of songs," she recalls, as she remembers the melodies with delight. *"Does your mother come from Ireland? Sure there's something in you Irish and I love those Irish eyes,'"* Martha sings. "Oh my, yes, we had lots of fun. Who has more fun than the Irish? Who is more handsome? No one, I think."

"The Irish, if you listen to their music," says Hoot McInerney, "the songs are sad. The ballads are sad. I know Joe got a kick out of 'The Bricklayer's Lament,' but one song Joe never liked is 'Danny Boy,'" McInerney recalls.

"He did not like 'Danny Boy,'" concurs WJR radio host Mike Whorf, "but he tolerated it. We used to have a big argument over who had the best version of 'Danny Boy,' because he would play a version by barroom singer Frank Duncan and never the quintessential versions by John McCormick or Robert White," teases Whorf.

"Make no mistake, he hated 'Danny Boy,' says Ford executive and friend David Scott. "He found it to be syrupy and overly dramatic."

"We'd go out and have a few drinks," remembers George Millar of the Irish Rovers, "and before you know it we'd even have J.P. yodeling an Irish tune. He wasn't the best voice, but after a Bushmills or two he'd loosen up and sing," insists Millar, "and we had many jokes and many singing nights in the pubs of Michigan."

"All Irishmen can sing—right!" laughs professional singer Larry Santos, while another close friend, John Schaefer, remembers singing with J.P. in Ireland. "Sometimes in the evening in the hotel bars, people will come in and start singing," explains Schaefer. "Joe and I both loved to sing, and we were right in the thick of it. When I'd try to sing with him, he'd say 'I work alone, don't get near me!'"

"The Irish are poets, good in literature, good in stage and theater," says car dealer Hoot McInerney. "There are no Louis Pasteurs among them . . . although Henry Ford was Irish and he put a car under your ass," Hoot allows.

"My dad really took pride in the history of the Irish and all the great Irish people," says McCarthy's son Kevin.

Michigan Attorney General Frank Kelley agrees. "Every year on his show J.P. would give me time to mention that three generations of Irish in this country have done very well, and I told him that he was living proof. We've grown from poor immigrants facing help-wanted signs that said, 'No Irish Need Apply,' to having more CEOs of Irish descent than any other group in America, and we have the highest income of any group in America. J.P. liked that," says Kelley.

J.P. with Steve Allen, on "The J.P. McCarthy Show," January 18, 1993

"Irish people tend to be funny, like Jewish people tend to be funny."

"Now a lot of blacks are becoming professional comedians, and what those three groups obviously have in common is restless servitude over long centuries, and that gives rise to a lot of muttering out of the side of your mouth."

"And also the ability to laugh at themselves, isn't that true?"

"Absolutely, because it's an emotional necessity."

♣

"On a trip to Ireland he wanted to look up Anna Mulcahey's record and find his grandmother's home," says McCarthy's wife Judy. "She was from a little town but the record was just too fuzzy." Bloomfield Hills golf professional Mike Kernicki also spent some time in Ireland with J.P.: "He would tell everyone he ran across that he was Joseph Priestley McCarthy and that his grandparents were from Ireland," laughs Kernicki. "He would even ask the bartender, 'Now would you know them in some way?' The bartenders would chuckle, 'Oh, another American with an Irish background!'"

J.P.'s pal Barry McGuire called J.P. from Ireland once to give him some important genealogical information. "I told him that I looked up the name McCarthy in the phone book and that most of the McCarthys I found were bookies! He got a kick out of that."

During a visit to the Blarney Castle, McGuire learned a bit of real history. "I found out that it was McCarthys who built the castle," exclaims McGuire. "I told one of the caretakers that I had a friend named McCarthy and he asked me if my friend had the gift of gab. I told him, 'That's how he makes his living,'" laughs McGuire. "He then told me that all McCarthys have the gift of gab!"

How else could McCarthy have pulled off "The Answer Man" segment of his radio show? When a listener would call J.P. looking for the answer to a trivia query or a need for information, they knew to ask for "The Answer Man." J.P., in a funny little voice, would assume the identity of the "Answer Man," and say, "The Answer Man here. Yes madam, what is your question?"

With no advance knowledge of even the subject matter, Mc-Carthy would listen to the oddball questions and somehow always have an answer. While I'd try to help him with my resources "behind the glass," he rarely needed help, because often he knew the answer, and if he didn't, he was, shall we say, adept with coming up with something to satisfy the listener.

"In Ireland they call it 'Blarney,'" says Irish Rover singer George Millar, "or in a nicer term they'd say, 'He could talk the leg off of a stool.' If you're going to tell any kind of story, especially an Irish story, you have to have that magic thing called 'timing.' Of course J.P. had that!"

Millar says McCarthy loved Ireland, everything Irish, and the Celtic tradition, remembering that McCarthy once told him the films *Finian's Rainbow* and *The Quiet Man* brought a tear to his eye.

Mike Whorf says he once played an Irish song for McCarthy that brought a tear to J.P.'s eye. "It was called 'Drink a Round to Ireland,' by Judy Collins." remembers Whorf, "and he got misty and kind of swallowed hard."

> ' . . . *Father was a singing man. Most of what he sang had to do with Ireland, the place from where he came. The Ireland of his childhood. Ireland of his spring. To return to Ireland was his dream. Drink a round to Ireland, boys, I'm home again. Drink a round to Jesus Christ who died for Irishmen.*'

"It made him think of his own father," says Whorf. "He was proud of his lineage. You can always tell the Irish, but you can't tell them much!"

Dr. John Murphy remembers some spirited lineage arguments between J.P. and John Schaefer on a trip they took to Ireland together. "We were traveling across Ireland by motor coach, and John Schaefer was always professing that he was Irish because his mother's maiden name was McGuiness. Finally, J.P. asked the bus driver, 'Are there any McGuiness in Ireland?'

To the horror of Schaefer, the bus driver answered, 'There may be a few up north . . . I think they're chimney sweeps!'"

"From then on," Schaefer gripes, "Joe loved to go along in this brogue and say, 'Johnny, Johnny, look at that little broken down shack over there. I believe that was the McGuiness family home!' Then he'd say, 'Do you see that big castle on the hill over there? That was the McCarthy family home. A family of kings . . . the McCarthys!'"

David Scott says he'd tease McCarthy. "I told him that he was in fact Scottish because anyone with a "Mc" on the front of their name was actually originally from Scotland," says Scott. "He'd hear none of that!"

♣

"Joe did love being Irish and traveling in Ireland," said Judy McCarthy, "but he never quite got used to driving on the wrong side of the road," she laughs, "and he scared us all!"

"He drove so close to the sidewalk," Judy remembers, "that he almost ran over this Irishman walking down the street. The Irishman turned around, raised his fist at Joe and yelled, 'You dirty fooker!' Joe turned to me and said, 'I think I know what he meant by that.'"

McCarthy's pal Trip Bosart remembers another clash with Irish custom. "It was a cold and bitter day and we went into the Lahinch Golf House for lunch and a beer, and we were absolutely starved," explains Bosart. "They had these little tiny grilled cheese sandwich squares cut into wedges and served with a pickle, like hors d'oeuvres.

"The waitress brought us a couple of pints of lager and Joe asks her, 'Are those your grilled cheese sandwiches?'

"She said, 'Aye, they certainly are,' and so Joe says, 'In that case, we'll have twenty of them, please!'

"'For the two of you?' she asked.

"Joe said, 'Yeah, and make it snappy!'

"We were acting like the original 'ugly Americans,'" admits Bosart, "but twenty of these probably equaled four American-sized sandwiches. The waitress was totally aghast, and the sandwiches were gone in about fifteen seconds!" laughs Bosart. All part of the 'Irish experience.'"

♣

"We'd go through these little towns," remembers John Schaefer, "and we'd find 'McCarthy's pub.' We'd even take pictures. One time we missed the ferry we were to take because we were in a pub drinking Blackbush with these Irish guys and playing darts," laughs Schaefer. "He loved the Irish people." In fact, a bit of Ireland is back in McCarthy's Bloomfield Hills home. "When we were building our home," explains Judy McCarthy, "we contacted some people we'd met in Ireland and told them we were looking for a panel for our bar. The front panel of our bar is actually an ornate door from a castle in Ireland," she reveals.

♣

Of course, McCarthy's trips to the auld sod included golf on some of Ireland's green rolling windswept golf courses. "We played at Waterville in the worst rainstorm and northern squall you could imagine," exclaims Trip Bosart of a golf journey made with some of the McCarthy cronies. "We had caddies, and the game of golf became secondary to the contest of 'who was tougher, the American golfers or the Irish caddies!'"

"The caddies were saying they'd never caddied in sleet like this," agrees golf pro Mike Kernicki, who also tried to brave the conditions along with Dr. John Murphy. "The rain was coming sideways," says Murphy. "In any other place we would never have gone out."

"It was raining so hard we couldn't see the group behind us," says Kernicki, and Bosart admits that "The weather kept getting worse and worse, but everybody was acting like it was nothing."

The golfers then encountered the twelfth hole, facing right into the Irish Sea, where the wind was blowing steady at about fifty miles per hour. "It was a 134-yard par 3 directly over a chasm," says Kernicki, "and I was hitting full three-irons as hard as I could with no chance of getting over."

"So Joe fades his tee shot a little bit," laughs Bosart, "and it started going right, got up into the wind, came back over us, and landed down the beach one hundred yards behind us!" Only then was the game called, and the caddies were happy the brutal contest was over.

"We were soaking," says Murphy, "and we quit on the hole that was the farthest from the clubhouse. It was the longest walk of my life."

"We got back on our motor coach and nobody had a change of clothes for the two-hour ride back to our hotel," says Kernicki. "Imagine all of our clothes spread out all over and J.P. sitting there in his underwear drinking a beer."

"Bosart already had a cold when he went over there," groans Dr. Murphy, "so we had to stop at the 'chemistry' to get him medicine. I went in and told the woman that I was a physician vacationing from America and one of our fellows was sick so I needed some penicillin. She seemed hesitant and went into the back and an old man came out and introduced himself as the chemist.

"'Can you write you a prescription for me?' he asked.

"'Of course,' I answered.

"Then he handed me a crumpled brown paper bag to write it on, so I wrote the prescription on a brown paper bag! The man behind me in line was waiting for ten gallons of sheep dip," exclaims Murphy, "and there we were standing at the same counter!"

J.P. played many of the famous Irish golf courses: Ballybunion, Lahinch, Waterville, and Tralee, which Arnold Palmer designed. Always curious, when McCarthy struck up a conversation with the golf starter at Tralee and asked how often Palmer visited his own course, he learned that even though Palmer designed it, Arnold had never even seen it! He'd sent the design in!

"He would invariably be the one who would strike up conversation with anyone," tells Kernicki. "He'd be asking the golf starters where in Ireland they were from and how long they'd been there and anything you'd want to know about them. He'd do that with the caddies too!"

"Drink a Round to Ireland, Boys"

Barry McGuire remembers hearing of an incident with a caddie in Ireland. "This guy had been caddying for McCarthy all day, and Joe came out of the clubhouse ready to leave.

"The caddie presented himself and said through his brogue 'Mr. McCarthy, I've cleaned your clubs up and all of your irons and woods, and put them in their proper places. I've taken your shoes and made sure the spikes were tight and the shoe trees were in properly and I've put them into the trunk of your car. If you don't mind, Mr. McCarthy, I'm ready for me pay.'

"Joe said, 'Gosh, I asked the caddiemaster and he said I was supposed to pay him.'

"'Mr. McCarthy, the caddiemaster is a rotten fucker,' grumbled the caddie!"

"McCarthy always stole all my good Irish jokes," says Schaefer. Here's one that J.P. liked to trot out his brogue to tell:

"Father O'Reilly was giving his sermon, a sermon intended to quell the natural Irish superstition. Father O'Reilly said to the gathered: 'There's been a lot of talk about spirits and sprites and leprechauns and ghosts. By a show of hands, how many of you have seen a ghost?'

Half of the congregation raised their hands.

Father O'Reilly continued by asking, 'How many of you have spoken to a ghost?'

About a quarter of the congregation raised their hands.

Amazed, Father O'Reilly challenged them further. 'How many of you have had sexual relations with a ghost?'

This time only Mulligan raised his hand.

'Mulligan,' Father O'Reilly gasped, 'you've had sexual relations with a ghost?!'

'Oh, excuse me, Father,' Mulligan answered, 'I thought you said 'goat!'!"

♣

Schaefer and his wife Sharon accompanied J.P. and Judy McCarthy on what would be their final trip to Ireland, staying at Adair Manor. "After a few days there I started to feel crummy," says Schaefer, "so I said to Joe at dinner, 'You don't like me, do you?'

"He said, 'What do you mean? What the hell are you talking about?'

"I said, 'You don't like me. You're trying to kill me!'

"He had me going from dusk until dawn," groans Schaefer. "We were getting up early and walking all up and down hills all day on these windy, rainy golf courses. The we'd go have lots of cocktails and a wonderful dinner and fall into bed and get up and do it all over again!"

♣

Back in America, McCarthy not only maintained his indefatigable schedule, but also his fondness for Irish spirit. It was in the late 1960s that he ran across a young group of unknown musicians who were in town to perform at the "Top Hat" club in Windsor and a place in Detroit called "The Living End." Jim Ferguson, Wilcil McDowell, Joe Millar, George Millar, Kevin McKeown, Will Millar, John Reynolds, and Sean O'Driscoll are now known collectively as "The Irish Rovers."

"The thing that strikes me about J.P.," says George Millar, "is that even before 'The Unicorn' became a hit, he would ask us to sing three or four songs and have a good talk, and leave someone like Robert Goulet waiting. It was amazing to me that he would do that for an unknown group of guys from Ireland! If we had walked in and handed him $10,000 for that kind of publicity, he would have thrown us out on our arses!"

McCarthy took "the boys," as he called them, under his wing and arranged special engagements for the Rovers whenever they came to town. "Jameson's Whiskey hosted an Irish coffee contest and we judged while J.P. emceed," remembers Millar. "It was a good thing none of us had to work that night!" A more serious occasion Millar recalls is when J.P. arranged for the Rovers to do a benefit to raise money for the children of Northern Ireland. "It was an event at Ford Auditorium he was emceeing with Belfast House of Commons Representative Bernadette Devlin, but he never got us involved in politics because he knew we were a mixed group, Millar insists. "He'd never embarrass us by asking if we were orange or green or what we thought of the troubles and bombings."

"Drink a Round to Ireland, Boys"

With sensitive Irish politics off limits for the fun-loving group, McCarthy still helped the Rovers network with local Irish American politicians like Detroit Mayor Jerry Cavanaugh.

"He'd take us to the Press Club and three or four nice lounges," remembers Millar, "and he took us to some private parties and showed us Detroit by introducing us to the Police Chief and the Mayor and all these important people. He knew all of these people and he'd trail us along, so all of a sudden here are these green kids from Ireland in all this great company and J.P. would always introduce us as his friends from Ireland." McCarthy would also introduce the Irish Rovers to the audience at their performances, whether it be the tiny old Raven Gallery or the Macomb Center for the Performing Arts after the Rovers made it big. "Without J.P. and the publicity he gave us," explains Millar, "nobody would have known who we were, and I wish he would have been our manager because to this day people are still saying, 'We heard you on the J.P. show!'"

The big break for the Irish Rovers may have been when they were guests on McCarthy's "Focus" show along with Arthur Godfrey. WJR newsman Gene Healy remembers the scene of Godfrey's reaction to being introduced to the Irish Rovers. "After the Rovers did their song, Godfrey said, 'Joe, where have you been keeping these lads? When I get back to New York I'm going to make arrangements to have them on my show," Healy remembers. "That led to about six of his radio shows," exclaims Millar, "which were very important to us because it took us to New York and places we hadn't been before and that was directly related to J.P.!"

Aside from Godfrey, the "boys" made contacts with many famous people over the years by appearing on the "Focus" show, including Robert Goulet, Johnny Cash, and Waylon Jennings. But there was one celebrity they did not get along so well with, as Millar recalls:

"We were just trying to make conversation with Billy Crystal before the show and he wasn't very responsive to us. Maybe we were too scruffy for him or not too well known," wonders Millar, "or maybe he was just tired or in a hurry. When he left the studio, it was our turn to come on and talk to J.P., and my brother Will says, 'Boy, Crystal seems like a real stuck up so-

and-so' on the air. Crystal heard this on the speaker in the lobby and he came running back in while we were on the air and berated us, shouting, 'Why don't you just go sing a whalin' song.' We haven't run into him since," laughs Millar.

McCarthy's interviews with the charming, impish Rovers were likely to stray into almost any topic, but almost always included an Irish joke, like this one told by Jim Ferguson in 1992:

> *"A man comes home crying one night and the wife says, 'What's wrong with you? What are you crying about?'*
> *"He says, 'The doctor says I'll be dead in the mornin.'*
> *"She says, 'Oh my god. You'll be dead in the mornin'? I'm gonna give you a lovely evenin' of a lovely dinner, and I'm gonna let you sit and watch all of your favorite television shows and we'll spend the whole evening together.'*
> *"He says, 'I've got a better idea. Let's go upstairs with a bottle of whiskey like in the old days and make mad, passionate love!'*
> *"She protests, 'That's okay for you. You don't have to get up in the mornin'!'"*

The Irish Rovers went on to have hits like "The Unicorn Song" and "Wasn't That a Party," and they looked forward to their yearly visit with J.P., never shying away from performing on his show. "Even after our hits," insists Millar, "we never got too big to trudge in our guitars and a tin whistle and be glad to play for him if he wanted. We were friends."

Even though the Rovers were on the road, they'd be sure to phone J.P. every St. Patrick's Day to offer a special Irish toast.

> *"All animals are strictly dry.*
> *They sinless live, and they swiftly die.*
> *The horse and the mule live thirty years*
> *and nothing know of wine and beer.*
> *The sheep and the goat at twenty die,*
> *they never tasted scotch or rye.*
> *The cow drinks water by the ton,*
> *and at eighteen it's nearly done.*
> *The dog at fifteen cashes in*
> *without the aid of rum or gin.*

"Drink a Round to Ireland, Boys"

The cat in milk and water soaks,
and then in twelve short years it croaks.
But the sinful, the ginful, the rum-soaked men,
survive for three score years and ten!
And some of them, a very few,
stay pickled 'til they're a hundred and two!"

♣

J.P. McCarthy always celebrated St. Patrick's Day on his morning show, but it wasn't always a big party. He would play some standard Irish tunes by the Clancy Brothers, like "The Bricklayer's Lament," and "Galway Bay." He had some special songs, like a duet of "It's Not Easy Being Green" by Kermit the Frog and Frank Sinatra. He even once played "I'll Take you Home Again, Kathleen" by Elvis Presley, of all people! He would chat with the Mayor of Dublin live from the St. Patrick's Day parade and yuk it up with Irish comic Hal Roach.

"J.P. knew that St. Patrick's Day was not just a day to imbibe and do the Irish jig," reminds frequent St. Patrick's Day guest Frank Kelley. "He knew that it had a serious significance in the history of Ireland, and he would always let me have a few moments to remind everybody that what we're commemorating here is a very troubled people who were persecuted for five hundred years and the reason why St. Patrick is so important is that they were persecuted, and if it wasn't for their faith in God and symbols like St. Patrick, they never would have survived as a group of people," says Kelley. "He knew that over here we can be light-hearted and gay, but he remembered that St. Patrick's Day is a time to commemorate our history, and most of it was kind of sad."

WJR newsman Gene Healy even remembers accompanying McCarthy to Father Russ Kohler's famous St. Patrick's Day Mass at Holy Trinity Church in Detroit's "Corktown" district, where J.P. was to serve as celebrity lector. "It's the only time I got to sit in the first pew," reveals Healy. After his show each year, McCarthy would be met by his friends to celebrate in his own way, until the party started coming to him in 1986. "His cronies and buddies started to slip up to the station and back into Studio D," says Hal Youngblood, who was J.P.'s producer at the time. "Professional Irishmen like Barry McGuire and Tim Johnson—all of them would come up," says Youngblood, "and it just grew."

McCarthy's secretary, Dorothy Powers, remembers that the radio-show-turned-party eventually moved to the lobby of the station, where just a small gathering was expected. "The elevator doors opened and I couldn't get off because people were jammed into the lobby," says Powers.

"I don't think they expected more than thirty people," said actor and J.P. pal Ed Oldani, who attended the very first "party."

It grew to become the masthead show of J.P.'s year. All of J.P.'s regular guests, face to face, all in one room. The juxtaposition was incredible, and very warming. It was like a reunion of the top people in their fields, all linked together by the common denominator of one very curious, powerful, and spirited radio host. Movie critic Susan Stark next to movie star Jeff Daniels, next to screenwriter Dutch Leonard. Latin correspondent José Marín teaching J.P. how to say "Happy St. Patrick's Day" in Spanish. Bob Talbert standing with Pete Waldmeier. Joe Muer talking with Jimmy Schmidt. Former Lion coaches Rick Forzano and Joe Schmidt having coffee with soccer expert Roger Faulkner. All contributors present and accounted for.

♣

When J.P. McCarthy's St. Patrick's Day Show became too big a party to hold in the lobby, it was moved to the Pegasus Restaurant in the Fisher Building, twenty-two stories below WJR. While invitees dressed in green ties enjoyed coffee, orange juice, and sometimes even stronger spirits, J.P. hosted his "Morning Show" from the dance floor, backed up by Richard McMullin's Irish band, called "Blackthorn." There was plenty of Irish music, and plenty of Irish guests. The "Maid of Erin" would perform a step dance, the Grand Marshall of the St. Patrick's Day parade would be on hand, and a leprechaun character would greet guests at the door, pinning them with a green carnation or handing them a coveted J.P. McCarthy St. Patrick's Day coffee mug. The mugs, which varied each year, usually featured a cartoon caricature of J.P. (reluctantly approved by McCarthy after careful inspection each year—no double chins allowed!) and an Irish blessing or toast:

> *"Let those that love us love us.*
> *May God turn the hearts of those that do not love us.*
> *If He cannot turn their hearts,*
> *Let Him turn their ankles,*
> *So we'll know them by their limping."*

"The Four Fifths" barbershop quartet would sing "When Irish Eyes are Smilin'," the "Sweet Adelines" would sing the Irish Blessing, and Frank Duncan, lounge singer from Lafrey's Bar, always caused the room to pause with his rendition of "Danny Boy."

Cardinal Adam Maida or Edmund Szoka would offer a St. Patrick's Day blessing, and one year, when St. Patrick's Day fell on a Friday during lent, Cardinal Maida issued a special dispensation allowing Irish Catholics to eat the traditional meal of corned beef and cabbage on a day they were normally expected to abstain from eating meat. The rest of the show, which ran from 7 a.m. until 10 a.m., consisted of McCarthy wishing many of his guests "Happy St. Patrick's Day" on the radio by wandering around with a wireless microphone. It was a completely ad-lib arrangement, with no scheduled guests or serious interviews. Whoever McCarthy happened to run into, he either spoke with or mentioned. Although most guests were relaxed and enjoying the atmosphere or the fantastic high-level elbow rubbing, McCarthy's hit-or-miss interview style could present problems when sometimes pushy guests did everything they could to get interviewed by J.P. This became even more of a problem in 1993 when the show began being simulcast statewide on cable television. Jeweler Doug Shubot was famous for his huff and puff, while one year Frankenmuth businessman Wally Bronner, dressed in green lederhosen, practically stalked McCarthy through the entire show. Gubernatorial candidate Debbie Stabenow wasn't the only politician who impatiently tried to position themselves in J.P.'s sightlines, and this became even more sensitive when WJR advertising clients were invited to the soirée. McCarthy always mentioned at the beginning of the show that he would not talk business and that "anyone who takes this day seriously just misses the point."

Governor Jim Blanchard explains why, surprisingly, he never came. "I got the idea that it was a lot of local politicians fighting to get attention, and I didn't want to be one of the people elbowing and pushing and shoving to get his attention," Blanchard says. "Joe probably always wondered why I didn't come, but I didn't want to be another struggling politician on his show. I offered to call in, and they said, 'Come or don't call.'"

Holy Trinity Pastor Russ Kohler recalls the scene. "It was the usual swarming of sharks hoping to be called to the microphone, but there was instant eye contact for this old pastor with the wink of his eye, a waving in and an assuring, 'Get you on right after the news, padre.'"

"It was tough to operate a radio show from that standpoint," says engineer Cliff Coleman. "My job was to watch the clock and try to make sure all of the commercials and traffic and weather breaks occurred on time. It was such a big crowd, and so many people wanted to get on the show, that logistics were difficult," says Coleman. "Only someone with J.P.'s poise could have pulled it off."

If it was tough to get interviewed on the show, it was even more difficult to get an invitation. The event was eventually moved from the Pegasus to the spacious and glitzy Fox Theatre lobby, and even when the extensive guest list topped one thousand, still more would try to talk their way in at the door. "People would always call asking how to get invited," explains Coleman, who helped Powers assemble parts of the invitation list. "It was a very hot ticket, and there were people who would want to be there, people who should be there, and some people we couldn't accommodate because of space considerations or some agenda they had to meet, greet, or get on the show," admits Coleman.

The bottom line was, it was J.P.'s party, and he never invited anyone for "political reasons." I sat with him many times when the list was made, and he always reeled off names from the top of his head of people he really wanted to attend—people he really cared about, even though they numbered in the hundreds.

I was always touched by his sincere modesty when, moments before he was to enter the location for the party, he would try to peek through the door and say to me, "Gee, I hope people decide to show up. I hope it's a good crowd." That was J.P. McCarthy and his Irish pragmatism and unpretentiousness. Moments later, the crush would be on and the huge crowd would pack the Pegasus Restaurant or the Fox Theatre lobby. "If you didn't go to that party, he knew!" shouts an incredulous Hoot McInerney. "I remember one year I didn't go, and you'd have thought I put a knife through his heart. I said, 'Joe, you had a thousand people down there!' I thought he was going to kick me right in the nuts!" insists McInerney. "That was one day—sick or sore—you went. There were no excuses; if you were his friend, you showed up on St. Patrick's Day!"

"It always struck me that it was probably the highlight of his year," says Wayne County Executive Ed McNamara. "He was so laid back, and you'd be standing in line behind the Cardinal, who would be standing in line behind City Councilman Jack Kelley, who was standing in line behind all of the other dignitaries—the governor, senators, congressmen, and mayors all went out of their way to be there. Some even came in limousines. Appearing on that program was a must for anyone who wanted to be seen," says McNamara. "I don't know of any other affair where more people of stature in the community showed up!"

"He'd have Judge Vince Brennan—may he rest in peace—and Bill Cahalan," remembers Frank Kelley. "Everybody wanted to be Irish on that day, because they wanted to be as happy as J.P. appeared on that day," says Kelley.

"Vince Brennan is with us today. Happy St. Patrick's Day, Vince."

"Congratulations on making the whole state of Michigan liven up their spirits today. In every life there's some tears and travail, but for some reason or another, today, J.P., you help lift them out of those tears for a few hours. The Irish have that knack, and you've got that knack, and that is to take serious events and traumatic events and look to the bright side and try to make their lives a little more cheerful."

"Vince, you're going to get me all choked up. Gee, if you ask an Irishman a question on St. Patrick's Day you get a speech and there isn't a dry eye in the house!"

♣

"The reason Irishmen cry at wakes is because their eyes are so close to their hearts," imparts meteorologist John McMurray, who spent many St. Patrick's Days with his friend J.P.

"He did such a wonderful job of bringing everybody together on that day," remarks Tom King. "At his party there were no adversaries. Republicans walked with Democrats, Jews walked with Germans, blacks walked with whites," says King. "Everyone became Irish for that day," says psychiatrist and attendee Dr. Emmanuel Tanay.

Advertising executive and J.P. pal Fred Yaffe changed his Jewish name to O'Yaffe and brought green bagels.

Another yearly party guest was Wayne County Sheriff Robert Ficano, an Italian who always brought green Italian food, like cannoli or lasagna. One year he promised to feed jail prisoners green spaghetti that day in honor of J.P., while City Councilman Gil Hill remarked that he heard the jail food is usually green anyway.

Black mayoral candidate Sharon McPhail danced an Irish jig one year, while Detroit Mayor Coleman Young and other African Americans became "black Irish," in a lighthearted reference to dark haired Irishmen versus redheaded ones.

Bigwigs from the auto companies—especially General Motors, perched right across the street—would always wheel into J.P.'s party. GM Presidents Roger Smith and Jack Smith, Marketing guru Phil Guarascio, and Cadillac General Manager John O. Grettenberger would stand right next to Ford executives Bob Rewey and Tom Wagner. Car dealers were in abundance too.

"Drink a Round to Ireland, Boys"

One year, the bar tab at the Pegasus rang up to $800 by 10 a.m., proving that Irish revelers were "fond of the jar," even at that hour . . . excluding J.P. Once during the show when he asked for orange juice, I brought him a screwdriver. He took one sip, thanked me for the sentiment, and said, "I can do a lot of things, but I can't talk and drink at the same time." Not to worry, local ad specialty man Tom Brooks took to handing him a beer the very second he signed off the air. After all, those television lights were very hot, and a man could get thirsty working a room like that. Even presidential candidate Pat Buchanan eschewed 8 a.m. coffee for a green beer when he made a campaign stop at J.P.'s party. "J.P.," Buchanan said wearily, "if you lost twelve primaries in a row you'd be drinking beer at this hour too!"

Wayne County Executive Ed McNamara was called to the St. Patrick's Day microphone one year and remembers telling J.P. this story: "I had gotten an invitation from President Clinton to go to the White House and meet Sinn Fein leader Gerry Adams. Unfortunately, my wife and I promised these people we would play bridge that night, so I called, checked with the White House, and sent my daughter in my place. In the meantime, the bridge game got canceled, and, rather than disappoint my daughter, I got hockey tickets and she still got to go.

So my daughter Colleen gets in the White House reception line, and when Colleen introduces herself to the President, Clinton asks, 'Oh, where's Ed?' and she says, 'He went to the hockey game!' J.P. loved that story!"

Irish wit and humor were in abundance that day. "At the last St. Patrick's Day party," says Father Russ Kohler, "I asked J.P. 'What have you been drinking—green Slimfast?' He said, 'Thank you Russ. You're the only one who noticed.'"

"I would show up in a green top hat and green sash," laughs Jack Mulcahey, "and do Irish cheers. I haven't worked a St. Patrick's Day in forty years!"—*"Hooray for Joe, Hooray at last! Hooray for Joe, he's a . . . real nice guy."*

♣

J.P.'s St. Patrick's Day excitement didn't stop when he went off the air at 10 a.m. In fact, some would say that's when it got started.

"Barry McGuire would bring this ugly green limo, a '50s vintage car," laughs Tom King, "and the driver, who knew nothing about Detroit, never knew where he was going, but we'd still get Joe to Jacoby's, Dunleavy'z, Nemo's, and Reedy's."

"We also went to a bar called 'McCarthy's Party,' recalls McGuire, "and one young lady took off her bra to show us that she had shamrocks on her breasts!'"

Corktown, so named because of the many Irish settlers from County Cork, has no shortage of Irish bars, including The Gaelic League and Nancy Whiskey. "The limo would come right up to the door of the Irish bar," laughs Frank Kelley. "J.P. wasn't so much interested in drinking as he was making his duty calls to every Irish bar he could that day, because he wanted to see everyone and they wanted to see him. You'd see big celebrities with him in the bars along Michigan Avenue, but at the same time there'd be humble, laboring people in these bars, and he'd be as nice to them as he was to the celebrities," Kelley insists.

"We'd run into everybody," says Tom King, "from Jerry Cavanaugh to Joe Schmidt to Ron Kramer to George Perles, to Brooks Patterson—all out having fun and migrating around Joe."

McCarthy's St. Patrick's Day pub crawl always included a stop to see Buttons Mulcahey, who bartended at the Lager House and Nemo's until he passed away in 1982. "He'd have J.P.'s drink on the bar before he even came in," says Buttons' brother Jack, who worked for City Councilman Jack Kelly. "J.P. always called us 'cuz' because his grandmother was a Mulcahey and he figured we were cousins." Mulcahey still talks about the time Pat O'Brien himself came into the Lager House for a shot and a beer and a sandwich.

I remember being with McCarthy at Nemo's one St. Patrick's Day when Ron Kramer bit a huge hole into the side of a beer can and guzzled it down. Fat Bob Taylor showed off his legs in a glorious kilt, and the sun shone warm upon downtown Detroit and J.P. McCarthy.

"He would start to fade because he worked hard early on the air," says Tom King, "but he'd never be the first to drop. I marveled at his tenacity and capability to run all day and well into the night, hitting the bars and carrying on with the Irish curse," remarks King. "We'd get home after midnight, and he'd be on the air and lively again at 6:15 a.m., when I'd get beads of sweat on my upper lip just trying to walk to my dresser at 8 a.m.!"

One St. Patrick's Day occasion with King wasn't quite finished after midnight, when they arrived back at McCarthy's home in Bloomfield Hills. "We got there very late, after having been served plenty of green beer, and we realized that we had forgotten to make our annual late night stop at the Lafayette Coney Island in downtown Detroit," King explains, "where two Stroh's and two 'with everything' always made great fortification for the late ride back to the suburbs.

"So Joe says, 'We missed our Lafayette. Let's go,' and Judy McCarthy says, 'You two aren't going anyplace!'

"To which Joe insists 'Judy, we never miss having a coney!'

"Judy says, 'You're right, and you know what? We're all going!'

"We all got in the car, and Judy drove us down. We all had our Stroh's and 'two with everything' and she drove us back. I'm sure we were terrible passengers, breathing on her, flatulating, making no sense at all!"

St. Patrick's Day in Detroit is still associated with J.P. McCarthy, and his reach still extends beyond Detroit, as Delphi Automotive President J.T. Battenberg recently discovered at a golf outing in Tampa with Lee Trevino and Al Kaline. "I pulled out a seven iron with a shamrock on it given to me by the J.P. McCarthy Foundation, and Kaline and Trevino both knew what that shamrock stood for," says Battenberg warmly. "These guys from two different walks of life immediately see the shamrock and start talking about him. It's his magic, you know."

Frank Kelley explains J.P.'s magic and reach:

"The Irish tend to be rather critical of their neighbors. J.P. wasn't that way. If J.P. couldn't say a good word about you he wouldn't say anything. J.P. was that way, and everybody knew it. If he knew something bad about you, and I'm sure he knew bad things about a lot of people in the city of Detroit, you never heard it from J.P.

"The reason the Irish worship saints is that there are so few of them. The old Irish nuns used to tell me that one of the qualities of sainthood was that if you never speak ill of another human being during your entire life, no matter how long or how short it is, that God will send the angels down and personally escort you to heaven. Because you never spoke ill of anyone, you'll automatically have a high place in heaven."

Irish Rover George Millar remembers getting a phone call from his agent to inform him that a friend of his had died:

"I said, 'No, no, he's a young man! Are you sure you've got the right name?' I was shocked and I had to call the other boys. He wasn't supposed to go that soon, and we didn't even know he was sick.

"We had just done his show, and we were the only guests. It was a reminiscing type show, a full retrospective. All about the old days and our career right to the present. The Irish are naturally superstitious, and we thought, 'Wasn't that an odd show we did?' It was like a premonition, as if he knew. It was eerie, almost as if it was full circle and it was done, like he knew something was going to happen and he was going to clean it all up and bring it to a complete end. The Irish are strange that way," says Millar.

"We finished the show, shook hands, and that's the last we ever saw of our friend J.P."

♣

The J.P. McCarthy Foundation to Fight Blood Disorders has raised over $400,000 by organizing two memorial St. Patrick's Day radiothons since his passing.

McCarthy's grave is decorated by his family with green balloons and flowers each March 17, and I make a visit there each year on that day with two beers. One to drink, and one to pour for my friend and mentor.

"Drink a Round to Ireland, Boys"

Although there is no more St. Patrick's Day party, some of McCarthy's close friends keep his St. Patrick's Day Corktown pub tradition alive. They still drink a round to Ireland, and they drink all their rounds to J.P. McCarthy.

It is now to J.P.'s memory that we dedicate the poem he dedicated to Irishmen gone before him at the close of his St. Patrick's Day shows:

"I've always read this poem, written many years ago by Hal Boyle, which expresses what it means to be Irish, and remember, on St. Patrick's Day everyone is Irish who wants to be:

"What does it mean to be Irish?

It is to have an angel in your mouth, turning your prose to poetry.

It is to have the gift of tongues.

To know the language of all living things.

On this day it is the music, the deep, deep music of the living and the low sad rhythms of eternity. You see, the Irishman hears the high song of the turning spheres, the dim lullaby of the worm in its cocoon.

All the world is in tune—a tune that only he can hear.

It is to live the whole history of his race between a dawn and a dawn.

On St. Patrick's Day, to be Irish is to know more glory, more adventure, more magic, more victory, more exaltation, more gratitude and gladness, than any other man can experience in a lifetime.

It is to walk in complete mystic understanding with God for twenty-four wonderful hours."

♣ J.P. McCarthy for President

On January 29, 1968, J.P. McCarthy stepped up to the podium in front of the influential Beavers Club meeting at the Detroit Athletic Club and announced that he had decided to run for President of the United States of America:

It's really a pleasure to be able to kick off my campaign in front of such a distinguished and happy group—the most hostile audience we've ever faced. I did have a terribly bright, articulate, and deep speech prepared for you, but by general agreement among my staff, it stunk, so with great reluctance I'm going to be very brief, state my cause, and answer questions from the members of the assembled press.

My stand is very basic and simple really, gentlemen: I'm against taxes. I'm against taxes and levies of all kinds and types. They will be abolished.

I'm for girls . . . and newspapers . . . and in that order!

I stand for unlimited and unchallenged expense accounts for all executives.

I'm for long lunches, and wet lunches.

I might add, and this is very serious, that I am for the breaking up of subversive groups in our country. Groups like the Green Bay Packers, the Los Angeles Rams, the Baltimore Colts, the Oakland Raiders, St. Ambrose . . . moreover, I'm for George Plimpton for quarterback of the Lions.

I'm for establishing Hugh Hefner as a National Park and his Chicago apartment as a National Shrine and recreation area.

I am also for solving our freeway traffic problems. What I want to do is close all the exit and entrance ramps first.

Gentlemen, I promise you that when I am elected, the very first thing I will do will be to deport Ralph Nader. Ed Cole lobbied for that one.

Now for some questions from the world press, which folded right after the *Daily Press*. Mr. Bob Reynolds will fire them at me and I will answer them in typical unrehearsed fashion:

Q: Mr. future President, what is your party, and what is the platform?

A: Bob, let me say this about that. Our party is one in complete keeping with the times. It will be more liberal than liberal. In fact, on the Libertine ticket, with solid coast-to-coast Playboy endorsement. Platform? I'm no expert, but I think this one is oak or maple or maybe even vinyl.

Q: What about civil rights, sir?

A: Let me say this about that. I believe you have the right to be treated civilly, even if you are white.

Q: Would you take a stand on public housing? Houses for people?

A: You might as well legalize the houses. What the hell. You can't fight it. Would you be my friend if I was going to put the houses out of business?

Q: That wasn't exactly what I had in mind, but I'm sure some of the people gathered here appreciate your stand, and I could point out a few . . . Now, what about foreign affairs, Mr. Candidate?

A: That's a ticklish problem. What's so hot about an affair with a foreigner? Why take it out of the country? We've got some good, red-blooded American girls right here in the good old U.S. of A.

Q: What about the atom bomb?

A: She opens next week at the Playboy Club.

Q: How do you rate Castro?

A: Castro-rating is not a very popular subject with the Libertine party. I want to tell you that.

Q: There is a lot of talk about honesty and immorality these days. How do you feel about honesty and immorality?

A: Mr. Reynolds, let me say this about that. We Libertines believe we should be more honest about our immorality. Be frank, be honest. There's nothing dirty in sex. For example, you are certainly a typical red blooded male. If you thought sex was dirty you'd certainly never indulge in it as much as you used to . . . Whoops! or do!

Q: What the hell do you mean "as much as I used to"? Seriously, what about the tremendous problem of taxes and fiscal responsibility?

A: You've been drinking again, haven't you? Taxes are out of the question. I've already stated my position on that very clearly. The Libertine Party is going to carefully investigate the claim that everything that is fun is either taxed, immoral, illegal, or fattening. We'll get to the bottom of this thing, I promise you!

Q: It seems we're getting to the damned bottom of the thing right now! What about the gold standard and devaluation?

A: I don't want to answer any of those hard questions. The treasurer will take care of all those deficit and devaluation problems. I think my record, Bob, clearly indicates that one of my strengths, and frankly comforts, too, is my willingness to delegate all responsibility and all work. Besides, don't link me with defects and devaluations. Give me a couple of home run balls, baby!

Q: I understand, Mr. future President that you are taking an unprecedented and forward step in naming your Cabinet and key appointees in advance. I think this is a forthright and bold innovation of the Libertine Party under your leadership. Will you tell us some of the composition of your Cabinet and your key appointees?

A: Yes. Ambassador to the United Nations: Sophia Loren. Personal and private advisor to the President: Raquel Welch. Secretary of Health, Education, and Welfare: Joe Don Looney. Secretaries of the Interior: Doug Sanders and Glen Johnson, because I understand Doug Sanders likes to double date. Secretary of Labor: Mrs. Robert Kennedy. Secretary of Defense: John Wayne. He's going to get all the wagons in a circle. My campaign manager Bob Reynolds has agreed to handle the sex determination tests for the next Olympics. We'd like to think he'd make a great chairman for the committee to keep America beautiful . . . lovely!

That's it. The rest will come to me when I see who has the most money.

Q: Wrap this first rally up by telling me just why you are running for President.

A: Bob, let me say this about that. I'm running for President because I've got 28,796 bumper stickers left. I've got 10,471 matchbooks left. Not only that, I've got buttons ordered, and I'm on the hook for all of it. That's why the hell I'm running for President.

The band struck up and the singing girls belted out:

J.P. days are here again
Jay Pee will pour the beer again
When he's our prez we'll cheer again
J.P. days are here again!

He'll play golf and he will ski
Hold Cabinet meetings on the 19th tee
Put a bunny under every tree
J.P. days for you and me!

Down with taxes, up with cheer
'cause J.P. stands for nickel beer
More holidays in every year
J.P. days are finally here!

Fred Yaffe, the advertising and marketing guru, carefully crafted the campaign theme song, had it recorded, and J.P. McCarthy became a Presidential candidate. The rally at the Detroit Athletic Club included entertainment by Fat Bob Taylor—"the singing plumber"—sassy clarinet player Bob Snyder, the Playboy Club's "Matt Michaels Trio," and singer Sue Chiles.

"He let it go for a few weeks," said McCarthy friend Barry McGuire, who witnessed J.P. toss his hat into the ring with that kickoff speech, "but then he announced he was dropping out of the race."

♣

It seems J.P. McCarthy would rather have been a kingmaker than a politician. Kingmaker he was, as his radio show grew in popularity and influence. Politicians knew the importance of being interviewed by J.P., and they knew just appearing on his show was good for their campaign and good to rally public support behind their causes or agendas.

McGuire insists McCarthy was approached on a number of occasions by well-meaning supporters trying to get J.P. to run for office. "He would have been a great politician," says McGuire. "He knew how to handle people and get them on his side in just about anything," McGuire explains.

One of the people in search of McCarthy's influence, according to political analyst Jack Casey, was Detroit Mayor Jerry Cavanaugh's purchasing director, Art Stone. "At that time Cavanaugh was recruiting candidates to run for City Council so he'd have a friendly council to work with," explains Casey, who was then Cavanaugh's political assistant. "Stone approached J.P. and told him that Jerry would like him to run for council. J.P. kind of idolized Cavanaugh and they were close like brothers. Even though J.P. was flattered by the offer, he wouldn't have been able to keep his career going, and it would have been disastrous for him," admits Casey.

♣

"He may have been fascinated by politicians," says WJR newsman Gene Healy, "but I don't think he ever would have aspired to public office. He never said, 'I want to be a U.S. Senator when I'm done.'"

McCarthy once made his real political intentions very clear when Irish Rover Will Millar once asked him this question:

"J.P., are you going to run for politics one of these days?"

"Never! Why would you wish that on me? I thought we were friends!"

"Well, J.P., I just thought every Irishman wakes up one day and either wants to own a pub or become President."

"You're right. It does grab a lot of Irishmen that way, but not this one!"

♣

"J.P. would have loved the campaigning, and he certainly had the campaign skills," Casey speculates, "but J.P. in a legislative body would have been bored."

Politicians seem to roundly agree that while they might not have been great radio hosts, J.P. could easily have crossed into their form of public service if he had been so inclined.

"He would have been a fabulous politician because he's a human being," says U.S. Senator Carl Levin, a Democrat from Michigan who also served as Detroit City Council President, "and he was connected with people, and he cared about people. It's one of the most important qualities a lawmaker can have," continues Levin. "You've got to listen to your constituents. You've got to be considerate and sensitive to what people's needs are and what they're trying to say even if sometimes they aren't perfectly artful in saying it. You've got to figure out what they mean, and that requires a great ability to listen. That is really what radio is all about, and what the best interviewers are about," explains Levin. "When you have that skill, you're going to be a great interviewer and a great public servant."

"In my travels, the two most engaging conversationalists I've ever met are J.P. McCarthy and former House Speaker Tip O'Neill," says pro golfer Evan Williams. "The best to play the 19th hole with."

Longtime Michigan Attorney General Frank Kelley draws another comparison in explaining why McCarthy would have been a great politician. "J.P. reminded me of a quality the Kennedys have, and JFK was the most impressive man I've ever known in public life. The thing about the Irish character-istic they shared is that the Kennedys enjoyed being them-selves," Kelley remembers, "and they enjoyed being what they were. J.P. was the same way—happy to be what he was, and he made you feel the same way."

"He didn't suffer fools, but he suffered them well enough," laughs former Michigan Governor James Blanchard. "He would have done it well enough to get the fools' vote."

♣

McCarthy may never have aspired to elective office, but he did serve as Governor of Michigan, even if only for a day. "I thought I'd do something special and appoint him 'Governor for a Day,'" explains Blanchard, "a clear recognition that he was more than a radio announcer, more than a talk show guy. He was a so-phisticated Johnny Carson."

Blanchard says he received no protest of complaint from others who may have criticized him for making such a move to curry favor with McCarthy. It seemed unanimous that J.P. deserved the recognition.

Barry McGuire, a Lansing resident, drove to the capitol building with McCarthy at 5:45 a.m., so that J.P. could do his morning show from the Governor's office. "We pulled in and parked in the Governor's parking space, and they had an honor guard with guns waiting, saluting him as we walked though. He looked at me and said, 'Not bad for a couple of privates. Right, McGuire?'"

"He did his radio show right from my desk," remembers Blanchard, "and he had both Republicans and Democrats calling in. He's the only one who ever did anything like that behind my desk."

"He was right at home behind that desk," insists Frank Kelley. "I'm sure he would have done all the right things and made all the right decisions." Following the show, Governor McCarthy held an impressive cabinet meeting. Blanchard says all of the cabinet members were excited. "They each gave him a little report and he asked questions because he was a quick study and very up on things." Blanchard also remembers that J.P. was very touched by the opportunity. "I thought he'd take it in stride," says Blanchard. "He didn't. He took it very seriously."

♣

James Blanchard began guesting on the "J.P. McCarthy Show" as a Congressman in 1975. "We worked at getting on his show," says Blanchard, "and I was very excited to be a part of it."

Few would deny that "boy guv" Jim Blanchard and J.P. McCarthy developed a special relationship. Blanchard's biting wit and frequent appearances on the show made him very candid and at ease with J.P., their conversations sounding warm, friendly, and productive.

"Over my twenty-two years in public life—eight as a congressman, eight as a governor, and two as an ambassador—I probably did J.P.'s show more than anybody," remembers Blanchard, who even guest hosted McCarthy's show in a case of friendly turnabout. "He helped my campaigns enormously because he had me on his show and people knew that we were friends," explains the youthful and charismatic politician. "In fact, he had me on so much that people must have thought I was a decent guy." While Blanchard made use of the publicity and exposure, and McCarthy enjoyed the cachet of a close relationship with a rising and popular political star, they grew to admire and respect each other, both gathering power and growing in popularity and stature.

"They were close as a matter of convenience for both of them," asserts Jack Casey.

Jim Blanchard with J.P., November 8, 1990

"Twenty-minutes after eight o'clock in the morning on WJR radio in Detroit. I'm J.P. McCarthy and Governor Jim Blanchard is on the other end of my line this morning. Good morning, Governor. Our condolences this morning. It was a shock to almost everyone. I think it was a shock even to Governor-Elect Engler. Nobody expected you to do anything but win. Your thoughts, twenty-four hours later?"

"I am just very grateful for having been Governor for eight years in Michigan and before that being a Congressman from Michigan. I consider myself one of the luckier people on the face of the earth and certainly in politics I have been. This may be a good turn for me and Janet. As you know, I'm in the second year of a new marriage. We're looking forward to a new life together. J.P., I don't like to lose, but it happens. You're not going to hear me complain."

"You're forty-eight years old with a lot of life in you. That's why it's difficult to imagine you staying out of politics. You loved being Governor."

"Most of the time, absolutely. It could be a love/hate relationship. When you're in that position, everybody expects to get what they want from you, but you have to say 'No.' After eight years of saying 'No' to people, you do collect enemies. There are a lot of special interests out there that weren't happy with me. There's always a time for someone new, and this is the time."

"Thank you for your accessibility. You've always been there. You never shied away from anything."

"J.P., I've always enjoyed being on your show and listening to it. Don't worry about Jim Blanchard. We're looking ahead, J.P."

♣

"Jamie" Blanchard lost to John Engler by less than one half of one percent.

"J.P. was a friend in victory or defeat," remembers Blanchard with a wince. "I didn't feel like talking to anybody that morning, but I made the call anyway. J.P. was great."

McCarthy's association with Blanchard did not end with Blanchard's loss. Although John Engler was just as accessible and friendly to McCarthy, listening in his car and calling in at almost any time, Blanchard continued to be a regular guest, reporting from Democratic National Conventions, the G-7 Summits, and offering political analysis and commentary.

"As Ambassador to Canada, I even called him from the magnetic North Pole," exclaims the Governor-turned-diplomat. "I was overlooking the Arctic Ocean, looking at icebergs that had not yet thawed and would eventually melt and run down into the Atlantic, and talking to J.P. McCarthy," Blanchard detailed.

Blanchard had planned to bring McCarthy to Ottawa and name him "Ambassador for a Day" in a nostalgic variation of his earlier honorary title given to J.P. by Blanchard.

When asked if a hypothetical "Blanchard Presidency" would have included J.P. McCarthy, Blanchard says that although he knows he could handle the job, he does not think of J.P. as a Cabinet member. "I would think of him as Ambassador to Ireland, except every Irish Catholic politician in America wants that job, including [Wayne County Executive] Ed McNamara, and J.P. wouldn't want to go away," Blanchard explains. "If I were elected President, his would be the first interview I would do, and then I'd appoint him head of the U.S. Information Agency. Radio Free Europe, Radio Martí. Edward R. Murrow did that."

♣

Blanchard was also instrumental in arranging interviews for J.P. with a Blanchard friend, another young governor, who was attempting to make a move from Arkansas to Washington D.C. Thanks to Blanchard, Governor Bill Clinton's first interview in Michigan as a candidate for President was with J.P. McCarthy.

McCarthy spoke to President Clinton after he was elected, too. "Joe was expecting a call at home from the President because Clinton wanted to talk to Joe personally before the interview the next day," remembers Judy McCarthy, "so he was trying to keep the line clear. So our daughter Kathleen called and she started to tell him something, and he cut her off, saying, 'Kathleen, you'll just have to call me back later. I can't talk right now.' She said, 'But Dad,' and 'clunk,' he'd hung up."

"Of course, I had no idea what was going on," says Kathleen McCarthy, "so I was flabbergasted!" Judy remembers the call from the President going fine, and J.P. calling his daughter back to hear her in tears. "Once I realized what had happened, I teased him that it better have been President Clinton, and no one of less stature for him to take my call second!" Kathleen laughs.

♣

Another President from the South sat across from McCarthy on his "Focus" show:

"My next guest in 'Focus' was the thirty-ninth President of the United States of America, the first President from the South since before the Civil War. A man who, more than any other President in American history, addressed himself and his administration to the always volatile, critical, and thorny issues generated by the Middle East, for time immemorial.

"The Holy Land. A land of turmoil and a land today that is still a cause for great concern. A tinderbox, if you will, as it has been for as long as any of us can remember.

"President Carter, I think the Middle East was his peril and glory, from the shining hour of the Camp David accord to the nightmare of Iran. Mr. President, you look well. Thank you for coming."

"I always feel good when I'm in Detroit."

"The last time you were on this show, we reminisced about the 1980 campaign and about the Democratic Convention, and you did say that you were going to 'kick Senator Kennedy's ass.'

"Those were your words, and you did. Have you ever buried the hatchet with Senator Kennedy?"

"We've never had any personal animosity or unpleasantness between us. As a matter of fact, I saw him last month in Washington and we had a pleasant handshake and a few words about our families, but we have been political opponents."

♣

Car dealer Hoot McInerney remembers traveling with J.P. to Washington, D.C. at the request of then President Carter. "Carter called J.P. to Washington as one of the most influential people in the country who were called to discuss important issues," explains McInerney.

"Another time in Washington we rode down Pennsylvania Avenue in a Cadillac limousine throwing beer cans out the window, when we decided to crash a Rockefeller party. The radiator blew as we pulled into the driveway," Hoot laughs. "It's raining like hell and we go inside and there's George and Lenore Romney wondering how the hell we got in there. The party was supposed to be for ambassadors and diplomats, and we were in there dancing around!"

J.P. interviewed Presidents Ford, Carter, Bush, and Clinton, and he interviewed just about everyone who campaigned for the job. J.P.'s secretary, Dorothy Powers, remembers coming across

Senator George McGovern in the elevator after a "Focus" appearance. "He was smiling and he said to the person he was with 'I've been interviewed all over the country and that guy ranks right up there with the best!'"

Gene Healy remembers a similar incident while working in the WJR newsroom:

"McCarthy had interviewed Democratic Party Chairman Lawrence O'Brien," explains Healy, "and I happened to be in the elevator after the show with O'Brien and his assistant as they were leaving the building after the show and carrying on a conversation. They didn't know who I was, and the assistant began talking to O'Brien about the interview.

"'Well, that was pretty good,' he said.

"'Good?' says O'Brien? 'That guy was great! He was terrific! As good or better as any I've been up against anywhere. That guy had me spilling my guts, and I loved it,'" Healy recounts.

"I was so excited," Healy says, "that I was tempted to go back up on the elevator and tell J.P. But I waited for the next day and went to his office, where I found him going through his mail.

"'J.P.,' I said, 'I've got some good news for you.' I proceeded to tell him the whole story, word for word, and then I said to him, 'Isn't that fantastic?'

"J.P. barely looked up from his mail, and casually said, 'Yep. That was very kind of Larry.' That's the essential McCarthy!" exclaims Healy. "Other guys would have made me tell them the story over and over."

♣

Vice President Hubert Humphrey spoke face to face with J.P. during Humphrey's 1968 presidential run.

"Mr. Vice President, what will you think about in terms of picking your running mate?"

"Well J.P., it's my view that in light of the tremendous pressures on the president and the presidency and the real uncertainty of life these days—I hate to say that, but that's fact, that you have to have a man in the vice presidency that you really believe has the potential to be president of the United States."

"That was not always so."

"No, indeed it was not so. As a matter of fact, I think we've been very lucky in the past in our carelessness. All too often the VP was selected for geographical reasons."

"Political expediency."

"Really, that's what it was."

♣

The presidential candidates converged on McCarthy, and politics really did make strange bedfellows, when in 1992, both far left Democrat Jerry Brown and far right Republican Pat Buchanan chose to attend J.P.'s St. Patrick's Day party. "Brown and Buchanan were both the mavericks running for the nomination of their parties," remembers Gene Healy. "I got a big kick out of the way Brown and Buchanan were both diametrically opposed, had nothing in common, and just gave each other a little nod of the head," laughs Healy.

McCarthy reminded the crowd and his St. Patrick's Day listening audience that both Brown and Buchanan were Irish, and Buchanan even enjoyed an early morning green beer while CNN and the national media showed clips of J.P. McCarthy's St. Patrick's Day party all over the country on the evening news.

"Someone told Jerry Brown to get rid of the 'sissy coffee' he was drinking and have a beer," remembers partier Ed Oldani.

McCarthy was always respectful of, and even protective of, the presidents. "He had some high-profile doctor on 'Focus' one time," Healy says, "and she was involved in some kind of protest movement. She began taking potshots at Ronald Reagan. Really insulting things.

"'Just a minute, Doctor,' J.P. interrupted, 'I must caution you that I cannot have any more of that. You're not even a citizen of this country and you're talking about the president of this country, so I must caution you to cease and desist,'" Healy recounts. "She made one more comment and walked out. He chastised her, and that was it. The interview was over."

♣

"Very few politicians tried to give him a poli-sci lesson," insists *Free Press* columnist Bob Talbert. "Most politicians will try to give reporters a poli-sci lesson and get a leg up on them. I never heard anyone do that with J.P.," Talbert remarks.

McCarthy had a very good relationship with President George Bush. While they never spoke in the White House or in Studio D, they did meet in some very interesting places.

"President Bush was visiting his mother, who lived around the corner from the McCarthys at Jupiter Island, Florida," explains McCarthy friend Tom King, who was visiting J.P. at his Jupiter Island home at the same time, "and he was playing golf at the Jupiter Hills Country Club."

"They had the course blocked for certain hours, but Joe and I teed off early, and we were already on the course when Bush arrived to play. We went up to the tenth tee, which is the highest elevation on the course, and there were two young fellows that were about the age of my belt," King laughs. "They had a special case across the front of their golf cart, and they were wearing fatigue pants and golf shirts. In order to accommodate the President, the club had to have two hundred phone lines put in, forty secret service people, and helicopters circling.

"Joe hit his tee shot off on #10, and the young secret service man looked through his binoculars and said, 'Good drive, sir. That's about two hundred and thirty-nine yards. In fact, it's exactly two hundred and thirty-nine yards.'

"Joe was so curious, he asked the agent 'What are you looking through?'

"'These are laser binoculars built for the military,' the agent answered.

"Every drive we took, he spotted the ball and told us exactly how far the shots were. The laser binoculars gave him distance and wind conditions. Off the property were some satellite dishes set up on the coast to protect the President from incoming air attack.

"The agent peered through the binoculars and said, 'Sir, you see those dishes? They are one thousand three hundred and seventy-four yards away, and the windage is twelve miles north by northwest. With this rifle, I could hit the exact middle of that dish. Therefore, our President is in good hands if anyone tries to come over that fence.'

"Joe asked where he could buy those binoculars and the agent said, 'You can't. They're forty thousand dollars a pair, sir.'"

Meanwhile, Judy McCarthy was just trying to get to the club. "Joe was at the golf course, and I was going over to meet the girls for lunch," she explains, "when the secret service stopped me and said I couldn't pass. 'Look,' I kidded them, 'I belong to the club, he doesn't, and I'm going.'

"They kept me waiting outside the club for forty minutes, and I finally got in. Joe was having lunch and George was sitting with him and chatting with him, and then came over to our table and gave us hugs and talked to us about our golf games," recalls Judy.

♣

McCarthy's other meeting with Bush came in a much more formal setting, thirty-five thousand feet above the ground! During the final days of the 1992 Presidential campaign, Bush invited J.P. to interview him aboard Air Force One as he flew from Washington to Detroit. So J.P. flew, tape recorder in hand, to Washington, D.C. and boarded Air Force One, spending quality time with Bush and taping an interview. They even discussed common friend Dan Burke, the former WJR General Manager who went on to become CEO of ABC and Bush's next door neighbor and tennis partner in Kennebunkport.

Judy McCarthy picked her husband up at the airport. "I got to see him come off Air Force One, and I was so proud of him," she beams. "He got in the car and was so excited. He said, 'Think about this, Judy: How many men get to fly on Air Force One and have a private conversation with the president of the United States?'"

It was a long way from the time McCarthy and Hoot McInerney stood in the White House mess during the Ford Administration wondering whether it was okay to snatch the pewter White House napkin holders!

Judy McCarthy said that during his flight and conversation with Bush, J.P. got the idea that Bush didn't realize how dire the campaign situation was, and never considered that he might actually lose the election.

One group of people not so excited about J.P. on Air Force One were the Democrats who ran the Clinton campaign in Michigan. Clinton campaign staffers called Jim Blanchard to complain that J.P. was being "duped" by President Bush. "I told them not to worry about it," says Blanchard. "'He's fair. He's got to do both,' I told them. 'We can get Clinton on there anytime we want!'

"The staffers agreed, but weren't eager to put Clinton on, griping that J.P.'s audience was Republican, and I said, 'Well, then don't complain to me! When you want Clinton on his show, call me!' They had a bunch of third-graders running his campaign at the time," says Blanchard.

♣

Blanchard was right about one thing: J.P. McCarthy was fair. In an age when right and left wing media personalities make their mark by championing personal causes, beliefs, positions, and candidates, J.P. McCarthy never interjected his ideology or political affiliation into his show. "People learned more from J.P.'s interviews than they ever got from those ideologue windbags," says Michigan Attorney General Frank Kelley.

Chairman of Crain Communications, Keith Crain, agrees: "One of the things I found fascinating about J.P. was that in all the time I heard him on the radio, he had a unique ability of never giving away his positions. He was extremely political," says Crain, "and he had extremely strong social positions, but the listeners were never able to figure out if he was a Republican or a Democrat. Was he liberal or conservative? He was able to draw out other people's opinions without ever getting into his point of view. I've never run across anybody who spent as much time talking without giving away his views," remarks Crain.

"Regardless of who he interviewed," says Dorothy Powers, "people on the other side would accuse him of being one-sided. I think he maintained a good balance."

"One of his great skills," says Senator Carl Levin, "was getting useful information by putting people at ease without interjecting his own politics. If he had done that, guests would be defending or discussing his views instead of accomplishing what he set out to do, which was to, in a very low-key, chatty way, get important or interesting information from the people he was interviewing," explains Levin.

"He was the most neutral Democrat and Republican I ever met," says Ed McNamara. "He always tried to run it right down the middle, and if you polled 5,000 listeners, probably 2,500 would say he was non-partisan, one quarter would say he's Republican and the other quarter say he was Democrat," hypothesizes McNamara.

Just where did J.P. sit on the political landscape? It's been debated by many, speculated on by some, and many listeners insisted he dropped just enough hints for them to know. I can tell you this: during election years and heavy campaigning, I would get as many complaint calls from Democrats as I would from Republicans. It's the nature of the media. Nobody is ever satisfied that their party is being treated fairly, and while J.P. never consciously matched Republican guest for Democrat guest, they always evened out. He never even gave in to noisy requests for equal time unless he thought there was information to be gathered to further clarify an issue.

If he had any bias, it was a bias toward excellence and accomplishment. There were certain legislators he refused to talk to because he identified them as "bad men," and that was that.

"He was bipartisan," says Frank Kelley, "and if he liked you, he'd say good things about you. If you're a politician and J.P. says good things about you, that's got to help you! Those people who liked J.P. felt an inferred endorsement."

Kelley remembers J.P. calling him and Congressman John Dingell only days before the election. "John Dingell would have three hundred thousand people listening to him five days before the election," exclaims Kelley. "You can't buy an ad like that! Then he'd find some issue to call me about! He helped a lot of candidates!"

"I do remember that he'd allow people on that were running for office," says Ed McNamara, "and party didn't make any difference. He just made sure listeners knew the person was a candidate and it never seemed like there was an equal time rule. He didn't turn the other guy down, but if they were interesting, that's all that mattered," observes McNamara.

"He reached one hell of an upscale educated audience. J.P. talked to an audience of voters, fairly wealthy, activists," says Jack Casey, "and you weren't going to get on that show if he didn't like you, and he wasn't going to give equal time because it wasn't that kind of program. He was right to do that," says Casey.

In 1965, Casey was Jerry Cavanaugh's mayoral campaign manager. "Somehow we convinced J.P. to do the voice-over for a thirty-minute television commercial for a campaign rally," recalls Casey. "Can you imagine? As a campaign manager I was happy he did it, and as a former journalist, I was surprised, and wondered how he could do it," Casey exclaims.

What then was J.P. McCarthy? What political ideals did he identify with? What is the answer to the question once and for all? Was J.P. a Republican or a Democrat?

Senator Carl Levin says, "I had the impression that he'd vote for whoever he thought was the best candidate, but he sure as hell never made it very clear to me if he had any party affiliation."

Says Levin, "I remember talking about tax issues and capital gains issues and I thought he had certain views in that area."

Here's Attorney General Frank Kelley's vote: "I think he was a Republican. To show you the measure of his fairness and humility, nobody knows for sure. Probably Republican Governor Bill Milliken best represented his views, and Democrat Jim Blanchard to some extent. Both of them were moderate guys, and that's where he stood. He didn't get too excited about the extremes of anything, because he was very intelligent and could see both sides of any issue, which a rational mind should do. I'd say he was either a moderate Republican or a moderate Democrat, happy in the company of Bill Milliken, and happy in the company of Jim Blanchard."

"Bill Milliken best represented his views," says Jack Casey. "J.P. was definitely a Republican. He'd ask me on-the-air for debate analysis and he always thought the Republican candidate won the presidential debates."

"I always thought I best represented his views," says Jim Blanchard. "We agreed on economics, and he was not conservative on social issues. He was a very tolerant man, open-minded, and humanitarian. When you grow up an average kid on the block in Irish Catholic Detroit, and you end up being the pillar of Bloomfield Hills Country Club making millions in entertainment radio, I think there's a belief you have to become a Republican, purely on taxation, or there's something wrong with you!"

Blanchard laughs about the best compliment J.P. ever paid him. "He said, 'Jim, you really should have been a Republican!'" Blanchard laughs. "I used to say 'J.P., you could have easily been a conservative Democrat.'"

Wayne County Executive Ed McNamara agrees. "I think people might have considered him a Republican because financially he had those kinds of friends," says McNamara, "but he was a good friend of Democrats Jim Blanchard, Carl Levin, and John Dingell, and I considered him a good friend. I don't even know if he was registered to vote! I never thought about that!"

"If I was going to pick a politician that best represented Joe McCarthy," states publishing magnate Keith Crain, "it had to be Ronald Reagan, who was 'the great communicator.' Joe was probably a fiscal conservative and a social liberal. He and I were both independents. We didn't have a party that we supported up and down the line, but I think he admired Reagan for his ability to communicate and get things done. Joe did that on the radio," Crain observes.

"One morning I called him because he was going on and on about Bush versus Clinton," says *Free Press* columnist Bob Talbert. "He had just come back from Air Force One, and we started arguing about taxing and spending, and our voices raised and I finally said, 'You rich Republicans are all alike,' and slammed the phone down on him. He called me back after he got off the air and was laughing his ass off," grins Talbert. He didn't really take politics that serious. It was like a game to him.

♣

J.P. loved talking politics on the air and off. "He would speculate for months as to what would happen," says close friend and attorney John Schaefer, "until it annoyed me. I thought, 'Why are we speculating about this, when we'll eventually learn it?'" gripes Schaefer.

"One day I mentioned privately to him at the midterm elections in 1994 that Colin Powell and Elizabeth Dole would make great running mates in 1996," says Ford VP David Scott. "The next day I heard him ask an analyst on his show what he thought of that pairing. It was sort of fun!"

On the air, political analyst Jack Casey was always ready to talk politics. "He loved politics, and he'd throw the format out if we got going on a subject," Casey recalls. "Sometimes on the morning after an election we'd talk twice on the morning show and do the 'Focus' show too!"

While politics can be dry fare, McCarthy could keep it lighthearted. "He used to bet me lunch or dinner on political outcomes," laughs Casey, "and I wouldn't have to buy a meal for a month if I would have collected on them." McCarthy and Casey disagreed often. "I could always tell when he was getting irked at me because he'd say, 'Oh Jack, you're letting your Democrat side show.' I was always respectful because I knew that it was his show, but I couldn't let it go by if I disagreed with him. A lot of people kissed his butt on the air, so sometimes he appreciated it."

Even "Lifestyles of the Rich and Famous" star Robin Leach talked politics in 1991 when J.P. asked him if he was as rich as the people he featured on his show:

"I wouldn't want to be enormously wealthy, J.P. I don't know that you can spend it in the first place, and most of it goes to 'Uncle Sam,' who spends it on a lot of things I don't believe in. Getting rich comes with awful responsibilities of what to do with your money. I'd sooner not be rich. There is nothing wrong with being rich. I do not agree with the current 'soak the rich' rumblings coming out of Washington. We need rich people in the system. Rich people are extraordinarily generous people. They dig deeper in their pockets than any other segment of society for charity and those less fortunate. They fund libraries, hospitals, and charitable activities.

"We must encourage wealth in the U.S., and not tax people and put people out of work, but rather encourage people to earn more money and spend it back into the system."

"That's the whole idea, isn't it? Wealth creates wealth?"

"It certainly does."

♣

McCarthy took his show on the road from time to time, and his remote broadcasts weren't always from golf tournaments, as some critics might charge. In fact, he hosted radio shows from some very significant locations. He spoke with U.S. Ambassador to France Pamela Harriman while in Paris, and the U.S. Ambassador to Japan while doing remote broadcasts from a hotel across the street from the U.S. Embassy in Tokyo. Keith Crain remembers being at the McCarthy remotes live from the Okura Hotel:

"There was a great deal of commotion," says Crain, "and Judy McCarthy and I go rushing out to discover that very nearby, the Emperor of Japan and his wife had entered the hotel to attend a formal dinner party. We went back to the conference room where Joe was broadcasting to report what had happened, and he was indignant that we hadn't brought the Emperor to be interviewed!" laughs Crain.

"Instead, we gave him a fashion report," chuckles Judy.

♣

Judy McCarthy found herself playing another important role when her husband hosted his show live from the historic Reagan/Gorbachev Moscow Summit.

"That was an exciting time for me because Joe was busy working on the show and he sent me out to do some investigation on the meeting between Raisa Gorbachev and Nancy Reagan. I learned all about the 'cat fight' Raisa and Nancy got in, so I rushed back to the broadcast site and started to tell Joe, when he stopped me and asked me to go type something up so he could read it," says Judy. "So I'm standing at this copy machine with my typed information and I can sense someone trying to read over my shoulder. I wheel around and Peter Jennings says, 'Tell me all about it.' He wasn't aware of what had happened between Nancy and Raisa.

"I said, 'I'm not sharing any of this. This is for Joe's show and you can't know any of this!'

"'You little brat,' he kidded!"

Working from the same hotel with all of the world media, McCarthy became friendly with NBC News anchor Tom Brokaw, who would share information and ask about the show each day. While Judy McCarthy describes Bryant Gumbel as "somewhat less than friendly," she remembers ABC's Sam Donaldson displaying remarkable graciousness when things didn't go exactly as planned:

"Joe was conducting a live interview with Sam Donaldson and feeding it back to WJR, and they were almost finished with the entire interview when the engineer with us stopped Joe and told him the feed back to the U.S. had been lost and the interview had not been recorded."

McCarthy, never one to lose his cool, maintained his composure, apologized to Donaldson, and asked him politely if he wouldn't mind starting all over.

"Donaldson was gracious," says Judy, "and not long after they'd restarted the interview the engineer lost the feed again and signaled Joe to stop. Well, Sam didn't notice the signal, so Joe just kept right on going and finished the interview as if nothing had happened. He faked the whole thing because he was not going to ask Sam to do it a third time," Judy says as she shakes her head.

♣

Working in Moscow was considerably less glamorous than Paris, London, or even Tokyo, and the McCarthys remember brushing their teeth with vodka and drinking warm Coke because the water and ice was not fit to consume and riddled with bugs. They also took jars of peanut butter in order to avoid eating the usual "gray chicken" offered for every meal. A Radio Moscow representative drove the McCarthys, in his thirty-year-old "new car," to the fruit market. "We each got an apple," Judy groans. "They were about the size of golf balls and filled with worms."

The Tiananmen Square massacre quelled McCarthy's ambition to broadcast from China, but his next desire was to broadcast his show from Fidel Castro's Cuba. Negotiations underway would have had J.P. McCarthy speaking with Pope John Paul II and broadcasting from Vatican City with Cardinal Adam Maida of the Detroit Archdiocese and Father Wally Ziemba of the Pope John Paul II Museum at Orchard Lake. Sadly, McCarthy's death precluded that interview.

McCarthy did interview international political figures like Sinn Fein leader Gerry Adams, the Netherlands' Princess Beatrix and India's Lord Louis Mountbatten.

♣

Politics were always interesting back in Detroit. Anyone interested in the mechanics of Southeast Michigan was sure to tune to the J.P. McCarthy Show, because it was the "water cooler" of the Detroit political scene. McCarthy's friendship with Detroit Mayor Jerry Cavanaugh (1962–1970) set the stage for on-the-air relationships with mayoral heirs Roman Gribbs (1970–1974), Coleman Young (1974–1994), and Dennis Archer (1994–).

McCarthy producer Hal Youngblood remembers getting chewed out by Cavanaugh for phoning him too early and waking him to be on the show. "I'd say, 'I'm awfully sorry,' and Cavanaugh would say, 'Well, that's terrific. Don't you people think anybody deserves to sleep? Goddammit!'" Youngblood says once J.P. got on the phone, Cavanaugh would always brighten up and tell J.P. how good it was to talk to him. "He liked Joe and Joe adored him," assures Youngblood. "Jerome partied with Joe often, too, and sometimes where he ought not to party," whispers Youngblood.

Everyone knew that the flamboyant Coleman Young, usually at odds with the media, was more willing to speak his mind to McCarthy, who escaped being classified as "media" because of his impartial, noncombative style. "They both liked each other because Coleman is a 'no bullshit guy,'" insists political analyst Jack Casey, "and J.P. admired a lot of things about Coleman, and Coleman was an interesting character."

"J.P. and Mayor Young were both raised in Detroit," observes *Free Press* columnist Bob Talbert, "and Coleman, who didn't listen to any show in particular, started hearing about J.P. and started listening," explains Talbert. "He felt comfortable with J.P. because J.P. was one of the first guys in the media who directly helped an inner-city situation when he started raising money for the Detroit Police Athletic League. Coleman Young always said that morning was for 'chewing people's asses out,' but he did his best to hear J.P.," laughs Talbert.

♣

"I think Joe had a love for the city," says Keith Crain. "He was a Detroiter through and through, and I think it made him sad to watch the deterioration of the city. I'm not sure he had a grand solution," says Crain, "but I know he was frustrated watching it go down the tubes and he was frustrated with the people involved."

J.P.'s thoughts about what he'd witnessed in Detroit sometimes became evident on his show, as they did during this 1990 interview with television news anchor Bill Bonds just after the city was ravaged with fires on Devil's Night:

"J.P., I was just telling the next guest that the top of the Fisher Building here was one of my earliest failures. We used to come down on a day like today from Blessed Sacrament grade school, take the elevator all the way to the top, and then climb around the 'golden tower of the Fisher Building' and call ourselves 'the mud balls.' We wanted to see how our mudballs worked, dropping them from the roof."

"Was this a street gang?"

"It wasn't a street gang. It was a group of altar boys, see. After a half an hour of that we ended up at the old Bethune Police Station with Sergeant Miller, and our lives changed forever."

"Well, listen, that's what it was like before 1980 when suddenly 'Devil's Night' became something that nobody ever dreamed of or imagined even in their wildest dreams. Isn't that about when the fires of 'Devil's Night' started?"

"I think it really started in '67, when whatever Detroit's identity had been radically changed, permanently changed, and is evolving into something else."

" '67, July, the start of the riots."

"Clairmont and 12th Street."

"Detroit changed certainly in our lifetime and over the last twenty-three years. It was during the riots that you, Bill Bonds, really made your mark as a newscaster."

"I had taken my mother to the Bronze Door for dinner, and I happened to call the station. Acting news director Barney Morris said, 'There's something happening in Downtown Detroit. There are columns of smoke rising into the sky.'

"I said, 'Well, what is it?'

"He said, 'Nobody seems to be able to answer that question.'

"So I started making some phone calls. Somebody told me, 'There's no riot,' but when I asked, 'Where's Jerry Cavanaugh?' they said, 'He's at the Command Center.' At that point, I knew something had happened.

"I took my mom home, went to the station on a Sunday afternoon, and didn't go home for the next six days."

"Devil's Night is a difficult night in Detroit for everybody, especially for the firemen, the police, the mayor, the whole city administration, and everybody in the media."

"I think Coleman Young said it best yesterday. He said, 'I don't understand the sickness it is that has human beings fouling their own nest. Burning their own neighborhoods.' I think what the mayor was referring to was a tremendous cultural and moral gap that exists between a forgotten and lost generation of young people in the city and the people who are trying to put it back together. I think it's incomprehensible to most responsible adults."

"I remember, Bill, back in 1967 talking to the people on the street, the kids on the street, asking, 'Why did this happen?' Never will I forget their utter despair, their complete frustration. There was nothing for them and nowhere to go. That hasn't changed, and maybe it's worse."

"Oh, I'm sure it's worse."

Judy McCarthy remembers living downtown with J.P. in the Lafayette Towers when the riots occurred:

"We were playing golf at Detroit Golf Club when all of a sudden WJR Program Director Jim Quello came out on a golf cart and said, 'Joe, the city is burning down around us! There's been a huge riot!'

"Nobody could get into downtown Detroit. Joe sent me to my parents' house in Birmingham and found his way to the radio station. The next day, the city was acrid with smoke. I insisted that my father drive me to Lafayette Towers so I could be with Joe. The whole apartment complex was surrounded by tanks.

"Joe was unhappy that I'd come home and nervous about my safety, so he told me, 'Don't you dare come out of this apartment. Whatever you do, you do not leave this apartment.' So in the afternoon, after hosting his morning show, he came home and took one of his catnaps. I figure he's never going to know, so I slip into Joe's car, go right around the corner to the store, get some things we need, and hurry back, trying to leave everything exactly as it was, except I'd moved the car seat way up because I'm shorter and Joe is much taller than I am, and forgot to put it back.

"The next morning, at 5 a.m., with gunshots still sounding all over town, Joe races down to his car to jump in safely. He pulls the door open to get into the car and drive away as quick as he can, and because the seat is so far forward, he hits his head and knocks himself cold, falls to the ground, and thinks he's been shot! He comes to, feels himself to see where he's been shot, and finally realizes what happened.

"He called me from work, saying, 'Judy, Goddammit, do you know what you've done?' When I realized he was okay, I just couldn't stop laughing."

J.P. McCarthy with WJR veteran city reporter Bill Black on the "Focus" show in 1991

"White flight really began in this city in the '50s, and it accelerated in the '60s."

"It began with the freeways."

"Sure it did. It was a way to get out. The Davison got you across town, but it didn't get you out of town. The Lodge Freeway was the first to get you to the northern suburbs, the Chrysler, and the Ford, and so forth. But the white flight began in the '50s, and accelerated in the '60s, and really took off in the '70s, to where now, in Detroit, you have essentially an all black city."

"Detroit in the 1990 census is seventy-six percent black. That means there are two hundred and fifty thousand white residents in the city of Detroit."

"Many elderly who can't afford to live anywhere else, isn't that a fact?"

"If you're talking about the Cass Corridor—"

"I'm talking about the city."

"The Cass Corridor has the largest concentration of elderly people in the state. They may be stuck economically, but in other situations, they are not marooned. Some live there by choice and some not by choice. The point is, Detroit's white population equals the second largest city in the state. It's larger than Grand Rapids, and a good many people discount Detroit's white population. They make a remarkable contribution, and they're dedicated to the city."

♣

J.P., despite his perceived wealth and social status, was one of the white contributors who was indeed dedicated to the city. He helped city charities, covered city issues, worked in the city, and often played in the city, as friend Tom King remembers:

"We went, in the heat of the summer, to Willie Horton's bar on Dexter and Fenkell in the ghetto," says King. "We went in the back door, and if we weren't with the mountain of a man that Tiger pitcher Earl Wilson was, we would have been scared to death because we were out of our environment. It was dark, and the whole place stopped when we came in because they thought we were police," King continues. "We were really just two guys who weren't normally there. They introduced Joe, and all of a sudden the whole place was around him and treating him great! Just like a regular," insists King.

> *"As I was looking out here I was really impressed with this audience. I think the size of this audience is a tribute to J.P. It's a reflection of his listenership . . . old fat white guys!"*
> —Detroit City Councilman Gil Hill at the "J.P. McCarthy Charity Roast," June 13, 1994

Detroit Free Press columnist Doron Levin remembers being interviewed by J.P. and being impressed with the depth of his interest in Detroit's condition and future. "I once did a piece on how we ought to get the U.S. Army Corps of Engineers to bulldoze all these old buildings. The column was meant half tongue-in-cheek, because I knew the army wasn't about to come into Detroit, but the point was that we had to stop delaying and thinking that there was going to be a lot of rehabilitation money for these buildings. It would be a lot better for everyone if we just knocked them down," explains Levin.

"We discussed the difficulties and expense of that in a way that elicited a lot more understanding than the original column," remarks Levin.

On many occasions, a better understanding of a given issue was the result of J.P.'s interviews. Issues would be cleared up certainly for the listeners, and on many occasions, the public officials involved ended up with a clearer picture of the subject they were involved in. Answering J.P.'s simple "everyman's questions" could challenge officials to take hard looks at their positions. "He might challenge your position one way or another," says Ed McNamara, "but that didn't mean that was his position. He might take you on, but it didn't mean that he disagreed with you—he just wanted you to defend yourself," explains McNamara.

Detroit Mayor Dennis Archer, February 8, 1995

"Mayor Dennis Archer is on the other end of my line—up early this morning. Mr. Mayor, how are you?"

"Fine, thank you. I had a great run out there. It was a little cold this morning, but not as cold as the other day, when it was a –37 wind chill!"

"You're running in this stuff?"

"Yes sir."

"Okay, you're keeping in shape. Well, you have to, because they're nipping at your heels! Coleman Young, in that story he did with George Weeks, really went after you. That was somewhat of a surprise. He called you a liar, said that you'd dropped the ball getting things moving in the city on the gam-

bling issue, and the stadium issue and so forth. Did he just get up on the wrong side of the bed, or what's the deal?"

"J.P., I have no idea. I was just as surprised as most people in terms of the viciousness with which he pronounced his thoughts, but hey, listen, that's life. The great thing about America is that you're entitled to free speech whether you're right or wrong."

"Well, obviously there's something in his craw that's upsetting him. Do you know what it is? Have you slighted him, or have you not spent any time with him, or what do you think?"

"I don't know, J.P. I think you'd probably have to ask him. I can't put a handle on it."

♣

"I could tell from conversations we'd have off the air that he was more tolerant of gambling and wasn't anti-gambling in any real sense," says Frank Kelley, "but he'd still interview me on his show and carry on for five or six minutes explaining all of the reasons I thought gambling was not acceptable and nothing for the government to promote. He let me develop the whole situation. That way the audience could make a decision. They either wanted to buy what I was saying or they didn't want to buy it," explains Kelley. "He didn't have to filter it for them. He let you rise and fall on the basis of your personality."

"He had a 'why not, let's try it, what do we have to lose' attitude about gambling," says Keith Crain. "I think he'd be excited to see big time Las Vegas casinos in the city."

♣

On rare occasions, McCarthy would champion a cause. His influence and arbitration helped return Salvation Army coin-collecting, bell-ringing charity Santa Clauses back to the fronts of department stores from which they had been banned. That bit of on-air lobbying and publicity made Christmas much nicer for many less fortunate Detroiters, and on another occasion Mc-

Carthy made the freeways much safer for many Detroiters. WJR Newsman Gene Healy reports the story:

"The Detroit freeways were very unsafe in the '70s," Healy says. "The City of Detroit's financial situation made it impossible for them to properly cover the freeways, and the State Police were not patrolling Detroit's freeways. People were speeding down the expressway at very excessive speeds, and there were all kinds of car bumping robberies once the bad guys figured out no one was patrolling," explains Healy.

"People were getting mugged, raped, and robbed," says *Detroit News* columnist Pete Waldmeier, "and there was no way anybody was going to help you because there was no police patrol. The opportunists realized this, and if your car broke down, by the time you got back from getting help the wheels would be missing, and then everything else would be stripped," Waldmeier laments.

Downtown businesses and restaurants were also being hurt because suburbanites were afraid to come in on the freeways, fearful that they'd be mugged or have their car stolen just trying to get to the symphony or baseball game. The frustrating situation came to a head when the countless victims were suddenly represented by a familiar face:

"I was driving home after my daughter's birthday dinner, and my wife and daughter were following in the car behind me," remembers Waldmeier. "Three guys blocked me off on the freeway and robbed me at gunpoint."

"Pete's wife and daughter saw this and drove to the police station for help," adds Healy.

"I managed to get away," recounts Waldmeier, "but they smashed the windows out of my car and everything else."

"J.P. interviewed Waldmeier," recalls Healy, "and Pete related the entire story on the radio. Then, anyone who'd had a nasty freeway experience called in," Healy continues. "In the course of one morning, J.P. questioned the mayor, the head of the State Police, and finally asked Governor Bill Milliken to please help out."

"It wasn't anything we'd planned," says Waldmeier, "but it worked very well to resolve the problem."

"Milliken offered to send the State Police in for temporary attached duty until everything settled down." Exclaims Healy, "They came in one week later, they're still there today, and probably always will be!"

Another crime-related story that drew McCarthy's ire and attention involved his friend Ben Gravel, who was murdered by teenagers who'd blocked his path with fallen branches when he attempted to drive out of the Bayview Yacht Club. He spoke frequently with the normally media-shy Wayne County Prosecutor John O'Hair, imploring him to capture and try the juvenile perpetrators—whom he labeled "jackals"—as adults. "He wanted to know every detail of that case," says McCarthy friend Tony Frabotta. To the disappointment of many, the "jackals" were tried as adolescents, despite having shot Gravel in the head in cold blood. One was released and the other served two years in a youth home.

♣

As McCarthy's morning newsman for ten years, Healy saw many successful examples of J.P.'s influence. "Did he know which political buttons to push? You bet," says Healy. "Did he have the entree with the politicians? Did they stand in awe of him? Yes, with plenty of respect, too. I think they liked J.P. because they knew he was plugged in and had the state of Michigan's and the city of Detroit's interests at heart. They knew he talked sense, and when he touched a nerve, they didn't hesitate to go on his show," Healy observes.

"J.P. used to talk to Councilman Jack Kelley three times a week," says Kelley's aide Jack Mulcahey. "He'd even call him and get potholes fixed!"

Sportscaster Dave Diles remembers a not so pleasant exchange between McCarthy and Kelley:

"One day, I was going home in the car, listening to J.P., and Councilman Jack Kelley called in and nominated me for 'loser of the day' because it had appeared in the newspaper that I had filed for divorce," groans Diles. "Because of that, this lush, this loudmouth, called J.P. and nominated me for 'loser of the day.'

"Well, J.P. was polite and said, 'I don't think we're going to do that.' I called Kelley later and was so mad I offered to drub the hell out of him, and was even thinking of suing him. J.P. called him, too, and told him that it was a classless thing to do."

♣

Federal Communications Commissioner Jim Quello once launched himself into a full-blown feud with radio "shock jock" Howard Stern by being interviewed by McCarthy. "I told Joe one time that I wouldn't be surprised if a lightning bolt came out of the sky and hit Stern right in the crotch," laughs Quello. "Well, someone at the *Free Press* heard it and reprinted the quotation right next to the television listings, and it ended up as *People Magazine's* 'Quote of the Week!'"

"Funny, I was always fining Stern," says Quello, who was once WJR Program Director and therefore McCarthy's boss, "but sometimes Joe and I would have our own raunchy exchanges. He'd ask me how I was doing and I'd say, 'Oh, I still get my semi-annual,' and he'd say, 'Oh, no, you get your annual-semi!'"

Quello was instrumental in having McCarthy adopt his famous two-letter moniker in place of his given name, "Joseph." "I knew 'Joseph Priestley McCarthy' was not going to make it," says Quello. McCarthy himself explained many times how he came to be known as J.P.:

"When I started as a staff announcer on October 1, 1956, I was 'Joe McCarthy' for one day. The general manager was a fellow named Worth Kramer. Remember, the memory of Senator Joe McCarthy was still very vivid. The trials had only been a few years before and he'd just died. Worth did not like him or anything that he stood for, and he said, 'No one named Joe McCarthy will ever work on my radio station.' So chief announcer Charlie Park said, 'How about 'Jack McCarthy? We can't call you "Jay McCarthy" because we already have a Jay Roberts.

"I said, 'How about my initials?'

"He said, 'J.P.? It has a nice ring to it.'"

J.P. McCarthy for President

"If J.P. McCarthy had started his radio career in the '60s with his given name of Joseph McCarthy, the same name as that icon of red-baiting demagoguery, Senator Joseph McCarthy, we certainly wouldn't be saluting him today as a famous celebrity thirty years later. Actually, Mr. McCarthy would probably be mopping up a showroom at one of Hoot McInerney's car dealerships."
—Michigan Attorney General Frank Kelley at the
J.P. McCarthy Charity Roast June 13, 1994

♣

How can you sum up J.P. McCarthy's role in the politics of Michigan? He was important to the politicians and important to the political process. He kept an eye on national politics, his finger on the pulse of state politics, and his heart in local politics.

"I thought he cared deeply about Detroit and had a great feeling for the city," says U.S. Senator Carl Levin. "He was one of the great community institutions which help glue us together. When you get a radio signal, it doesn't stop at Eight Mile Road. When you have an audience that cuts across geographic and racial lines, you've got someone that holds it together," Levin continues. "We have him in common. City and suburb have him in common. Black and white and Hispanic have him in common, and it's that commonality which makes a community. It's that community institution that all people hold onto or connect with or listen to or know about. It's things we have in common. That's what J.P. was."

♣

"This town does not honor inadequate people. This town does not pay tribute lightly. I don't care what you say about Detroit. Detroit's idea of a mixed drink is a shot and a shell. This is a little town with a lot of people in it, and nobody has been better to Detroit than Joseph Priestley McCarthy."
—Sportscaster Dave Diles at the
J.P. McCarthy Charity Roast, June 13, 1994

237

♣ Station Break

"Why do I love boating and spending so much time on my boat? It's a perfect family activity. And even in Detroit, the fifth largest city in the country, it's only necessary to go a few miles offshore in 15 minutes and be in the middle of nowhere. One can in a short time be as remote from civilization as one would be in the farthest tip of the Upper Peninsula. And yet the top of the Westin Hotel is still vaguely visible.

"It's my way of getting back to nature, and I know that feeling is shared by several thousand other Michigan boaters. Michigan's magnificent waterways are one of the country's best-kept secrets and treasures, though we need more harbors and docks soon.

"I began my love affair with boating in a sailboat and enjoyed the peace and quiet. But my work limits the time I can

spend on the water and so I got into powerboating, which increases our range."

♣

As "Captain McCarthy" told AAA *Michigan Living* magazine in March of 1988, range was important because he liked to skipper his 44-foot Ocean Yacht Sports Fisherman *Station Break* through Georgian Bay, up to Canada's North Channel, a remote body of water at the top of Lake Huron that separates Manitoulin Island from the mainland.

"Joe loved boating, just like his dad did," Martha McCarthy explains about her son. "As a boy, he'd go fishing with his uncle up in Nova Scotia."

By all accounts, McCarthy was as passionate about boating as he was about any of his other endeavors, including golf. While flying lessons, horse racing, skiing, and some of his other hobbies were short-lived, boating was a mainstay in his lifestyle.

"Once you get on a boat, boaters are all the same," says McCarthy pal Tony Frabotta. "It doesn't matter who you are, how important you are, how big your boat is. None of that matters. From Joe's perspective, it got him back to the real people. There are no airs out there," Frabotta insists, "In golf there are airs."

"He was torn between his two passions: golf and his boat," says Tom King, "so he got into playing golf after work at 10:30, then he'd get the hell out to Miller Marina by 3:00. He loved his boat, and it was away from all of the 'Bloomfield stuff.'"

Although he claimed that solitude and escapism were benefits of boating, perhaps it was the social nature, like that of golf, that drew him to the water. He loved to engage in "boatspeak," and enjoyed the comradeship in the breed called "boaters," both "stinkpotters" and "ragbaggers"—powerboaters and sailors.

♣

"Joe's first interest in boating was with a sailboat," says Frank McBride, a longtime McCarthy pal and WJR boating reporter, who has covered the Port Huron to Mackinac Yacht Races for almost 40 years. "He loved the freedom to cast loose from everything in the fresh air and sunshine. He couldn't totally get away unless he was on the water." McBride, who serves on the Department of Natural Resources Waterway Commission, says McCarthy didn't really have the time, though, to keep a sailboat up, and Judy McCarthy agrees: "I was never really crazy about the sailboat. I can remember the kids on this boat, and Jamie was young, and they'd all put their life preservers on and Joe would make them stay below because he was afraid that when the boat heeled over, they'd fall off. They'd yell, 'Daddy, we're getting sick down here! Can we come up for air?' They'd be green!

" 'Stay down there,' he'd say. 'Judy, don't let those kids come up.'" Judy laughs.

Even though Judy didn't care for the sailboat, McCarthy named it after her. "Joe used to tease me that I was a detective because I knew where he was every single second of the day," laughs Judy, "No matter where he was, I could find him anywhere. So he called me 'J. Edgar Buttorf,' because Buttorf was my maiden name. Then he named the sailboat 'J. Edgar Buttorf,' and people would ask, 'Wherever did you get that name?'"

"We finally sold it, and graduated, thank heaven. That sailboat even made me sick, and it took too much time to sail, so we began looking for a powerboat," Judy explains. Says Susan McCarthy, "We were only one year away from the Port Huron to Mackinac race when he sold it."

♣

"I was a boater all my life," says McCarthy pal Tom King. "Joe was interested in powerboating, and began to ask me questions about it. His first impulse was to buy a 30-foot Scarab open boat with twin screws (two propellers). I told Joe that was the wrong boat for him. He needed something a little more domestic.

" 'Joe, that boat is a hotrod that would be good if you have a pair of Lucky Strikes rolled up in your sleeve, and tattoos!'"

" 'Nah, you're just making me old,' McCarthy disagreed."

He ended up buying a 34-foot SeaRay from Bill McMachon, but he didn't know a damned thing about how to run a twin screw," King continues, "so we would take him out after he bought the boat and go into Anchor Bay or the Grosse Pointe Yacht Club and work on his hand-eye coordination. He was very sincere about wanting to navigate this boat."

"We had to go to power squadron school," says Judy Mc-Carthy. "I could handle the smaller boats, but as he got bigger boats I could not. I could just see myself wiping out docks and buildings! I was insecure about docking, but I could drive once we got into the lake," Judy claims.

McCarthy did end up with "boat fever," and as King says, boat fever is about growth, so the next McCarthy boat was a 41-foot Egg Harbor. "That was a wonderful boat, a sports/fish," says King, "but on one occasion, we took our boats to Cedar Point, and the winds blew up on Sunday afternoon on Lake Erie when we were headed back. Lake Erie can be a helluva lake to navigate when the winds kick up. Joe had his family on board, and our boat was a little bigger and could run a little better, so while we moved forward through the rough water and huge waves, Joe didn't move so well and got bounced around like hell. That upset him tremendously, because he was in danger of becoming the 'pickle boat,' or last to finish, and being as competitive as he was he didn't like the idea of that. We talked back and forth on the radio, and the mileage spread. We got further and further apart," says King.

"When you traveled with Joe, he was always on the ship-to-shore radio. Every five minutes he'd be calling us on our boat," laughs Frabotta. "He'd say, 'What's your speed?' I'd say, 'We just talked about this five minutes ago, and we've already checked five times!' He couldn't stand not talking to somebody, so we'd chat and chat, and he'd always give his call numbers and sign off in an official way. King and I never would, but he always did," Frabotta grins.

McCarthy and the Egg Harbor known by the name *Station Break* plowed back home from Cedar Point after everyone else. "When we got back he sold that boat and bought a higher-powered boat that would never allow him to be the pickle boat again," laughs King.

♣

Station Break II, a 44-foot Ocean Yacht Sports Fisherman, would be McCarthy's next upgrade, which he had custom built. "It was a bigger and faster boat built at the Ocean factory in New Jersey," says McBride, who, with his wife Gerri, traveled with Joe and Judy to the plant in New Jersey to "sea trial" the boat. "When we went out on the boat, I knew something was wrong with it," McBride insists, "I could feel it in my feet. The captain went through all kinds of antics and I finally said, 'Look, Captain, you and I both know there's something wrong with this boat. I'd already mentioned it quietly to Joe. The propellers were not in pitch, so they changed the prop for us, but we lost a day on our nautical journey back to Detroit."

The McBrides and the McCarthys picked up the repaired boat the next day and headed north, stopping at an Atlantic City casino for lunch before heading up the coast. "We didn't make very good time because there was a lot of debris in the sea after Hurricane Kate," McBride explains, "plus Joe had a lot of relatives in New Jersey and so he entertained them on the boat."

They made their way up the Hudson River as far as Albany, but then J.P. and Judy flew back to Detroit so that he could be on the air, and the McBrides continued moving the boat up the Erie Canal until Joe and Judy rejoined them days later. "We then made our way through Lake Ontario to the Welland Canal, which collapsed right after we passed through and closed the lock for a month. It was big news at the time and had a big impact on shipping routes."

McBride says McCarthy made frequent calls to John McMurray at the WJR weather center to check conditions, and when they finally made their way home across Lake Erie, other boaters, who had heard J.P.'s position on the radio, pulled alongside to wish him well.

♣

Now, McCarthy's boat fever doesn't end there, but there were plenty of boating stories that occurred during his "exploration" and "navigation" of the Great Lakes area.

Free Press columnist Bob Talbert remembers an adventure with McCarthy and car dealer Hoot McInerney. "We finally found an afternoon where we could all take time off, and J.P. and Hoot wanted to show me the Detroit River," Talbert recalls. "They bragged, 'We know this river up and down. We know the river, we know the lakes, we know it all!'"

"We get out on the boat, and nobody's drinking, and they decided to show me Bob-Lo Island."

"We couldn't find Bob-Lo Island," McInerney howls.

"They never could find Bob-Lo," Talbert agrees. "They did all this talk about skippering and sailoring, and they couldn't find Bob-Lo. I wrote about it in my column, and it took a long time for those guys to live that down!"

Many, including Talbert, remember McCarthy actually skippering the historic Bob-Lo steamships in riverboat races down the Detroit River on a number of years as a fund-raiser for the Police Athletic League. Fans and donors could ride aboard McCarthy's boat or choose his rival, WXYZ TV's Bill Bonds, who skippered the other twin steamer. The *Columbia* and the *Ste. Clair* were giant three-level ships that normally ferried passengers and tourists to the Bob-Lo Island Amusement Park, which somehow evaded McCarthy, McInerney, and Talbert as it sat in the south end of the Detroit River at the edge of Lake Erie with its rollercoasters and thrill rides poking hundreds of feet over the horizon into the skyline.

♣

McInerney remembers laughing even harder than the Bob-Lo incident. Judy McCarthy was witness this time. "Joe was really safety conscious, and he always told us, 'No matter what you do on a boat, you do everything slowly and carefully. You don't make any fast moves, you make sure everything you do, you do slowly and carefully.'

"So Joe backed the boat in the way he normally would," Judy details, "I'm throwing lines, and Hoot is in the next well. Hoot and Joe are yelling back and forth, and Joe is not paying attention, and he turned and missed the whole step."

"I heard a big splash," Hoot says, "and I never heard anybody laugh harder than Judy!"

"He fell right into the water," Judy laughs, "and I thought he was going to be crushed because the boat wasn't secured. Of course, he came up blubbering, and we both looked down at him and said, 'Remember, you told us, move slowly and carefully!' He was so mad but we were laughing so hard!"

McCarthy got his revenge on his next boat ride with McInerney. "He made me go with him because he was entertaining some people from the Campbell-Ewald Agency on his boat," says McInerney. My doctor had given me some pills because I had a bad knee at the time, and McCarthy found the pills and threw them overboard. I couldn't walk without those pills!

During the cruise, McCarthy sat on his knee so he could see over the windshield, and accidentally strained ligaments in his knee!" McInerney laughed at the irony of McCarthy asking Hoot for the name of the doctor who gave him the pills at the end of the cruise! "He threw mine over and then he wanted me to give him the doctor's name!"

The doctor was Robert Nestor, who would become a very close friend of McCarthy. "He was boating and kneeling," says Nestor, "and going up and down on the waves forced his knee back to the point where he could barely walk. We had to do surgery on a Sunday morning because he wanted to get it over quickly."

Nestor, a boater himself, helped McCarthy on many occasions. "He fell through the hatch one time, and Judy called at 2:30 in the morning," Nestor recalls.

"Bob," Judy pleaded, "Joe can't get upstairs!"

"The name of my boat was *Housecalls,*" laughs Nestor, "so I ran down to his house and helped him upstairs and he came out all right."

Dr. Nestor remembers being with Joe and Judy in the Bahamas with three or four other boats. "We all went into Turtle Key, and had bad lobster. I was giving out medicine like crazy! Everybody got sick!"

It was Nestor to the rescue again when McCarthy's "turf toe" began acting up in Martha's Vineyard, where Nestor happened to be traveling the next day. "He called and said, 'Bring some medicine, Doc!' So I brought some cortisone, and we were driving a rented brand new white Cadillac Brougham, and I'm in the back seat injecting Joe's toe! We put the needles and syringes in a bag and threw them away. We were all laughing that anyone watching would think we were drug dealers!"

On a boat trip to the North Channel, King remembers needing Nestor's help. "He brought along B-12, and once in a while he'd give us a shot of B-12 to keep us going. B-12 was our hangover remedy," says King. "Once Joe administered a shot to Dr. Nestor, and put it in crooked. Nestor howled!"

Nestor, who then kept his boat at Miller Marina in St. Clair Shores next to McInerney and McCarthy, says they founded their own club, called the "International World Yachting Association." We had our own burgee on the bows, and he'd sometimes talk about it on WJR, announcing, 'IWYA meeting this week for the annual trip to the North Channel!' "

♣

The North Channel trips included lots of fun, and also some excitement, as Tom King remembers during a trip that included his boat, *The Venture, Station Break II* with McCarthy, and Dr. Bob Nestor's *Housecalls:*

"Nestor's boat was the only one that had radar at the time. The fog had settled in across the straits. We were traveling from the Canadian North Channel to Mackinac Island, which is about 50 miles," King continues. "We were radioing back and forth, boat to boat, and since Nestor had radar, he could tell us if we were going to run into anything, but he could also tell us how far we were apart. That's how close this fog had settled in. We could not see over 20 feet, and yet we were running at fairly decent speeds—over 15 knots—and Bob Nestor was like an air traffic controller. We were talking at all times."

"With visibility decreasing rapidly," McCarthy told *Michigan Living* magazine, "we gathered together abreast, with 50 feet or so between us, and ghosted along. Radar was the only means of contact for a time, and with it, Loran, and the VHF, we made our approach to Mackinac Island in zero visibility conditions."

"Joe and I made it to Mackinac, but we were on the wrong side of the pier," says King. We spoke to the attendant at the Mackinac docks on the radio and we could hear the foghorn, but we couldn't see anything. When something came into sight, we told the attendant we could see the lighthouse. The attendant said, 'You're on the wrong side! You'd better turn around quickly or you're going to be on the rocks!'

Frabotta and King remember what trips to Mackinac Island with McCarthy were like. "Grand Hotel owner Dan Musser and his public relations man Bill Rabe literally rolled out a red carpet, arranged for quick docking, and had a horse and carriage waiting at the dock with champagne chilled!" Frabotta exclaims.

"Joe never took cuts, but he never had to wait in line," explains King.

"When it was time for dinner, the Grand Hotel would send a carriage down with a guy in a top hat" says Frabotta. "We'd put on jackets and ties and go meet the Mussers, and they'd have cocktails for us at the Cupola Lounge on top of the hotel. Then we'd go downstairs for dinner."

J.P. enjoyed hearing the big band sounds of the Bob Snyder Orchestra at the Grand Hotel, and frequently talked to Snyder on his radio show. Snyder was a member of the WJR Orchestra in the late '50s and '60s, and had backed up some major recording artists in the "Motown" heyday.

"After dinner, we'd grab a bottle off the bar, get back in the carriage to go back to the boats, and just have a riot," explains Frabotta.

McCarthy friend Trip Bosart also remembers seeing the red carpet rolled out for McCarthy, but this time at Beaver Island, not Mackinac Island. "We were on his boat, going over to Beaver Island, and Joe had radioed ahead, so the townspeople were really excited to have him. We were going to spend the night on the boats in the harbor, and there were about five boats going over there, but when we got there, it was not exactly what Joe expected.

"All of the townspeople are out to meet him, and they take him around and take him in some old hotel that was really old. It was very rustic there, and Joe got it in his mind that he didn't like it there and he wanted out, so he called Judy Coy at the WJR weather center.

"'Judy, call me and tell me there's a storm coming and I've got to get the boat back to Harbor Springs.'

"So she waits about half an hour and she calls.

"'Joe, there's a storm coming and it's going to set in for about two days and you're going to get caught on Beaver Island.'

"'Okay, Judy.'

"He then makes an announcement and explains the weather situation.

"'We're out of here!'

"We'd been there two hours, the townspeople were prepared for us for two days, and they had everything but the high school band out there, and we get back in the boat and steam out just as fast as we steamed in, and they just stood on the dock and waved good-bye. I felt so sorry for them!"

♣

As fate would have it, McCarthy actually did get trapped on another Great Lakes island, this time while paying a visit to Domino's Pizza chairman and Tiger owner Tom Monaghan, who owned a resort on Drummond Island. McCarthy, Frabotta, and King steered their boats to the island, as King recounts:

"Tom Monaghan invited Joe to stop, so we did," explains King. "We had a wonderful place there, but we got weathered in there, and we spent four days with Monaghan, his wife, and his bodyguards, with our boats locked into his shore. He kept two unarmed bodyguards that worked out everyday and he would cycle them through different fitness tests every 30 days. If they could do enough sit-ups and climb the ropes enough times, they made the cut and were his bodyguards.

"We toured the island, viewed the island from airplanes, but the big thing was going to the dump to watch for bears. He had a tremendous workout center, and he gave us Toyota 4×4's to get around. Why he didn't have a Detroit product up there I'll never know.

248

"We were his guests, so we'd dine with him, and then he'd come down to our boats with his bodyguards, and he'd drink Perrier water, and Joe and I drank a beverage that looked like water. It was called vodka. We talked about different things. Children, family, or whatever, and as we were giving Monaghan more water, Joe and I were sipping on vodka and he thought we were all drinking water. Of course, Joe and I were beginning to feel no pain while talking to Monaghan!"

King says that Monaghan was a very gracious host, but after a while, they got bored, and in order to respect the fact that Tom was very religious, they had to sneak away to the only bar on Drummond Island. "Monaghan generously offered to fly us back if the weather hadn't lifted," King adds.

♣

Bosart also saw the red carpet rolled out at Put-In-Bay when J.P. would call and let Pat Dailey know they were headed for the popular south Lake Erie island resort. Dailey was somewhat of a local legend—a boozin', fishin', singin' bearded character that performed salty songs for rowdy bar crowds on the island. It had been said his show was "for mature adults and boaters," and Dailey, as a favor to J.P., would visit Detroit's Roostertail Club during the winter and perform a fund-raising concert for the Police Athletic League. McCarthy would introduce him every year at the event, and the joke was that Dailey had made his way through Lake Erie and up the Detroit River in his 12-foot outboard skiff, dodging the January ice flows.

"Dailey would arrange a special dock for us," says Bosart, "and he had a '68 Mustang that he kept on the island that he made available to Joe, and we'd visit Pat Dailey's restaurant and get seats right in front of the stage for Pat's show. We just had a great old time."

"Joe was always treated well by Pat Dailey," Tom King agrees. "We had a great time going to his show and going backstage and dancing in the aisles, doing the 'half-time,' and the 'jitter' to the '50s stuff. We'd visit every bar, restaurant, or Dairy Queen on that island!"

> *East coast, West coast, no need to roam!*
> *The North coast is better and it's closer to home!*
> *Bye bye bye bye babe, I'm going to Put-in-Bay!*
> — Pat Dailey

Meeting "characters" was just a part of boating. McCarthy's friend Tim Johnson liked to tell a story about a man J.P. encountered on a dock: "One year, we were shooting pool with two fellows in a bar up in East Tawas."

"One of the guys, not recognizing Joe, asks him, 'Say, what do you do, anyway?'"

"'Well, I'm in radio,' Joe answered in his usual, self-effacing manner."

"'Radio?'"

"'Yes, radio.'"

"'Well, listen, I've got one down on my boat that's not working too well. Would you mind coming down to take a look at it?'"

J.P. always liked chances to talk to people who didn't recognize him, but he didn't mind running across fans, either. "We were in Chatham, Ontario," recalls Tony Frabotta. "We'd gone up the Thames River. We were walking down the street in Chatham, and cars pulled up and they would stop and say, 'Hey, J.P.!' Joe would just keep walking and turn and look at me and say jokingly, 'They love me here too!'"

WJR meteorologist John McMurray, a veteran sailor, remembers visiting the Old Town Pub in Harrisville, Michigan. "Joe had been there two months earlier. They had a life-ring from his boat on display behind the bar, and they still talked about him!"

McMurray, while in the weather center, would often get early morning calls from the vacationing McCarthy to check the weather for his charted plan for the day. "He'd have continual conversation with John McMurray," says King. "Joe advertised that McMurray didn't forecast the weather, he created it! If

John said that it's going to calm down or get better, Joe took that as gospel and commanded the group to go ahead!"

♣

There were some occasions that didn't work out exactly as planned. "We got caught in some really rough rides and a few extremely dangerous situations on Lake Michigan," King allows. "Coming out of the Collins Inlet in the North Channel around Killarney on his 41-footer we ran into terrible weather. Heavy winds blowing, the boat was rocking 30 degrees, and it was all we could do to hang on. Joe navigated that boat back to the George River and into Killarney, and it was 17 miles of hell. We always had an itinerary, and Joe was not reckless, but he would always try to keep moving. He was 'Custer!' Almost fearless," says King.

"I never felt exactly like Columbus," McCarthy said, "and we arrived home salty but none the worse for the wear!"

"Joe loved boat adventures, and I loved adventures," says Judy McCarthy, "but the waves were huge and Joe gripped that wheel so tight that his knuckles turned blue. He was so patient and so competent and so knowledgeable about operating that boat. It took us a long time, but we made it safe and sound. We could have been killed!"

King remembers another example of McCarthy's safety conscious attitude and patience. "Joe came to my house with his whole family on his boat. My house is on Anchor Bay. He pulled his boat in, and secured it with Jamie and Kevin. We had a good time and were barbecuing steaks at my house when a severe storm came in. The boat was bouncing so much, and because of the waves, he could not get it loose. It weighed about 35,000 pounds.

"Joe said, 'The hell with it, I don't want anyone getting hurt.' The intensity of the storm was great, and the boat was getting damaged as part of the decking and hull took a beating. The swim platforms cracked off. It never upset him. His boat was his pride and joy, but he recognized the fact that salvaging it would be dangerous. You could see him watching the boat bounce around and saying, 'Oh, boy,' but it wasn't that important to take a risk," King explains.

At the helm, King says McCarthy was equally cautious. "Joe always took the lead until near the shore, and then he would wave me ahead, saying, 'Go on ahead, Eisenhower,' because it got dangerous with regard to bottoms and such. I had to tie my boat first, and all the other boats would raft off," King shrugs.

♣

"McCarthy was a very devoted captain. In the mornings, he was extremely serious about getting the navigational charts out, plotting the day, entering the points into the computer, and he would set up the trips," admits King. "He loved electronics and satellite systems. He wanted 'the latest.' He had fun with it, always remarking, 'Look at this! We came within a quarter of a mile of where we planned to!' "

The North Channel trips always required some planning and charting. "We stayed up past midnight going over our charts, plugging in the Loran (a computer navigational device), and full of great enthusiasm, camaraderie, and spirit," McCarthy said of the North Channel trips.

Port Elgin was the first stop on the North Channel trips, which basically circumnavigated Lake Huron. "We always had a cocktail party when we got to Port Elgin," says King, "and there was always a great debate over where to have dinner. We'd go through a lot of decision making, and there was usually only one restaurant in town, but we still made a big deal about it," King laughs.

"The main sport for locals in this small Canadian port seems to be walking on the docks at night to check out the day's fleet of boats," McCarthy said of Port Elgin.

The North Channel tour, according to McCarthy's charts, would then leave Port Elgin and proceed north along the shoreline of the Bruce Peninsula toward the Cove Island light, turning east around Cape Hurd. After passing through the Cape Hurd Channel, the Little Tub Harbor in Tobermory becomes the jumping off spot for Manitoulin Island.

It's past the Bear's Rump Islands that the course turns due north between Club Island, Lonely Island, and the east end of Manitoulin Island, the largest freshwater island in North America. At the top of Georgian Bay, a 90-degree turn west leads to the narrow Killarney Channel, where the group of boats would tie up at the Killarney Mountain Lodge for a few days.

"Joe always promoted a fishing contest in Killarney," explains King. "In this part of the country, if you had a gold ring on and you waved it over the dock, the fish would jump in your hand. Catching fish was not a problem. The ladies would always go out and buy a knickknack item from the area to use as a trophy. The tournament was for one hour. Size didn't matter. It was quantity, not quality. We had double hooks, and we were pulling in perch as fast as we could drop lines in," says King, and the next part of the story is open for debate. "Joe, in his exuberance, stepped and fell into the water."

"I was either pushed or fell into the Killarney Channel," said McCarthy at the time, "and with a water temperature of 55 degrees Fahrenheit, it's one of the most bracing dunks I've ever had!"

"He fell in and came out of that cold water like a jack-in-the-box," laughs King, "and his pole went right to the bottom. Dr. Nestor is a swimmer, so he dove all the way to the bottom, got Joe's pole, and swam back up, saying 'Ah, it's a little chilly!' "

On another occasion, McCarthy dropped his designer sunglasses in the water while looking over the side, and actually hired a diver to retrieve them. "The cost of the diver was half the cost of the sunglasses," laughs King, "so it was an investment well made!"

After the Killarney stay, McCarthy's group continued their voyage, heading west through the Landsdowne Channel, north to McGregor Point, and into the Baie Fine Fjord, one of only two or three genuine fjords in North America. The channel is narrow, and cliffs of white, bald rock jut straight up a couple hundred feet in this very remote setting.

"The pond we settled in in the back of the Baie of Fine was about the size of a city block," King details. "We tied our boats up to the shore, and we'd put plastic bottles on the lines to keep snakes from climbing on board. It was wild and woolly!

"We'd cook on our boat because we had generators. The ladies would cook and the guys would wash all of the utensils in the water, sitting on the back of the swim platform. Dr. Bob Nestor was an aquatic freak, so every morning we'd awaken to the sound of Nestor diving off the boat. We'd hear a splash, and it was like a rooster crowing. Time to get up! Bob dove in!

"Well, I'm sitting on the back of the swim platform washing the pots and pans while the guys relaxed, and a snake swam around past my leg and back up onto the rocks, and Nestor saw that. He never dove off that boat again for the entire trip! He dreamt about those damned snakes!"

After this portion of the trip, McCarthy's chart takes the boat past the northern tip of Strawberry Island, under the Little Current Bridge, and on to Drummond and Mackinac Islands before hugging the eastern Michigan shoreline back down past Alpena, Oscoda, Tawas, Port Austin, and again, Port Huron— eight hundred statute miles when complete.

♣

Boating was in McCarthy's blood, as he himself wrote in this 1986 WJR promotional piece that was supposed to be about his radio show:

"It's just possible that my audience has heard enough about my boat . . . about dodging hurricane debris on the way to picking it up in Atlantic City . . . about traversing the St. Lawrence Seaway, barely clearing the ill-starred Lock Seven of the Welland Canal just before the bloody thing collapsed—backing up hundreds of ships in the seaway! What a saga!

Can it be that you want more?

Can it be that you're waiting for every detail of my trip to Killarney, then on to the Bay of Fine (where the only sound to be heard at night was the sound of snakes slipping off the rocks and into the water around my boat)? Then, of course, it was on to Mackinac in a zero-zero fog. Surely you want more?

No? Well, what kind of loyal WJR listener are you if you don't want to hear more about my boat?"

♣

If McCarthy didn't talk about his own boat on his morning show, he was talking about other people's. As the end of each winter drew near, he'd remind boating listeners that better days were ahead by counting down: "44 more days 'til launch," he'd optimistically proclaim. Anyone who launched on the day he counted down to ended up with frozen fingers on the tiller, I can assure you!

"He never launched on 'launch day,'" King admits. "The Michigan weather was too bad. Instead, we had four or five launch days until the middle of June when the weather was great!"

J.P. might get the weather from John McMurray in the WJR Weathercenter, but John was an accomplished sailor, so there were many questions to ask about his trips into the Saginaw Bay aboard *The Edge,* his 30-foot Tanzer sailboat. J.P. even called on McMurray for boating help from time to time. "I went with McCarthy on a boat cruise with clients and sales people," says McMurray. "Since it was a 'flying bridge,' Joe drove from on top of the boat and I was down below, in charge of mingling and making sure nobody fell overboard.

"It was a long, long evening, and we went to Brownie's afterward. We both had to be on the air early in the morning, so at about 1:30, I said good-bye to him, and he said, 'I'll talk to you in the morning!'"

The WJR Weathercenter is located in Flint, with McMurray's home nearby.

"So I'm driving home," McMurray continues, "and I'm exhausted and trying to stay awake. I got all the way to Baldwin Road, and there's a Big Boy Restaurant, so I stopped, got out of the car, had breakfast, and it's already 2:45 a.m. and I've got to get home!

"I figured, 'I'll just go right back to the Weathercenter,' since I had to be on the air at 5. I'm still trying to stay awake, trying to stay awake, and I ran right into the back of an abandoned car. I came to a dead stop, and my hand slipped off the steering wheel and went right through the dashboard. I break two fingers, and I can tell they're broken because they're just hanging there.

"I called the office and said, 'You've got to come and get me because I've got a little bit of a problem here.'

"I get out of the car, after managing to get off I-75 at Dot Highway, and someone comes and picks me up and takes me to the Weathercenter. At 6:15 McCarthy comes on the air and says, 'Good morning, world. Good morning, John, how are you?' There I was, reporting the weather with my broken fingers taped together!

"I finally get home at noon, and my wife Mary Ellen says, 'What the hell happened to you?' She never minded when I went out with J.P., though. Anyone else, she'd get angry, but with J.P. it was okay," McMurray explains.

♣

Smoother sailing were the annual Port Huron to Mackinac Races, which McCarthy covered every year, whether doing his show from the Black River starting area or getting the reports from his boating correspondent and expert, Frank McBride. "We did the show from the back of Joe's boat, and I would help bring Mackinac sailors over as guests," says McBride, who says that sometimes Hoot McInerney would fly J.P. to Mackinac to catch the finish of the race.

McBride would provide race reports and updates to J.P.'s show while covering the progress of the racers from an airplane. McBride, who also gave J.P. a weekly boating report all season long on his show, got his start on WJR one fateful day in 1959. "I was in charge of the Patrol Committee for the Mackinac Races," McBride recounts, "and WJR sports director Bob Reynolds had permission from the Coast Guard to come aboard the icebreaker and cover the race. He was out there for the first time and had written his story on a yellow note pad. He handed it to me to read before he went on the air, and I read it a couple of times and I thought, 'How do I tell a guy like this that he doesn't know where he is or what's going on?'

256

"I finally looked at him and said, 'Mr. Reynolds, would you mind if I made a suggestion or two?'

"He threw up his hands in typical Bob Reynolds fashion and said, 'I haven't the faintest idea where we are or what's going on, but don't go away!'

"I took Bob into the radio shack behind the pilot house of the boat and got his radio channel back to WJR so he could do his report. He started the report with his usual opening line:

"'This is Bob Reynolds, sports director at WJR, covering the Port Huron to Mackinac Race for the first time. It's a beautiful day out here on Lake Huron, and standing here with me to tell you about it is Frank McBride.'

"He shoved the microphone in my face," laughs McBride, "and that's how I became WJR's boating correspondent!"

McBride, the stereotypical eastside Yacht Club commodore type, traveled with McCarthy to cover a much more significant yacht race, the America's Cup races in Freemantle, Australia, in 1987. "J.P. and Dennis Connor got along well," says McBride.

The trip to Freemantle was long and could be considered arduous, until you consider that J.P. made the best of it in his McCarthy fashion. After flying to San Francisco and connecting to Hawaii, where they refueled in the middle of the night before traveling ahead to Sydney, Australia before changing planes to go on through Melbourne and the Great Barrier Reef. "Joe wanted to do some diving," McBride admits, "so while he was diving, I worked on the show."

The McCarthys and McBrides stayed there for three days and then went back to Sydney for a few days before flying on to Perth, in Western Australia. "Flying from Sydney to Perth is like flying from Detroit to LA," says McBride. "It was a long flight along the Indian Ocean, and we'd look down out the window and McCarthy thought it resembled the moon because there was nothing there. Just a highway and a beach for all those hours."

Once in Perth, the group stayed at the Esplanade Hotel, just a short walk from the America's Cup Press Center. "We each had an outside balcony," McBride explains, "and on the other side of the privacy screen, I noticed a man on the balcony with gray hair reading the paper, and the next day when Joe interviewed him, I found out it was Walter Cronkite!"

"Walter Cronkite and his wife are the loveliest people in the whole wide world," Judy McCarthy insists. "I was coming upstairs in the hotel and I came up with his wife in the elevator. We were standing in the hallway chatting, and she introduced me to Walter when he came out. I told him who we were and explained that my husband was broadcasting back to the United States. Walter came to our room and sat on our bed and taped an hour-long interview with Joe! He was so warm and friendly."

The McCarthys' room was next door to the Cronkites', and Judy remembers sitting with J.P. and having coffee on their balcony. "Walter would stick his head around and say, 'Good morning, you two! How are you?' What a voice to hear as a wake-up call!"

McCarthy broadcast three hours a day from Freemantle. "We'd go on the air at 7 p.m. in Australia because of the 13-hour time difference," explains McBride, who helped arrange interviews for the show.

"Nobody could get any interviews with Alan Bond," explains Judy McCarthy of the man who financed Australia's America's Cup bid. "He was being incognito, but I got close to him because I knew tennis player Margaret Court from the Virginia Slims series, and her husband was Alan Bond's right-hand man. I was introduced to Alan Bond, and I used my maiden name and told him that I was Joe's producer.

"'Mr. Bond, Joe McCarthy has a big show in the United States, and it's heard by millions in over 59 states.' I made up this big thing," Judy admits.

"'You know, this guy is lucky to have you as a producer,'" Bond told Judy. "'You are a good talker! For you, I will do an interview.'

"We loaded into the car and he had so many sycophants that I ended up having to sit on his lap," Judy groans, "but when we got to the live interview site, Joe was already on the air. He looked up and saw who I was bringing him, and his eyes got as big as saucers! Bond sits down and does the interview with him, and when the commercial is on during the break Bond tells Joe, 'You know, you wouldn't have gotten me over here if it wasn't for your producer. I haven't been doing any of these, but she is some talker!'

" 'Producer? Thank you,' Joe said. 'She's my wife!' "

♣

"We are here in Freemantle, and just about an hour ago, down in Dennis Connor's headquarters, inside the Stars and Stripes *compound, we observed the victory bedlam and saw Dennis Connor soundly dunked in the drink along with all the crew.*

It was a very quick series. Four wins in five days, the quickest in almost one hundred years. The biggest margin was today . . . almost two minutes. Frank McBride watched every turn around every single marker, and fills us in. Francis?"

"Well, Joe, the start was the best we've seen in a while. Ian Murray and the *Kookaburra* crew did the finest job that they've done. They were very aggressive at starting time and it looked for a while after the gun went off that he was going to be able to tuck the *Stars and Stripes* away, force them outside the line and make the start. But the cagey little pelican from San Diego . . .

"Excuse me Frank—'little' is not an adjective that one uses for Dennis!"

♣

McCarthy and crew watched Dennis Connor make history on February 4, 1987, in the first successful American reclaiming of the America's Cup in the long history of the series, after being the first American skipper to lose it, when the Australians beat him in 1983. As Dennis Connor prepared for his title defense back in San Diego in 1992, he visited J.P. in the studio:

"Hey, J.P., nice to be here. I'm looking forward to getting you out in San Diego for a ride on the new America's Cup class boats."

"I will be there with my whole crew."

"I'm counting on you."

"Tell us about the new boat."

"It's about ten feet longer than the 22-meter, so it will be around 75 feet long. Instead of eleven in the crew there will be sixteen. It's a very high-tech boat. As opposed to aluminum, the new construction encompasses carbon fiber and honeycomb, much like the Stealth Bomber and the Space Shuttles. The whole project is very, very high-tech. We're using computer design as opposed to the old-fashioned way of just drawing it up and testing it in a test tank."

"Most of the syndicates have corporate financial backing. How else could you do it?"

"Fortunately for me, I've been able to secure the help and support of Cadillac Motor Car. They've been terrific, not only financially, but they've actually helped us in the wind tunnel, and the Tech Center helped us to build a faster boat, so I'm really indebted to them."

"Did they really? Has General Motors assisted you in the design of this boat? I didn't know that."

"Well, they have the best wind tunnel in the world."

"I've been in it."

"As you know, it's really fabulous. This enabled us to build a large-scale model of our boat and then run the wind over it and see how the flow attaches at various angles of attack on our rudder and keel, and this verifies our computer code. That's really how boats are designed now is in a computer, and this really gives some real, live, tangible evidence that the codes are right. It's a key part of our design program right here in Detroit."

♣

At the San Diego races in May of 1992, Connor and *Stars and Stripes* lost the chance to defend to Bill Koch and the *America 3* syndicate, but Connor was a guest on J.P.'s show, and spent some time with McCarthy while he broadcast from the Harbor Marriott. "Dennis Connor really liked Joe a lot," says Judy McCarthy. "We went to his home for cocktails, and Dennis arranged for Joe to be on a chase boat right near the races."

It was very stirring to be at the kickoff party at the San Diego Yacht Club, drinking champagne on the dock with McCarthy, when a large yacht pulled up and the enthusiastic *America 3* crew filed off the boat, dressed in red, white, and blue, toting sports' oldest trophy: the America's Cup.

The McBrides were along again, and *Yachting* magazine publisher Oliver Moore guested a number of times during the three days of broadcasting, as did Miss America Carolyn Sapp, who attended the races and promised J.P. a dance at the America's Cup Ball, and Tom Ehman, an Ann Arbor man who held the post of Director of the America's Cup Organizing Committee. Since the time difference made it impossible to host his morning show back east, J.P.'s America's Cup San Diego broadcasts ran from 6 until 8 p.m., in place of the WJR "Sportswrap" show.

Patriotic as he was, J.P. and our small crew couldn't help but root for the Italians in the finals against *America 3* so that we could broadcast from Italy at the next cup defense. *America 3* went on to beat the Italians four races to none.

♣

Though McCarthy was often criticized for doing too much "boat talk" on his show, he became somewhat of a spokesperson for the boating industry and an ambassador for the sport in the Great Lakes area. "I should have appointed him to the Waterways Commission," says former Governor Jim Blanchard, who recognized McCarthy's popularity as a leader in the boat community.

"I got it into my head that I wanted to trace the shoreline of the state by water in July of 1989," Blanchard explains. "The Shoreline Tour was a celebration of the Great Lakes that took six days. We started down in New Buffalo, and at each stop I did different things. At one point I signed 'dunes legislation,' for Coast Guard safety. At another stop we dedicated a new marina in Grand Haven. We did 34 stops, and traced the entire shoreline of Michigan by boat and helicopter.

"Each time we went into a port, local boatsmen would greet us. We'd come into a channel and they'd all be honking their horns and holding signs and escort us into a marina, where we'd land, and a high school band would be playing. The mayors would be there with a key to the city and the local leaders would be there while tourists would look on," Blanchard continues.

"New Buffalo up the western side of the state, to St. Joseph to South Haven to Holland to Grand Haven to Muskegon to Ludington to Manistee to Frankfort to Leeland to Traverse City, over the top to Mackinac, and down the east coast to Alpena, Oscoda, Tawas, Lexington, Port Austin, Harbor Beach, Port Huron, Marine City, St. Clair Shores, on to Detroit and Monroe. We did the Upper Peninsula on a different leg.

"We had different hosts on different boats, and when we did the St. Clair Shores to Detroit leg, I was on J.P.'s boat. He escorted me to Hart Plaza in Detroit, where we were going to be greeted by Mayor Coleman Young. That was not the most quaint stop. All around the state I had been met by throngs of smiling, happy people, and I'd talk about what a great state it is and how blessed we are, but when we got to Detroit, there was a big group of environmentalists screaming and yelling and throwing things and shouting about how awful Coleman Young was and how bad I was to be seen with him. They were protesting the Detroit incinerator.

"I remember saying sarcastically to Joe, 'This is really a great job I've got!'

"Joe was feeling bad because I was coming in on his boat and he was kind of presenting me to this mess that was really directed at Coleman Young, but I had to be gracious about it because he was there to greet me.

"I said, 'This is how I earn my pay, Joe!'

"He felt sorry for me but he was laughing about it," Blanchard chuckles.

262

♣

McCarthy's shining hour as a boater came in May of 1994, when an opportunity to test his years of boating experience and expertise presented itself. In a variation of the infamous "Cannonball Run Road Rally," Brock Yates, who originated the actual Cannonball Run and also wrote the screenplay, founded a 1,200-mile Miami to New York Cannonball Offshore powerboat race.

"When I first proposed the Cannonball Offshore, who knew how many people would think it was inside the envelope of rational behavior?" Yates would later ask.

McCarthy's version of rational behavior was to assemble his "dream team" boat crew to make a run at boat racing legend Gar Woods' speed record on the Miami to New York run. Captain McCarthy's crew would be:

- Tom King, longtime friend, Chairman of TEK Sales & Marketing, and captain of his own *Venture*, a 47-foot Egg Harbor.
- Oliver Moore, Publisher of *Yachting* magazine.
- John McMurray, the WJR meteorologist and sailor who would be helpful with reading weather conditions and charting courses.
- Tony Frabotta, Chairman of the Executive Committee at Follmer & Rudziewicz Accounting, seasoned boater, partner in *Venture*, and McCarthy pal.

This four-man crew and their captain called upon Pete Beauregard at Colony Marine in St. Clair Shores to help secure a brand new 44-foot Sea Ray with 420-horsepower Cummins diesel engines. The powerful boat was christened *Longshot*.

Frabotta accompanied McCarthy to Daytona for some pre-race "sea trials" with the brand new boat. "We get to the factory, and we see the boat with 50 guys all around it detailing it and cleaning it, and the Cummins people are down in the engine. Joe introduces me as his 'first mate,' and tells the guy from Cummins that I'm a diesel expert. The guy then takes me down into the engine compartment for an hour and shows me everything, and I have no idea what he's talking about," Frabotta grins.

"Okay, Captain, take her out for a run and see if you're ready," the man from Cummins tells McCarthy. "As we pull away from the Cummins dock, they're all watching." First mate Frabotta winces. "Joe looked at me and said, 'I just hope I don't ram that dock on the other side. All these people are watching!'

"He was nervous because the whole factory was watching, and we were their team. After we got away from the dock, the factory guys were whooping it up and throwing their hats in the air," Frabotta exclaims.

McCarthy and Frabotta did three days of sea trials and shakedown cruises with the gleaming new *Longshot,* but they were careful when they passed a certain shoreline house. "The Cummins people told us they test boats in those waters all the time," Frabotta explains, "and that the woman who lived in the house didn't like fast boats, and so she shoots at boats going too fast or making too much noise!"

So far, race preparations had gone smoothly, and the equipment was world class. Budweiser Racing provided the refreshments necessary to make such a grueling effort, and the crew was outfitted in monogrammed blazers, hats, jackets, and complete uniforms by Hoot McInerney. "We must have had 19 meetings to get our uniforms right," Frabotta laughs.

Apparel man Tom Brooks even set the team up with tear-away T-shirts so the team could show off and intimidate competitors at the Miami starting line by showing off their bare chests and gold chains.

"We were getting ready at the starting marina in Key Biscayne," says Frabotta, "and all of the other boat racers were loading in Evian Water and Powerbars. Then, our Budweiser truck pulled up and the driver wheels in sixteen cases of beer onto our boat." They fit the sixteen cases in the gunwhale below deck.

The competition was stiff. Entries included major players like Buzzi, Shaun Hall from Donzi, Ed Szilagyi from Volvo Penta, Craig Barrie from Cigarette, Bud Lorrow from Hawk, and Ted Sabarese with his Fountain. Nine boats started the race. Five made it to the finish in New York Harbor.

The crews woke up early on race day the next morning. "Everyone was excited, and the anticipation was so great that nobody could sleep," Frabotta remembers. "I kept thinking 'Hey, we're really in a race!' Up until this point, it was all sort of a joke!"

At the starting line, a camera boat filmed the start of the historic race on a beautiful morning. On the advice of McMurray, however, the crew decided to run up the intercoastal waterway instead of speeding up the coast in the ocean as originally planned. "It was bright and sunny," McMurray explains, "but with southeast winds all the waves shoal so that you get six- or eight-foot waves right at the shoreline. If you get two miles offshore, you might get past that, but it's not easy to get out there!"

"All of the teams raced 'inside,'" Frabotta adds, "but the Italians in the mad yellow Donzi boat didn't understand the 'no wake' laws in the waterway. They didn't speak English. The Florida Patrol had their guns out, and the Italians had their hands in the air as they were taken off their boat! We cheered as we went by them!"

"That's the spirit of the 'Cannonball,'" McMurray insists.

As the team approached Jupiter, where McCarthy had a home, J.P. called ahead to a place he liked and ordered lunch. "Lunch was two hamburgers and a few chicken sandwiches," McMurray details, "and so I said I would buy lunch. The bill came to $97.00!"

"That's the last time you'll buy lunch, eh!" King kidded McMurray.

While McMurray went alone on that pricey lunch bill, the crew's policy was to rotate, every hour, through the positions of driver and navigator, then three hours off.

McCarthy wanted to run the boat through the night, but the crew convinced him to tie up in the evenings for cocktails, dinner, and sleep. "Other than that, we were running all day," Frabotta explains. "Our goal was to be the first non-production boat to make New York Harbor."

The *Longshot*'s first night was spent at the Cape Canaveral Yacht Club near the NASA launching pads. "We had to stop because we ran out of vodka and supplies," McMurray jokes. "I put some ice in a glass and poured some scotch in it and handed it to Joe and he looked at it and handed it back to me:

"'Give me some more ice,' he ordered. 'What are we, at war?'"

Day two of the Cannonball Offshore provided more excitement, and even danger, as the *Longshot* ventured out into the ocean at the Ponce de Leon Inlet near St. Augustine to try to save time and make it to Charleston, South Carolina that evening for a party at Cummins headquarters being thrown in their honor. "We were going out into the ocean and a huge wave crashed over and soaked all of our instruments," Frabotta says. "After the first wave crashed over and I saw the second one, I started passing out life preservers because I thought we were going down!"

"The further out you go, the calmer it was," says McMurray, "but the problem was, we were running out of gas!"

They finally made it to the party in Charleston two hours late, after battling the sea and nearly hitting a breakwall on the way in after a navigational dispute among the crew. McCarthy settled the tense moment of indecision with his strong leadership.

"There's only one captain and only one navigator and only one helmsman. Everybody else, be quiet!" he yelled.

Weatherbeaten and exhausted, the *Longshot* crew made an appearance at the Cummins party. "These guys started telling us all about diesel engines, and I was fading fast," McMurray allows. "We stayed in a hotel that night and were up again at 5 a.m. to do it again."

"At that point, whether he really knew it or not, Joe claimed we were leading the race," Frabotta recalls, "as we headed up the coast past Frying Pan Shoals to Oriental, North Carolina." Running low on fuel, with darkness approaching, team *Longshot* put in for the night.

After Oliver Moore got a tip from the locals in Oriental, the *Longshot* crew decided to head up the Alligator River as a shortcut to Norfolk. "The locals claimed we could run wide open and still be inside, and not have to worry about the wake," Frabotta explains. "This canal system was developed by the U.S. Army Corps of Engineers during World War II because they didn't want submarines knocking our ships out. The locals said, 'If you're looking at the shore and you see sand, it's too shallow. Head for the tree side of the river, and be careful.' We thought we'd make up time because John said the weather was going to turn bad."

The locals didn't tell Moore that there would be stumps everywhere. "There were stumps all the way along," Frabotta groans, remembering the crew trying to get to Cape Henry, which was the inlet into Chesapeake Bay. "I was the helmsman and Oliver was the navigator," Frabotta continues. "He kept telling me to go faster, and I was not comfortable going that fast in that tight river. I was getting nervous in that canal, and at the end of my hour at the helm, I was very happy to turn the wheel over to Oliver, who had Tom King as his navigator."

Meanwhile, McCarthy was calling in reports to WJR and letting the listeners know about the *Longshot* progress. "Joe wanted to know how far we were from Norfolk," McMurray recalls, "so I went below and sat down to look at the charts and map out the distance. All of a sudden, the lights went out and I'm bouncing around like a rag doll! The refrigerator opens up and all the beer cans come flying at me!

"I look around and I hear McCarthy yell at Moore, 'You son of a bitch! You ran us aground!'

"Joe was so mad," Frabotta reveals. "I'm lying on my back on the back deck because I went forward, hit the dashboard, cracked a rib, and landed on the floor. I wasn't breathing real good," Frabotta admits. "McMurray comes running out of the hold and he's got blood running down his face. As the navigator, King saw it coming, so he braced himself. Oliver was on the wheel when it happened, and Joe was on the phone. With the engine no longer running, everything was so quiet, except for Joe, who was thinking about having Oliver walk the plank."

It was a sobering moment as McCarthy and Frabotta stood together in the water, preoccupied with surveying the damage to *Longshot*.

"Are we going to sink?" McCarthy asked Frabotta.

"We're standing in water up to our ankles, Joe. We're buried on a sandbar."

"Say, Tony, why do you think they call this the Alligator River . . . ?"

Fearing the answer, the two men jumped quickly back in the boat and McCarthy got on the phone to call for assistance.

"Joe calls and says that we ran aground," McMurray says, "but I interrupted him, saying 'No, no, don't tell them we ran aground. Say that we hit a submerged log!' Meanwhile, I look over and see that Tom King had gotten the emergency distress buoy out of the box and was getting ready to throw it over the side. It sends out a distress signal when you throw it over so that if the boat goes down they can still come and find you.

"'No, no, no,'" McMurray stopped him. "'When that thing hits the water you'll have Coast Guard helicopters coming from everywhere!'

"We weren't sinking," says McMurray. "We were sitting!"

Even though mechanics worked all night to fix the boat, and a hired captain took them safely the rest of the way through the Alligator River and two locks, a deeply disappointed team *Longshot* gave up in Norfolk, where the wind was "blowing like hell," and the crew realized they wouldn't even make New York Harbor in time for the Cannonball Awards party. The group made a pact never to reveal who was driving when the *Longshot* met its unglamorous fate.

McCarthy ended up buying the *Longshot* and could from then on be seen racing around Lake St. Clair, plotting his next Cannonball race. "Joe had been thinking about buying the boat," says Frabotta, "but after the accident he felt a little required to buy it. He loved the boat. It was the best boat he ever owned."

"That boat could really get up and go," says McMurray.

♣

McCarthy certainly enjoyed his days with *Station Break* and on *Longshot* in Lake St. Clair, spending time at the "Little Club" and the "Old Club," and frequenting Eastside establishments like Bobby Moore's Blind Fish and Jack's on the Water in St.

Clair Shores and Mac & Rays at MacRay Harbor in Harrison Township. "'The Old Club' is on Harsens Island," says King. "Sometimes we'd overnight there, and Joe liked to run up there for lunch during the week." The lakes and waterways were J.P.'s playgrounds, and the *Station Break* boats and *Longshot* were his high-powered tricycles.

After J.P.'s death, Judy McCarthy sold the *Longshot,* and donated the proceeds to help found "The J.P. McCarthy Foundation" to fight blood disorders. Maybe now, beating a rare blood disease will no longer be such a longshot.

> *Sweet mother Michigan*
> *Father Superior*
> *Running down from Mackinac and Sault Ste. Marie*
> *Blue water Huron fall down to Lake Erie*
> *Fall to Ontario, and run on out to sea.*
> — Pat Dailey and Shel Silverstein

Just Don't
♣ Tell 'Em
Where I Am

"I've been doing this for a very long time. I never thought I would do one thing for this long. I thought it would get boring, get stale, get old, and that I would, too. To be around as long as I have in this business is remarkable, but frankly, I enjoy doing what I do, and I hope to do it for a good deal longer."

— J.P. McCarthy, October, 1992

It had been a somewhat ordinarily exciting 1995 for J.P. Mc-Carthy. After his annual Christmas break at his Jupiter Island home, he returned to Detroit a few days after New Year's Day and began his week of extensive automotive industry interviews leading up to his television appearance in Cobo Center at the North American International Auto Show. His St. Patrick's Day Party at the Fox Theatre, shown statewide on cable televi-

271

sion, had been his most successful yet, with well over one thousand people in attendance. The eventual syndication of his morning show was at hand. He'd cut the "Focus" show out of his daily routine, and begun to really make use of his free time, departing the radio station at 10:30 nearly every day.

He'd taken a trip to Las Vegas with his old pal Hoot and sat ringside to watch local middleweight boxer James Toney fight at the MGM Grand, and traveled once again to Ireland with Judy and the Schaefers. He and Schaefer were planning to build new homes in Florida on the Loblolly Pines Golf Club, which they had recently joined.

Meanwhile, J.P.'s annual Police Athletic League Pro-Am golf tournament was again a smash success, raising over $125,000 in the single-day event attended by his old Tour pro friends Jim Colbert, Fred Couples, and Lee Trevino.

He enjoyed watching the Red Wings make it to the Stanley Cup finals from his lower bowl seats, and his impressive *Longshot* boat was primed and ready for another full summer on the lake.

The excitement of his youngest son Jamie's engagement and brand new job at BBDO Advertising made him confident that, like the others, his last child's career and life were on track and successful.

The heaviness of the fact that Tim Johnson, his charming and loyal friend of forty years, had suffered a debilitating stroke, was compounded by the death of his other longtime "rat pack" buddy, Fat Bob Taylor, who had suffered a massive stroke on Father's Day morning. J.P. eulogized him on his show:

"We are all saddened, obviously, deeply, with the news yesterday of the death of a friend and colleague, Bob Taylor, affectionately known as 'Fat Bob' to one and all. Bobby died yesterday after suffering a massive stroke this past Sunday. Our condolences and sympathy to his wife Carol, whom he loved desperately.

"I first became acquainted with Bob when, during my morning show back in 1967 I played a recording, by an opera star, of 'Vesti La Giubba' and explained that this was something I had sung in my garage the night before and what did ya think of it?

"Well, I got a phone call from a listener who said 'I thought you were a little sharp.'

"'I said, 'Well, come on the air and tell me that.'

"He did, and went on to explain that not only was I sharp, but that he could do it better.

"So I said, 'Well, go ahead!'

"He said, 'Right now? I'm a plumber on a construction site here in Ann Arbor, and I'm on the phone!'

"I said, 'Sing it on the phone!'

"He did. He was quite good! I asked his name and he said, 'I am Fat Bob the Singing Plumber.'

"And for the next twenty-eight years we remained friends. We got to know him, Bob, as a fixture on WJR as a personality. He kept right on singing. He performed everywhere at public and private functions—did the 'National Anthem' for Tiger, Red Wing, and Lions games more than anyone else in history.

"Bob Taylor was an extraordinarily talented and very, very funny man, and a very giving one. Never once did Bob say 'No' when a friend asked him for anything.

"He sang at my father's funeral, at my children's weddings. He was a good friend, and I will miss him terribly."

While, at Fat Bob's request, there was no funeral, J.P. McCarthy seemed noticeably saddened and profoundly stunned by the death of the man who was so loyal a friend and so completely full of vigor and life. The cheery voice with the dirty jokes who gladly served as punching bag would ring J.P.'s line no more. No matter the seriousness of any occasion or setting, Fat Bob Taylor's daring wit could always be counted on to transcend the situation and add a delightful humor and charm to any circumstance. He was the elegance between chivalry and chauvinism. He was as original as a man can be.

Twice a widower himself, he nevertheless maintained an eternal cheeriness that evoked smiles all over Michigan. He was the voice that whispered in the mighty McCarthy's ear, never allowing J.P. to take himself or his show too seriously, and he was gone.

J.P. McCarthy

Make a joke out of your heartache and tears,
a funny face out of your sobs of pain . . .
Laugh, clown, over your shattered love!
Laugh over the pain which is poisoning your heart.
—"Vesti La Giubba" — Pagliacci

McCarthy sat in his chair in silence during the commercial breaks and stared blankly out the window at the horizon. He spoke very little during the news, and played "As Time Goes By" and "If I Ever Had to Say Goodbye to You" from Fat Bob's albums.

Whether or not the death of Fat Bob and the bad fortune of Tim Johnson made McCarthy think of his own mortality is uncertain, but perhaps it explained to him why he himself had been feeling down and sluggish at the time. Or maybe he was pushing himself too hard. Burning the candle at both ends. Maybe just overcommitted to charity appearances. J.P. was clearly not himself.

"Joe ran hard," explains Hoot McInerney, "and when his body started giving him signals, Joe thought he was tired from running hard."

"I've never seen him look like that," remembers Barry McGuire. "I've never seen his color like that. He was gray. He just didn't look good at all," says McGuire.

♣

As the month of June moved on, J.P. became frustrated with his sluggishness, and began to seek medical advice, beginning with his old friend Dr. Gary Knapp, frequent show guest and family physician from Grosse Ile.

He sat with longtime friend and confidant Tom King at the "Blind Fish" restaurant near their boats.

"Tom, I don't feel good."

"Get some rest, Joe," said King.

"No, it's more," said McCarthy. "I just don't feel right."

J.P. had blood drawn a few days earlier, and pulled up his shirt sleeve to show King the startling black and blue result.

"That's never happened before," he told King.

John Schaefer also remembers McCarthy complaining of bruises. "He told me, 'Boy, have I got a bruise on my ass that you wouldn't believe. It looks like a major league pitcher nailed me from about twenty feet with a fastball.'"

McCarthy then called Dr. Murphy, Chief of Surgery at Beaumont Hospital in Troy, whom he'd known for twenty-five years. "He said he didn't feel well, didn't have any energy, and had a nosebleed that wouldn't stop," says Murphy. "He came to the office and we did some blood work."

♣

While waiting for his test and lab results, J.P. continued hosting his show and carrying on with the summertime events he loved so much, including a boat trip on the fabled *Longshot* on the Fourth of July weekend. His charted course was to head north out of Miller Marina in St. Clair Shores and hug the coast through Lake Huron all the way around the lower peninsula, pass through the Straits of Mackinac into Lake Michigan and down into Little Traverse Bay to put in at Harbor Springs for a few days. On the way back home, he would stop at Mackinac Island for a short visit, and make his way back home in order to be back on the air Tuesday morning. The McCarthys would be joined by their friends Alex and Val Morton. Alex was an advertising executive at DMB&B who managed the Senior PGA Tour promotions for Cadillac.

"I remember the day he was going to Harbor Springs with Alex Morton," says McCarthy boating pal Tony Frabotta. "He wanted me to go. I told him I couldn't go, and even though my wife wouldn't go, he wanted me to come by myself, but I just couldn't do it."

Frabotta went to the boat anyway to meet J.P. as he was getting set to cast off. "Joe's running around, getting things ready, and he calls me over and shows me his arm and it's all black and blue. He said, 'I'd really feel better if you were coming along.' I repeated that I couldn't, but when I got home I felt terrible. I thought something was wrong with his arm," says Frabotta.

The McCarthys and Mortons set out for Harbor Springs, and it so happened that I was also heading to Harbor Springs, but by car, for a golf weekend. After I arrived at nearby Boyne Highlands, I met Boyne COO and longtime McCarthy pal Art Tebo for a drink. I asked Art if he'd seen J.P. in the area.

"Yes," Art said, "I spent a little time with him down at the Harbor Springs marina."

"How was he?" I asked.

"He was good."

"No, I mean, how did he look? Was he okay?" I inquired further.

"He seemed fine to me," Tebo answered again.

I told Art that I was worried about him and that he hadn't seemed himself lately. I explained that I wondered what the toll would be on him after traveling so far by boat. At that point, we were now both worried.

A. Council Darling, known as Count Darling by most, was another DMB&B ad executive and McCarthy friend who owned a home in the Harbor Springs area. He had seen McCarthy during the weekend trip. Count Darling remembers that he spoke to J.P. by radio as his longtime friend piloted his boat out of Little Traverse Bay and back into Lake Michigan to begin his voyage back home. When J.P. said goodbye and signed off his radio, it would be the last time Count would ever speak to him.

♣

Meanwhile, back in Detroit, Dr. John Murphy called the hospital from his car phone to check on McCarthy's test results. "Talking to the woman in the lab, I asked what his hemoglobin was and she said, 'Thirteen something,' which is normal," explains Murphy. "Then she asked me if I wanted the rest of the results and I said, 'No, I'll look at them on the computer when I get in tomorrow.' She then said, 'Well, his platelet count is only 50,000.' It was like someone had hit me between the eyes," Murphy says. (A normal person's platelet count should be over 100,000.)

After the Fourth of July, I was unpacking the car after the Harbor Springs trip when I answered the portable phone on my deck. It was Judy McCarthy alerting me that J.P. would not be in to do his show the next morning. She didn't give a reason, but I didn't ask for one, and quickly told her not to worry about it and that I would call WJR program director Skip Essick and arrange for a substitute. I wasn't surprised to get her call, but still it seemed ominous.

"I went over to Joe and Judy's house on the Fourth of July to give them the diagnosis," says Dr. Murphy.

Tony Frabotta got a call later from Dr. Murphy. "Murphy told me Joe needs a friend," recalls Frabotta.

"What are you telling me, John?" Frabotta asked.

"I can't tell you any more, but he needs a friend."

Frabotta says he then called McCarthy and asked what was going on.

"I'm having a problem with a lack of platelets, but they're looking to see what the reason is," McCarthy answered.

"I told him to hold on, and got out my Mayo Clinic book," says Frabotta, "and as I'm talking to him I'm looking it up and I said, 'Joe, that says leukemia to me here!'"

"I don't have leukemia," McCarthy answered, "and I don't want you talking to anyone about this."

Frabotta, confused, called Murphy back and learned what the McCarthys learned on the Fourth of July. "Murphy said it was a 'pre-Leukemia,'" says Frabotta, "and that chemotherapy wouldn't make much of a difference."

"Joe's reaction was very stoic," Murphy reveals. "He wanted to know the details. Basically, there is no treatment. There's no way of predicting what's going to happen, but generally speaking, people do live for a period of time, sometimes five to ten years," Murphy explained. "I tried to be as upbeat as I could, but Judy took it very badly. I remember she sat there and sobbed."

"Well, we're going to lick it," McCarthy told Murphy and his wife.

"Typical of Joe," Judy says, "As soon as he found out he had the disease, he went and got all of the information he could get. All of these doctors' journals, which you had to be a doctor to read. He brought home volumes," Judy explains, "and he told me, 'I don't want you to read any of this.'

277

"I said, 'You know I'm going to read it!'

"Of course, I know why he didn't want me to read it, because as soon as I read it I knew what Joe's diagnosis was. He had the worst form of it."

Murphy says McCarthy probably had the disease for a while without knowing it. "There's a period of time where it develops, and when he started to have nosebleeds and bleeding from the gums, his platelet count was only 50,000," explains Murphy. "He was fairly far advanced at that point. It had been there for a while, but he appeared to be healthy as a horse until the symptoms showed up."

♣

J.P. McCarthy next gathered his family together for a meeting at his home one evening, with his daughter Diane in Arizona on the speaker phone. "My father informed us of the bad news," says daughter Kathleen McCarthy Dunlop," and my sister on the phone was speechless, my brother John was angry, and I was shocked."

"Each child handled it in a different way," remembers Judy McCarthy. "John is the most stoic of everybody. I think he felt like he had to be because he was the oldest and somebody had to be strong."

Kathleen was so upset, and afraid to let her father see so, that she cried uncontrollably in the car on the way home. "The first thing I said to my husband when I got home was, 'I think my dad is going to die,'" she remembers.

Judy McCarthy didn't want her husband to see her cry either. "Most of the time when I got sad, I'd go to the laundry room and do laundry and cry. I figured if he can be that courageous, I can be strong, too. But it was tough. He'd say, 'C'mon, Judy. You can't do that.'"

J.P. asked his family not to mention the news to anyone they knew at work or outside the family. "He was so brave and strong the way he told us, and he asked us to please live our lives as though nothing were wrong because he was going to fight this disease and he was going to beat it. He was determined."

♣

"I was in the car with Trip Bosart," recalls John Schaefer, "and Bosart had Dr. Murphy on the speakerphone discussing another issue when Trip then asked, 'How's Joe?' After a silence, Murphy said, 'I think you should ask him, and I think he should tell you.' Well, that sounded pretty ominous to Trip and me." The two McCarthy pals drove on in silence.

Later, McCarthy called Schaefer and asked him to come over and have a drink. "I thought, 'Geez, it's four o'clock in the afternoon,'" says Schaefer, "but I went right over because I knew he was concerned about this. I was concerned, but not very concerned, because Joe was sort of indestructible in a way. I remembered when he thought he had a heart problem and tossed himself into Beaumont, only to learn after testing that he had the arteries of an eighteen-year-old," exclaims Schaefer.

♣

The heart problem incident, while it had a funny ending, had been scary when it happened two years before. It was during the morning show that I noticed J.P. on the telephone through many of the commercial breaks. During the nine o'clock news, I got a call from Dr. Murphy, who told me that Joe needed to come to Beaumont Hospital immediately because he might be experiencing serious cardiac problems.

"I don't care what he tells you," Murphy insisted to me, "Don't listen to him, and get him off the air and on the way here. Drive him if you have to."

J.P. hadn't mentioned anything to me about experiencing discomfort, and I knew he'd be furious if he knew Murphy called me, so I eased into the studio during a break and innocently asked, "How are you feeling, Joe?"

"Fine," was the brief and dismissive response, as I expected.

This time, I asked the question more intently. "Are you feeling okay?"

He stared at me, figuring out that Murphy must have called. "Yeah, I'm okay."

He stared at me, figuring out that Murphy must have called. "Yeah, I'm okay."

"Why don't you let us play some tapes and you can get out of here early," I nonchalantly suggested.

"We'll see," he allowed.

That was as far as I needed to push it. I then called Murphy back and he told me to keep a close eye on him. J.P. stayed until the end of his show, skipped hosting "Focus" and went to the hospital just after 10 a.m. After a tense day of worrying, we learned that the problem was gastrointestinal in nature. "He'd had his usual huge steak with red wine and it turned out he had indigestion," says Murphy. "After the heart catheterization, they told him he had the arteries of an eighteen-year-old!"

♣

Now, though, Schaefer sat across from "the indestructible McCarthy" with a scotch in his hand.

"I just came from the oncologist at Beaumont," J.P. told his best friend, John Schaefer. "I should have thirty months to live."

"Bullshit," Schaefer snapped. "You don't have only thirty months to live. That's the stupidest thing I've ever heard in my life. Let me tell you something. How the hell does he know?"

"He told me," McCarthy answered, "and I've been thinking about it. If I can feel halfway decent, thirty months doesn't sound too bad. I could have a pretty good time in thirty months."

"Oh, come on Joe, don't talk like that!" I said. "This can't be, we have to get you to a better doctor or something."

"Would you ask your guy, Dr. Lester, to kind of quarterback this thing for me and supervise all of this testing?" McCarthy asked. "Otherwise, I'm afraid I'm going to go in so many different directions."

That evening, John Schaefer put in a call to Dr. Melvin Lester, Internal Medicine Specialist, Associate Professor of Medicine at Wayne State, and Trustee and Chairman of the Medical Advisory Committee.

"I had suspicions that something was going on because he was off the air so frequently," says Lester, but Schaefer told me that J.P. was ill, had seen a number of doctors, and that he was confused and was looking for someone to 'captain the team' and tell him where to go."

Lester then spoke with McCarthy by telephone. "He told me where he'd been and who he'd seen," Lester recounts. "Then I asked him how his schedule was for the next day."

"I want to do my show, but I'm free right after," McCarthy told him.

♣

J.P. McCarthy continued coming through that door at six-fifteen every day, wishing the world 'Good morning,' and talking about the important issues of the day, all the while never discussing the most important issue of his life. Some mornings, he was just too weak to get out of bed, but more often than not, he was at the microphone, acting as if there were nothing wrong.

Although I had a sense of the seriousness of his struggle, we did not discuss his health. I remained loyal to his wishes, and figured that if at least one part of his day could be normal, if there was at least one part of his day where it was business as usual, if there was at least one part of his day where he was completely in control, it should be his radio show and his work. I know he appreciated it, and I approached it much like I did the faux heart attack two years earlier—assisting without questioning or prying, and allowing him the possibility that I did not know about his condition. At this point, his needs during the show changed to include large amounts of Kleenex to quell his nosebleeds, and he had also taken to drinking bottle after bottle of purified water to soothe his bleeding gums. J.P.'s voice became more hoarse by the day, but since he would leave the radio station immediately after his show, nobody knew what was happening to him.

"He was trying to go to work, and he sounded like hell," observed John Schaefer. "There was something different in his voice."

"He sounded rough on the air," says Hoot McInerney. "I had buddies call and say, 'Hey, your friend must really be staying out late at night. Here it was dried blood in his throat. He sounded like Marlon Brando in 'The Godfather' near the end," McInerney says.

♣

I remember being with J.P. that July when he broadcast his morning show from the Bo Schembechler Celebrity Golf Tournament at the University of Michigan Golf Course. The mobile studio we broadcast from was parked about one hundred yards from the clubhouse. During one of the commercials, he wanted to go into the clubhouse to get some orange juice and look around. We began to walk down the path and talk. Walking along, I turned to say something to him and he was gone. I looked back, and he was about five paces behind me. He said to me sheepishly, "I'm afraid you'll have to walk a little slower for me these days." I swallowed hard.

He wore a bandage on his chin that day to cover a shaving nick that would not stop bleeding, and begged off from playing in the tournament, telling Schembechler that he had "turf toe." Schembechler, having no idea of J.P.'s condition, kidded him by saying, "I never let any player out of a game for giving me that weak of an excuse!"

J.P. did no more remote broadcasts after that one, cancelling an appearance at one of his favorite events, the Roger Penske Golf Tournament in Jackson. He told me he just didn't feel up to it. Organizers of these canceled appearances and golf tournaments seemed initially exasperated, but I did my best to explain to them that they were not being carelessly disregarded, without revealing the seriousness of the situation.

♣

Golf, his life sport, was unfortunately becoming less and less accessible to him. "I had a golf date with him at Bloomfield Hills Country Club on a Saturday morning, when I got a call at the club," says Anthony Franco. "He never canceled a golf date, but this morning he said, 'I'm not going to make it today.'

"'You not going to make it? Get the hell over here!'

" 'No, I was out late last night and I really don't feel good today.'

" 'Joe, sleep for a couple of hours and then come out and play nine.'

"No, I can't make it," McCarthy told his friend Tony, who finally relented.

"Judy and Sharon and Joey and I were playing golf on a Sunday afternoon," Schaefer remembers, "and I was real pleased that he was going to play because he hadn't been playing much. It was hard. He was having trouble with his nose bleeding, and it was driving him nuts. He was annoyed that he got some blood on his shirt. We got to the #3 tee and he hit a shot that went nowhere. 'Hit a mulligan,' I told him, and he gave me a look that said, 'Normally, you'd never let me hit another ball. You'd be rolling on the ground howling with laughter after a shot like that.' I felt so sorry for him," says Schaefer.

"We went out for nine and on the backside we tried to convince him to ride along," Schaefer continued, "and we played #10 and #11 and he said, 'I'm sorry, I'm just too tired,' and he went back in."

J.P.'s close friend Trip Bosart had a similar experience. "I played with him in a husband/wife nine-hole match, and he played most of the holes, and he had a couple of darn good holes, but it was obvious he didn't have any strength," says Bosart. "He had a hard time hitting the ball, but was a good sport. He'd miss a shot and we'd give him another, but he didn't want to take it.

" 'Oh, c'mon, hit another,' we'd say.

" 'No, that's not the way the game is played,' he told us."

Not long after, McCarthy attended the wedding of Bosart's son Brad, and Bosart remembers seeing J.P. as he came back up the aisle in church. "Joe was on an end pew, and he looked really tired. We just sort of looked at each other," says Trip. "He stuck his hand out and I grabbed it. It wasn't a handshake, it wasn't a high-five. I can philosophize now that it was a goodbye."

♣

During his illness, McCarthy spoke with another longtime friend and supporter, FCC Commissioner Jim Quello.

"'Jim, if it had been my lungs . . . I smoked to much at one time and don't smoke anymore. If it had been my liver . . . well, I drank a lot at one time but I don't drink that much anymore. What do I do about bone marrow?'"

J.P.'s efforts to quit smoking were well documented. Dr. Art Weaver, professor of surgery at Wayne State University, was outspoken in his effort to warn people of the dangers of smoking, sometimes scaring patients by showing them the actual "pickled lungs of a smoker." Weaver was a regular guest on McCarthy's show since 1966. "He tried to quit two or three times," says Weaver, "and he'd get so frustrated he'd be kicking over cabinets. When he finally did have some success in quitting, he puffed a cigar one day, and that little act started him smoking again!"

"We both went to a hypnotist," laughs Judy McCarthy, "but it didn't work with Joe."

McCarthy would always celebrate the "Great American Smokeout Day" on his show, featuring anti-smoking experts like Dr. Joe Arrends and Jim "The Mouth" Purol, who would break his own Guinness Book record each year by smoking over 150 cigarettes at one time. J.P. would also play Phil Harris' "Smoke, Smoke, Smoke that Cigarette" song, and Jerry Reed's "Another Puff." He'd also chosen that day to tell everyone how he did finally kick the habit in 1985: "I was being driven to Toledo in a limousine," he related, "and it was a nice sunny day and I was lighting up a cigarette and it finally struck me. What the hell was I doing? I put the window down, threw the whole pack of cigarettes out, and just never, ever smoked again."

"Cold turkey," says Judy, "he never smoked again. I started sneaking cigarettes about eight years later, and he'd get furious with me and make me smoke outside . . . even in the rain!"

♣

That kind of determination was bringing J.P. to work every day during his illness. WJR "Kaleidoscope" host Mike Whorf would see McCarthy because he was often in early. "I knew something was awry big time," says Whorf. "He looked tired and, not knowing anything, I said jokingly, 'Ah, you're burning the candle at both ends. When are you going to stop doing that nonsense?'

" 'No, it's more than that,' J.P. told me somberly. 'Much more than that.' "

"He was going to try to keep working," says Judy McCarthy, "and I said 'Joe, don't do this to yourself! You're so weak.' His cough had gotten so bad. His voice became a problem, and that was his livelihood."

To keep their minds off the illness, J.P. and Judy pursued one of their most favorite activities . . . going to the movies. Judy and J.P. also went shopping for a new TV. "When he got sick," she explains, "he said, 'Okay, if I'm going to be sick and I might be in bed with chemotherapy, our TV upstairs is really old. We'd better get a new one.' So off we went to buy a TV."

Judy remembers her husband grabbing her hand at the movies. "He looked at me and said, 'I'm so glad this is me and not you. I couldn't handle it if it were you, Judy.' "

J.P. and Judy did the best they could to celebrate their thirtieth anniversary, quietly, at home, alone together.

♣

Meanwhile, Dr. Lester's medical efforts continued. "J.P. was optimistic, and I thought he ought to be optimistic," says Lester. "In medicine, there's always time for a patient to recognize that things aren't going well. If it's a matter of getting your affairs in order, then I think you have to tell the patient. This was not the case. While the outlook was grim, it didn't appear to be imminently grim. We thought we had lots of time to deal with the issue, but to try to be optimistic and fight the thing in the hope that we were wrong, and that he would respond to the treatment.

"You can't tell, when you make the diagnosis of myelodysplastic syndrome, the direction that it's really going to go in. What you can tell is that there are five defined types of myelodysplastic syndrome. He had number four on a scale of one to five, with five being the worst."

J.P. McCarthy

"He was finally so sick," says Judy McCarthy, "he went downhill so fast. He got weaker and weaker, and he was bleeding horribly. Every night he would wake up with blood coming out of his nose and mouth. I know he was frightened."

♣

It was a Friday morning, just before ten, when J.P. finished an interview with political analyst Gerald Faverman, and signed off for the day. Bing Crosby crooned his usual "Have a Nice Day" theme song, and McCarthy wished listeners the same, saying simply, 'We'll see you Monday.' But J.P. McCarthy's frequent absences from his "Morning Show" were about to become permanent, and his very private struggle was about to become public. McCarthy telephoned *Free Press* columnist Bob Talbert.

"Bob, this is the hardest phone call I've ever had to make."

Talbert, thinking that J.P. was quitting radio or that someone had died, asked "What's going on?"

"I've decided to go public and want you to tell my story."

As McCarthy explained myelodysplastic sydrome to Talbert, both men started to cry.

"I'm a smart man, and I knew that was a death sentence," says Talbert. "He called me because he knew I would handle it well. He knew I would be writing his obituary, and he wanted to get it right."

Before Talbert's column was printed, J.P. released a memo to WJR staffers, which he dictated on the telephone to Dorothy Powers, his loyal, longtime secretary. The memo, dropped into the inbox of every WJR employee, read like this:

August 2, 1995
TO MY FRIENDS AND COLLEAGUES:
ON OR ABOUT JULY 7TH I WAS DIAGNOSED WITH MYELODYSPLASTIC SYNDROME, A BONE MARROW DISORDER WHEREBY THE MARROW DOESN'T PRODUCE ENOUGH OF THE RIGHT STUFF — I.E., WHITE CELLS, RED CELLS, PLATELETS. THERE IS NO KNOWN CAUSE FOR THIS MALADY, AND THE TREATMENT FOR IT SEEMS TO BE MORE ONE OF OBSER-

*VATION THAN ACTION. ALTHOUGH I AM ON THE LIST
FOR A BONE MARROW TRANSPLANT AT THE UNI-
VERSITY OF MICHIGAN BONE MARROW TRANS-
PLANT UNIT, IT MAY BE DIFFICULT, SINCE I HAVE NO
SIBLINGS, TO FIND AN EXACT MATCH, I AM TOLD.
MEANWHILE, I AM PURSUING OTHER AVENUES OF
CURE.*

    *IF THE GOOD LORD IS WILLING, I LOOK FORWARD
TO A COMPLETE RECOVERY AND EXPECT TO BE
BACK ON THE AIR IN THE MORNING SOON. SAY A
LITTLE PRAYER FOR ME . . .*

J.P. McCARTHY

The Detroit area, most of whom had never heard of this disease, became very concerned about the condition of J.P. McCarthy. Few really knew the severity of his condition, but the news of his illness was widespread. The newspaper articles, television coverage, and word of mouth reached McCarthy's mother Martha at her Florida home.

"He didn't want to tell me he was sick," Martha says. "A friend of mine in Belleville heard of his illness on the radio and called and told me what was wrong with him and that he was not on the air. I couldn't talk. I dropped the phone and fainted away. When I came to, I thought, 'What's happened to Joe?' So I called Judy and Joe, and poor Judy broke down.

"Joe was so mad. He wanted to tell me in his own way. He didn't want some lady to tell his eighty-five-year-old mother that he was dying.

" 'Mother,' he said, 'she had no business telling you that!'

" 'Joe, don't be mad at her. Nobody expects you to be sick,' Martha told him. 'It's all right for the rest of us, but not for you!' "

♣

Letters, cards, offers of medical assistance, and signs of support came from everywhere. Dave Bodkin, who guided J.P. through auto shows in Japan and Europe, left a bottle of spirits on Mc-Carthy's porch, with a note promising to share the bottle when

J.P. recovered. "I gave him a rosary," says Hoot McInerney. "I didn't know how he was going to take it. I didn't want to take it over to the house, so I called his son John and asked him to take it over. He gave it to him. Later, when Judy told me how they wore it out saying it together and how it is with him now, it was real touching," McInerney sobs.

"I showed up in my kilt to present him with a bottle of scotch from the smallest distillery in Scotland," says pal David Scott. "I told him we'd finish the bottle when he got better." Scott now sips from that bottle only once per year, and only in toast.

I was shuttling cards, letters, important papers, medical bills, and messages from J.P.'s Fisher Building office to his home every day, and there was even some talk of putting a studio in his home so that he could go on the air from there during his recovery.

"In the beginning, he thanked everyone on the phone and he'd ask them to say prayers for him," says Judy, "but after a while it became too tough for him."

Dr. Mel Lester called Dr. Bill Peters, President of the Karmanos Cancer Institute and a renowned expert on bone marrow transplantation. "He told me he didn't know if Joe would be a candidate for transplantation because of his age, but agreed to see him," Lester says. "I suggested at that time that we not have Joe go to Karmanos Cancer Institute, and I told him why. I asked Bill, if someone had this problem, and was not going to Karmanos, where would they go? He said there were three places. One was the Mayo Clinic, one was the University of Pittsburgh, and the other was Sloan Kettering in New York.

"The reason I didn't want him to go to Karmanos is because he was such a well known person in our community. Well-meaning people would say, 'Why didn't you go to Sloan Kettering' or places that have reputations that lay people would know. Karmanos and the people there are as good as anybody, anyplace. The scientists at those places all train at the same places and come out of the same mold, but our community might not know that. If we sent him someplace else like Freddie Hutchinson at the University of Washington or Mayo Clinic or Sloan Kettering, people would say he went to the best places, because at that point I knew the outlook was grim," explains Lester.

288

It so happened that the Sloan Kettering appointment came first. McCarthy was scheduled to go to the Mayo Clinic after the trip to Sloan Kettering Hospital in New York. The night before McCarthy left for New York, Tom King and Tony Frabotta visited him at home. "Judy called," says King. "She said, 'You've got to get over here. He's down.'"

King remembers that, "He was coughing a lot, and he told us that he was going to Sloan Kettering and then the Mayo Clinic, and then he was going to pick what treatment he was going to do."

"Our visit was sad because he was exhausted," Frabotta recalls. "He had his hat on, and he hadn't had a drink in three or four days. He asked Judy for a scotch and he was sitting in his chair in front of his big TV. Tom and I killed a bottle of Crown Royal and he barely took a sip of that scotch. We were telling him stories, he was laughing, but he was coughing and bleeding through the nose.

"Judy was smoking and having a drink. We sat with him for three hours, but he couldn't keep his eyes open. We had one more drink and we left."

Out on J.P.'s front porch, Tom King began to cry. "He didn't believe he'd ever see Joe again," says Frabotta, whose wife Cheryll asked him why he looked so bad when he got home that night. "I think Joe is gone," Tony answered.

"I had a bad feeling when he left for New York," John McCarthy allows. "I don't know why I felt that way. In my mind, when he told me he was going to New York, I was thinking, 'He was born in New York, and he's going to die in New York.' That's what I thought. It was a bad thought, that he's going there and he's not coming back."

Former WJR General Manager Bill James arranged for a private flight to New York for J.P. and Judy. "Joe would never have been able to fly a commercial flight," says Judy.

"He was sick," says Dr. Lester, "but not that sick, when he left Detroit. Twenty-four hours later in New York he was sicker than hell."

"The night before we'd gone to the hospital," says Judy, "I was awake all night long bathing him because his fever was up to one hundred and five, and that's so dangerous. It took me all night long to get that temperature down."

♣

When the doctors at Sloan Kettering learned of McCarthy's fever and examined his condition, they called Dr. Lester back in Detroit. "They told me that he was so sick, they didn't think they could let him leave the hospital," says Lester. " I told them not to let him go, to admit him right then and there. 'Take care of him,' I told them. 'Do the best you can.'" McCarthy went to Sloan Kettering only to meet with the doctors, and never expected to be admitted.

The stay at Sloan Kettering was a lonely one for Judy. "I was in New York the first eight days all by myself. Joe was so concerned. I'd be at the hospital and he'd say, 'Judy, it's ten at night. You have to go. I'm so worried about you taking a cab back to that apartment at night.' Of course, I hated to go."

While J.P. was in the hands of Sloan Kettering in New York, Detroit wasn't willing to let the treatment be one of "observation rather than action." McCarthy needed a bone marrow donor. He needed a perfect match, and as yet, none was found. Dr. Bob Nestor, old boating friend, and his wife Maryanne, fund-raising director at St. Joseph's Mercy Hospital, sprung into action. Nestor realized that a marrow match and transplant was the only thing that could save his friend J.P. Without siblings, finding a perfect match has been described as "trying to find a needle in a haystack," but Nestor knew he had to try.

"I called the Red Cross to find out where people could go for marrow testing," says Nestor, "and they were not too friendly. I felt like I got the runaround, and they said, 'We don't have time for this!'

"I called Joe back to tell him how difficult it was," remembers Nestor, "and I was crying when he said, 'Please, Doc, help me. If you can get this thing going, do anything you can.' After that, says Nestor, "I wouldn't listen to anybody who told me a marrow testing drive couldn't be done."

♣

Bob and Maryanne Nestor, in five days, organized a bone marrow testing drive after the Red Cross said it would need three weeks to implement one. St. Joseph's Mercy Hospital in Pontiac was the location for the two-day drive, and 160 volunteers manned the converted lobby to move as many people through as possible. Karen Clark was certain to round up support from the members of Bloomfield Hills Country Club, and many well known personalities staffed the registration table, including many personal friends of J.P., like Luann Battenberg, Val Morton, Christa Fortinberry, and Rick and Betty Forzano. Anthony Franco and Kmart Chairman Joe Antonini donated the money to fund a speedy valet parking system for people coming to be tested, and the Detroit media, including Bob Talbert, rose to the occasion, frequently reminding people of the location and times of the August 10th and 11th marrow match drive.

In a column written by Bob Talbert to spread the word about the marrow match drive in the *Detroit Free Press* on August 7, McCarthy was quoted as telling Talbert, "I sincerely believe I am going to make it. I'm real positive about this. If it can be done, I am going to do it. I am going to be back on the air doing my morning show."

Each individual test cost $22.50 per donor. Hoot McInerney and Tom King arranged for funding of what came to $62,000 almost immediately. That money allowed two thousand Detroiters to have their blood tested to see if they could save J.P.

"Don't worry about it, honey," Maryanne Nestor says McInerney told her, "I'll take care of the costs." Joe Schmidt, Tom Clark, and Marv Gillum all helped make it possible for anyone who wished to be tested to do so for free.

"Hoot tried so hard to help J.P. during his illness," insists Michigan Attorney General Frank Kelley. "If giving his right arm would have saved J.P., Hoot would have given his right arm in a minute. People who were close to J.P. were very loyal, loved him, and couldn't do enough for him."

People from all walks of life drove to Pontiac, stood in line, rolled up their sleeve, and gave enough blood to provide a test sample. The large majority of the donors had never met J.P. McCarthy, but had known him for almost forty years on the air, and felt moved to try to help their morning companion.

"I couldn't believe what was going on there," says John Mc-Carthy. "I had several of my employees from my dealership go down there, and it was very touching."

♣

Personally, I was most impressed with the perfect organization and efficient manner in which the testing was conducted. It was warming to see the familiar faces of the volunteers, the large amount of response, and it wasn't until I was alone with the medic in the private blood draw area, as the needle plunged into my arm, that I became emotional about why I was there and what this all meant. I knew that J.P. would never assume that people would line up like this to help him. I remember how he would so sheepishly and unassumingly ask for a favor when he needed something simple. Once he asked me for a ride to pick up his car that was just shipped from Florida. He was so grateful and must have asked me three times if I was sure I didn't mind driving him. Of course I didn't mind. Now I sat giving blood, the only thing left that I could do as his producer and friend, and again, of course I didn't mind. I cried and prayed that my marrow might somehow match, as I know countless others did. A national and worldwide search was under way for a marrow match, and WJR meteorologist John McMurray and Art Tebo were busy planning marrow match drives for the Flint area and northern Michigan locations near Boyne.

"Joe knew they were doing this for him," explains Judy Mc-Carthy, "and he was very touched. He also knew that things were not going well and that it wasn't going to be in time," she adds. "He didn't say it, though. He tried to be positive."

"He was optimistic at times," remembers John McCarthy, "but with what he had it was tough, and there wasn't much to look forward to."

"The chance of finding a match quickly was remote," says Dr. Lester, "plus the fact that his age was against the likelihood that he could survive a transplantation. Once you pass the age of sixty, most centers will not even consider transplantation. The patient's body won't tolerate it."

One can only imagine the grueling bravery McCarthy displayed as he gathered enough information to learn that his life was slipping away. "He made sure all of his life was in order to make it easy for me and the children," says Judy. "As soon as he found out how sick he was, he met with everyone he needed to get his life in order. He was always careful about planning ahead."

"Everything was failing," says Lester. "Every possible complication occurred. Liver failure, kidney failure, bleeding, severe anemia, and finally pneumonia, which is a common complication and is the cause of death about thirty percent of the time from myelodysplasia."

"He was a tough, tough guy," says Dr. Murphy, "and it was hard to see him wither away."

♣

Ironically, McCarthy and Lester were scheduled to play golf as partners at Bloomfield Hills Country Club in a match involving John Schaefer. "I went to Bloomfield and I played with somebody else," says Lester, "and we got our clock cleaned. Schaefer took every bet, so I called Joe at Sloan Kettering to cheer him up and tell him what happened:

"'You and I were supposed to play golf against Schaefer. He got me out there and changed all the bets and beat me every way,' Lester prodded, 'and where the hell are you? You're lying on your ass on some bed in New York!'

"'Mel, we'd have killed them,' McCarthy told him.

"That was it," says Lester. "I never spoke to him again."

"The last conversation I had with him on the phone from New York," Dr. Murphy remembers, "was him saying 'Murph, this is a bitch. I can't talk much. I've gotta go.'"

"The last time I talked to him, he said, 'Hooter, I'm not doing so good,'" says McInerney.

"At times, actually, the last time I talked to him, I actually thought he was doing better," says John McCarthy, who by this point had flown to New York with his brother Jamie to be near their father. "He was bright, but as it turned out that was the last time I talked to him."

♣

In New York also, Jamie gave blood for a helpful transfusion, and spent many hours at his father's bedside, where J.P. tried to comfort his youngest son with a message for all of his children. Tugging the oxygen mask from his face, he insisted firmly:

"You know, I've done everything anybody ever could have wanted to do. I've gone everywhere I wanted to go. I interviewed everybody I ever wanted to interview. I've tried everything. I've seen everything. I've tasted everything. I didn't miss much. I don't think many people can say that. I've had a very full life and I've got no regrets. I'm the luckiest man in the world."

J.P. McCarthy also had a telephone conversation with Cardinal Adam Maida, who later said that in their conversation, J.P. had made his peace with God and seemed calm.

John Schaefer, about to leave Detroit for a vacation with Keith Crain and his family, called the hospital to speak to his best friend "Joey."

"How are you doing?" Schaefer asked.

"I'm not doing very well."

"Look, I don't have to take this trip to Montana. I could cancel it and come out there to New York."

"No. I'll be back in a week," J.P. assured him, "Give me a call tomorrow."

"We probably would have gone home if Joe hadn't got so sick," says Judy. "The doctors said it was too dangerous to fly home. That was a Monday, and by Wednesday, his lungs had turned to what the doctors called 'garbage.' At that point, they had to use a ventilator, and Joe said to me, 'If they put me on this, I probably won't come off of it.' But he was willing to try.

"I felt so sorry for the kids. John and Jamie got a chance to see him, but the rest of them all arrived the next day. They all saw him, but he was unable to talk because he was so heavily medicated," Judy explains.

John Schaefer, by then in Montana, called McCarthy's room in the hospital and learned that he could not speak to J.P. because he was now in intensive care. Judy McCarthy stunned Schaefer with the request she made when she returned his call.

"John, Joe asked me if I would ask you to do his eulogy."

"I will not," Schaefer exclaimed. "He's gonna do my eulogy! I am not doing any eulogy for him."

"I don't think he's going to make it, John."

Silence.

Hoot McInerney was stunned when he called the hospital on Wednesday and Judy came to the phone sobbing. "I just said good-bye to him. The kids are in now saying good-bye to him," she told Hoot.

Doctor Murphy was in contact with Judy, and with no chance of survival, Murphy advised that it was appropriate that J.P. be taken off the respirator. "He had full-blown leukemia when he died," says Dr. Lester, "and the form of leukemia he had is totally unresponsive to any form of treatment."

♣

Joseph Priestley McCarthy passed away early in the afternoon of August 16, 1995 at Sloan Kettering Cancer Center in New York City, with his entire family present.

McInerney, King, and Frabotta, three of McCarthy's closest friends, gathered at Arriva Restaurant, a spot J.P. loved, upon hearing the news. "Hoot and Tom were crying," says Frabotta. "Joe's gone! What are we going to do about this?"

Meanwhile, two time zones away in Montana, Keith Crain and John Schaefer returned to the ranch they were staying at after a morning of fishing. They were met by the owner of the ranch, who had been trying to reach them all morning.

"Why don't you sit down for a minute. I'm sorry I have to be the one to tell you that your friend has passed away."

"We all cried," says Crain, "and he deserved our tears. We weren't prepared for that news."

♣

Back in Detroit, where no one was prepared for any such revelations, the news began to surface, and while the television stations began to break in to local programming with live continuous coverage, WJR News, with cameras moving in on the Fisher Building and the phones beginning to ring, had to report the death of their colleague. Once Dick Haefner, WJR News Director, opened his microphone at 4 p.m. and spoke the virtually unspeakable words, confirmation was made, and Detroit media began getting stunned reactions from everyone in the community.

WJR's afternoon show, featuring Joel Alexander and Dana Mills, began airing phone calls from newsmakers and community leaders who wanted to express their grief. Governor Engler, Cardinal Maida, the United States senators and others called the show, and so did saddened WJR listeners.

I listened as I instinctively left home and drove to the Fisher Building. When I arrived at J.P.'s office, I found Dorothy Powers, for many years his loyal secretary, still at her post, answering the phone. "Oh, Michael. What are we going to do?" she cried. I hugged her, and wondered the same thing myself. It most certainly did not seem real. I suppose our sense of duty took over in order to muffle the grief.

I called audio engineer Russ White at home and asked him to come in as soon as he could, and went to WJR program director Skip Essick's office, where I found him puffing a cigarette with General Manager Mike Fezzey, and ABC Vice President Don Bolukas, who happened to be in town. After hugs and words of encouragement, they asked me if I would be able to produce the next morning's show and what I thought we should do with it.

"I'd like to give him his show one more time," I said. "I'd like to play as much tape of him as possible. He never got to say goodbye, and I think the listeners will want to hear his voice one more time."

♣

Russ White and I began our evening at 7 p.m. at the Pegasus bar downstairs, site of many St. Patrick's Day parties and afternoon "meetings" with McCarthy. We had one drink in his honor to steady ourselves, and headed up to the production studio where we would spend the night listening to boxes and boxes of forty years' worth of the collected tapes of J.P. McCarthy's historic career. We listened, we laughed, we reveled in the chance to hear his voice—young, lively, and healthy. We had ten hours until broadcast time at 6 a.m. Mike Whorf and Frank Beckmann would be there in the morning to narrate the final "J.P. McCarthy Show."

At about 2 a.m., we were surprised but glad to find Mike Whorf opening the door to our production studio three hours before we expected him.

"I couldn't sleep, fellas."

He looked around at the reel-to-reel tapes and cassettes scattered and spread all over the floor and tables. "I've been awake, and I've written a little poem tonight that I'd like to offer for use on tomorrow's show," he said as he pulled out a piece of handwritten legal pad paper. "Want to hear it?"

We indeed did, and Whorf shut the door, and put some moving instrumental on the turntable to run behind the poem. Before he read it to us, I asked him if he had read it out loud yet. He told me he hadn't, and the music came over the speakers. Russ and I sat back for the first time in the evening as Whorf stood in the middle of the room and read the poem as the lonely flute and harp music strained.

It was then, as Mike Whorf choked his way through his first reading of the poem, stopping frequently to collect himself, that our tears flowed openly, and we realized once again the real reason we were there, working so frantically through the night. We wept, and Whorf, in his dramatic but shaken voice, read on . . .

Have you ever known an Irishman who couldn't make you cry?
Have you ever known an Irishman without a twinkle in his eye?
There is one such man I knew for years with gifts and talents
    true
And the thing that did amaze me most, was that he gave it all to
    you

Each day he'd sit himself behind a microphone
And tell you things you hadn't heard or things you hadn't known
He spoke a flattering speech, he did, and treated all as friend
He questioned and he queried the kings and common men

J.P. McCarthy

Have you ever known an Irishman that couldn't make you smile?
Who was always there with his support, who'd walk that extra
   mile?
There is one such man I knew for years, so young and full of zest
And in his life he'd climb each hill, 'til he became the best

It's not so much what he became
But how and why he did attain
A sense of fairness, a sense of right
The things that help us sleep at night

It's not to say he was perfect, no,
For perfection there is none
But he knew the battles that he fought
Were battles to be won

He tilted windmills daily, but there was one day in the year
Out came the pipes and fiddles, on that day that was so dear
He'd go and throw a party where everyone was seen
He'd welcome all as brothers, for the wearin' of the green

He loved the game of gentlemen, and he sailed on ocean's crest
Other than his family dear, these things he loved the best
He savored life and filled his life with really simple things
A stout, a song, a book . . . the joy that these things bring

I knew this man, this Irishman, for one score years and ten
There was an elegance about him, and sure, a touch of sin
He'd not approve of all this sentiment, he'd call it so much mush
I remember jokes he told me, they would make a sergeant blush

At times he'd express a gentleness, a true sincerity
And every time he spoke to all, it was with clarity
And what is it that's been left to us in this time of grief and sor-
   rows?
Where will he be as each day passes in all of our tomorrows?

I suppose it's time for trust and faith, with the passing of this man
Knowing he's at peace, and this man's soul is in God's dear loving
   hand

Once we collected ourselves, it took Whorf four or five takes to get the reading down on tape without breaking down. After that moving moment, we continued editing tape throughout this dark night.

As 6 a.m. drew near, the control room began to fill with TV cameras and reporters who wanted to see what would happen in J.P.'s studio, on J.P.'s show, the morning after his passing. Newsman Dan Streeter, who had been on vacation in Ohio, drove all night to make it back in time, and broke down when he came into the studio. His first news report at 5 a.m. was so heavy. It was very hard for Streeter to make it though the copy he'd written about the death of the colleague he'd looked up to so much.

It was almost showtime, and I began to prepare just like I would on any other morning. I left J.P.'s chair and microphone empty and readied the studio as I would if he were arriving. I hung his headphones on his microphone, placed his glasses and the newspapers on his little desktop, and even put out his required mug of decaffeinated coffee. Frank Beckmann and Mike Whorf sat in guest chairs, and J.P.'s theme song played to its entirety, as it always did when he was late.

Russ White and I wept often during that show, and I remember feeling grief over the death of my boss and mentor, and feeling the weight of ushering out the meaningful and significant era of J.P. McCarthy and his impact on the radio industry and the community.

Many fine highlights and memorable McCarthy interview tapes aired that morning in retrospective fashion, and there was an interview with J.P.'s old sportscaster, Dave Diles, whom I phoned to awaken and break the news to. "When the call came that he had died, it was a devastating feeling of unbelief," says Diles, who went on to give this interview on that show:

Diles: "When you consider the immensity of his talent and the scope of it, he really was so remarkable that I don't think we'll see the likes of him again. He absolutely was the best interviewer in my time that I have ever known in the business. I really think if you look at it and try to wonder why he was so good, I think it's very clear. First of all, he was exceedingly bright. He was not just some disc jockey or some personality. He really was a very bright guy and very well read, and so he was prepared.

"Secondly, and maybe this is the most important factor, he was a very attentive listener. Absolutely nothing got by him. I hear people do interviews today, and you can just tell that they have prepared their questions, and if they were interviewing Ronald Reagan, and suddenly in the middle of this seven- or eight-question interview Reagan said, 'You know, I almost dropped the atomic bomb on Canada,' the interviewer would just ignore that because they just have to get on to their next question! The slightest little thing, J.P. would pick up on.

"Then you add to that how generous he was with his time. He never forgot the words of Shakespeare that 'The play is the thing.' As big a star as he was, and he knew that he was—there's no question about that—he was so generous with his time. He touched many, many lives.

"Maybe the best thing about him is that he was not destructive with the immense talent that he had. He had a very good sense of how many people he reached and how far his influence was felt. He was so conversant. He could talk about sports, politics, religion—he was very much at home in any field. There aren't too many people that you can say that about.

"Maybe the test of J.P. is like the test of a Ted Williams. He wasn't one of those guys who came out with one record and got on the Ed Sullivan Show and went to the top of the charts and disappeared. He made it over the long haul, and isn't that really the mark of a real champion? Did he do it over a protracted period of time? And the answer, of course, on J.P. is 'Yes.'"

Beckmann: "It wasn't that long ago that you and J.P. mourned the passing of Howard Cosell, and there was a very poignant moment during that conversation between Dave and J.P.:"

J.P. Tape: *"Dave Diles probably does the best eulogies of anyone on the face of the earth. I've said that before. When I go, if Dave is still around, it would be my fondest wish that he does mine."*

Just Don't Tell 'Em Where I Am

Diles: "Oh, what am I to say to that?"

Beckmann: "It's been a very difficult time for you, Dave. With Mickey Mantle's passing, with J.P.'s passing, with Howard Cosell's passing—a lot of friends leaving you."

Diles: "Yeah, it really has. Pardon me . . . I'm having a little difficult time here. He was a class act. It's just very difficult. You don't want to second guess God. It's a very human part of our frailty to say, 'Why me, God?' but today we're saying 'Why J.P.?' Because I know in the book of Ecclesiastes, 'There's a time for everything. A time to live and a time to die,' but this morning you want to say, 'God, are you sure you did the right thing?' It really wasn't J.P.'s time. Our calendar doesn't have anything to do with God's calendar. You just have to accept it and go on and try to be stronger because of it and use J.P.'s life as a positive."

— August 17, 1995 WJR

While John Schaefer did the actual eulogy at the St. Hugo funeral service, Diles eulogized McCarthy on WJR and on the television coverage leading up to the funeral service, which was carried live in its entirety on Detroit television stations and on WJR radio. "When you lose someone like that," Diles would say, "you begin to realize how carelessly we use the words 'superstar,' and 'legend.' Very few things are 'great.' How many 'great' Presidents have we had? Not very many. How many 'great' actors are there? De Niro, Streep, Pacino, Hackman. 'Great?' There are thousands of actors, but we are too careless using terms like 'greatness.' J.P. had true 'greatness.' "

As the radio show wound down, and many of the reporters and television cameras had left, "The J.P. McCarthy Show" came to a dramatic finish. I left the control booth and went into the empty studio, knelt down at the spot where J.P.'s desktop microphone was and spoke a prayer for the soul of J.P., wished him Godspeed, thanked him for all he'd done for me, and wondered if he was pleased with his final show.

The Detroit News and *The Detroit Free Press,* publishing a combined issue that day due to the newspaper strike, ran a banner headline on the front page above McCarthy's photo: "DE-TROIT RADIO LEGEND FALLS SILENT . . . Longtime WJR broadcaster victim of blood ailment."

Meanwhile, on that Thursday, Judy and the kids returned to Detroit from New York, and their father was flown back home only moments later. "I drove to the airport when he came back," says Tom King, "and I saw Judy and the kids getting into the cars, so I jumped out and hugged them. They told me that Joe was being flown in on another plane. I drove over to the cargo terminal and they told me that his plane had just landed. As I got to the plane, the engines were shutting down. I helped them move his body into the car and the funeral people asked me who I was.

"'I'm his friend,' I said. I welcomed him home the best I could."

After this quiet, profound moment with his fallen friend, King realized the media was present.

"I told the paparazzi that if they didn't get out of there I was going to rip their heads off," King grimaces. "They didn't need pictures of this. That was a tough time. I didn't feel it was right."

♣

Regardless, the media was a big part of the McCarthy mourning. Television cameras were positioned outside the funeral home to speak to mourners and videotape them entering and exiting after paying their respects to the closed coffin with the smiling photo of McCarthy placed in front. It was finally decided that permission would be given to have Saturday morning's funeral service broadcast live by the local television affiliates and WJR radio. "That kind of took me aback a little bit," admits John McCarthy. "I really don't know in my heart if he would have wanted us to do that. I know that's what the public wanted us to do, and it was better than having people trying to jam into the church to watch."

"They would have had to have J.P.'s funeral at Tiger Stadium to accommodate everyone," says Michigan Attorney General Frank Kelley.

Daughter Kathleen McCarthy remembers Judy struggling with the tough decision and trying to comfort the grieving children. "She told us that we had to remember that he was a public figure, and that we almost owed it to the fans, because they helped make him what he was," Kathleen explains. "I watched a biography about Elvis Presley's life, who died on the same date my father did, and it made me think of my dad, the way he started as an unknown and made his way up the celebrity ranking. During the end of the film, they showed Elvis' funeral and how many people adored him, idolized him, and even during his funeral they showed thousands of fans mourning," Kathleen recalls.

On that sun-drenched August morning, WDIV TV had built a complete TV set outside St. Hugo's church in Bloomfield Hills, with Mort Crim anchoring the telecast. Dan Streeter anchored the WJR broadcast, while all of Detroit's community leaders came with heads bowed. "Joe's funeral was sad because he was so young," says former Governor Jim Blanchard. "He was so vital and enjoying life so much. I still have a hard time accepting his death. I always envisioned a friendship with him that would last another twenty years," says Blanchard, who was in attendance that morning alongside U.S. Senators Spencer Abraham and Carl Levin, Governor John Engler, Cardinals Adam Maida and Edmund Szoka, Wayne County Executive Ed McNamara, Oakland County Executive Brooks Patterson, and Mike and Marian Ilitch.

"Most people, in their grieving times, are pretty private," John McCarthy continues, "and having so many people with such an outpouring of feeling, on the other hand, was pretty spectacular."

"I was at Bobby Kennedy's funeral and many other funerals of prominent people" says Frank Kelley, "but never any bigger than this. As my Irish relatives would say, with two Cardinals praying for you, you've got to get into heaven. You can't miss!"

"It was a funeral that would have been reserved for kings, politicians, and captains of industry," says Keith Crain. "He was an icon of our city, and I think some people expected him never to die."

"He was like royalty," says McCarthy pal David Scott, "and it was like a state funeral."

J.P. McCarthy

Detroit News columnist Pete Waldmeier says McCarthy's funeral was five times bigger than any he's attended. "It was similar to the Mafia funerals I've attended where everyone has to come and show their respects when an old 'Don' dies. The only thing missing from Joe's funeral in comparison to theirs was the FBI guys."

"His death was a kick in the head," relates *Free Press* columnist Bob Talbert, "and discovering how big he was in death was an incredible experience."

"Focus Hope" leader and Detroit's most notable charity leader Father William Cunningham gave a homily, Jamie McCarthy read a Bible passage, and near the end of the service, John Schaefer stepped to the lectern to deliver the eulogy he prayed he'd never have to:

> *Is it hot in here or is my malaria kicking up?*
> *I am not sure I can get through this, but I will try because Joe asked me to do it. Please be charitable if I stumble from time to time.*
> *Joseph Priestley McCarthy, the subject of this eulogy, is like trying to get your arms around a mountain.*
> *How can I presume to eulogize this great man? It is a task too large for this humble old pal. I know each of us would do this differently, and throughout this past week the multitudes of Joe's achievements have been memorialized; however, a few of his achievements as a broadcaster, a son, a father, a community leader, a husband, and a friend should be recognized again today, even if only in a cursory manner.*
>
> *As a broadcaster:*
> *He is probably the preeminent broadcaster in the country, a true giant in his industry.*
> *That fact is partly evidenced by his recent induction into the Radio Hall of Fame, an accomplishment of which he was very proud, and I am so happy some of us here could be in Chicago to share that honor with him.*
> *In truth, for some years into adulthood, I actually believed the slogan "The Great Voice of the Great Lakes," stood for J.P. McCarthy, not the station.*
> *Will we ever forget his interviews with President Bush on Air Force One, shows from Russia during Perestroika, in-depth*

conversations with heads of state, senators, governors, ambassadors, generals, football coaches, architects, CEOs, physicians, authors, even lawyers, concerning esoteric subjects about which most of us wouldn't be able to frame a question? He did it with aplomb, style, and a real interest that made the subject matter fascinating to anyone listening, irrespective of his or her background. Somehow he, magically, made the listener as involved in the interview as himself and the interviewee. I would opine, he was, without question, the finest interviewer extant.

As a son:

How well I remember Joe's admiration for his father, and the fine mind he had. Whenever Joe and I couldn't remember some obscure fact or person, we always knew if we consulted his father, Priestley McCarthy, that we would have our answer. It was from the sage Priestley that we received the following advice: Never tell a young man: (A) that he is handsome, or (B) that he hits the golf ball a long way.

After Priestley died, Joe made arrangements for his mother, Martha, to move to Jupiter, Florida, to be near him and Judy. Just last fall Joe drove a car to Florida, principally so he could spend time alone with his mother when he got there.

He was a fine son, and always a joy to Martha and Priestley.

As a father:

Each of Joe's six children—John, Susan, Diane, Kevin, Kathleen, and Jamie—have their respective precious and treasured memories and thoughts of their father, which fortunately will endure and provide great solace for them for the rest of their lives. I can only confirm that which they know, which is he loved them deeply, individually and collectively, and was enormously proud of them, as well he should have been in light of their significant accomplishments. Each child is a reflection of wonderful parenting and the imbuement of qualities we all hope for in our own children.

As a community leader:

Mr. Detroit. Joe was Detroit, and its most important ally.

Many of you don't know the number of things Joe did gratuitously for various and sundry worthwhile organizations. Whether it was emceeing the Country Day School "Blue and

J.P. McCarthy

Gold" Club Dinner, the Leukemia Ball, for one of the hospitals, or the Detroit Historical Society—the list is endless—often five or six times per month with substantial preparation required in each instance.

Probably his proudest achievement was his PAL Golf Tournament, from its infancy at Wabeek with the Tour pros, to its lean years at BHCC, to today at TPC. Joe nurtured the tournament and was properly proud of the money it generated for inner city kids, to help cops help kids.

His greatest legacy may be the awareness which has been created relative to bone marrow transplants, and the potential donors who now exist as a result of the groundswell of people anxious to help Joe.

As a husband:
Anyone who knew Joe well knew how he felt about the "blonde bombshell"—he adored her. He never spoke of her without love in his voice. He was never rude or disrespectful—in short, he loved her deeply. Traveling with Joe and Judy, as Sharon and I have so often over the years, was without the petty bickering which so often contributes to unpleasantness traveling with another couple for long periods. He was wonderful to Judy and she reciprocated—more than once being rousted out of bed at 3 a.m. by her devoted husband and this eulogist to make fried egg sandwiches.

As a friend:
Joe had many friends. Friends with whom he enjoyed playing golf, sailing and skiing in the old days, and in more recent years, powerboating.

He was jovial, good-natured, rarely caustic or combative, but always ready with a quick-witted quip, one of my favorites: "It's not the money, it's the amount."

The first time we went to Ireland to play golf, my first tee shot was a large, looping hook which was last seen out over the Irish Sea—Joe turned and said in his best Irish brogue: "Johnny boy, that one's headed for America; your game may not be entirely suited to this wind."

He was a knowledgeable sports enthusiast with an incredible memory for sports trivia. Who else, for $1 million dollars, could guess the 1964 Heisman Trophy winner?

306

Just Don't Tell 'Em Where I Am

As many hours as we spent together—and they were indeed countless—I never tired of talking to Joe. We would often joke on the golf course that Judy and Sharon never stopped talking, sometimes not even to hit the ball. Frankly, we were just as bad.

Joe's election to the presidency of Bloomfield Hills Country Club was a proud achievement for him, but more symbolized the regard and friendship his peers had for him. Joe could be trusted with anything—we shared many confidences, often during long walks on the beach or a swim in the ocean, which he loved.

If Joe were here today he would say we have him pretty well canonized at this point.

Was he perfect? I'm not sure what perfect is. He loved good whiskey, particularly good whiskey that was free. When leaving on a 27-hour flight to Singapore, he turned to me and said, "I imagine we have the opportunity to be drunk and sober twice before we arrive." We didn't disappoint ourselves.

Joe loved life, and he hated hanging crepe, so I want to try to be upbeat.

Flying back from Montana Thursday, I was struck by the vastness of our country, and how interesting it is because of its differences and diversity. That was Joe—have you ever met a more interesting person?—because he was so interested in everyone and everything around him, which in turn made him so diverse.

I promised myself not to personalize this too much . . . but he was my best friend, and while we didn't always agree, and those of you who know both of us well will say that is one major understatement, Joe took positions in which he fiercely believed, and most often with substantial factual basis for his conclusion. But even so, he was a very fair man. He was a very fair man. He was smart, really smart, intensely loyal to his family, his friends, his city and his country—not a good idea to unjustly criticize or attack any of the above. Joe didn't take himself all that seriously; surely, he had an ego, but he never lost his sense of humility.

Why is he gone? In the final analysis I figured the ratings on God's radio station were so low, he pulled out all the stops and decided he had to have the best broadcaster in the world. It is also now confirmed that God is a golfer.

J.P. McCarthy

Joe's father used to say, "Don't wear your Irish on your sleeve"—he never did, but made no secret that he liked certain things Irish, like this little blessing, which, coincidentally, Judy selected for the Mass card independent of me:

May the road rise to meet you
May the wind be always at your back
May the sun shine warm upon your face
May the rains fall soft upon your fields
And, until we meet agin
May God hold you in the palm of his hand
So, to my best friend, godspeed, may you rest in peace, and
*   may perpetual light shine upon you.*

"John gave the perfect eulogy," says David Scott. "Humorous, a little ribald. Joe would have loved it."

Hoot McInerney agrees, insisting that McCarthy would not have wanted to hear endless accolades. "Joe would say, 'Time out. I don't want to hear this. You're embarrassing me!' He shouldn't be eulogized as a saint. What kind of guy was he? I've been asked that by a lot of people. He was just like you and me. He was mad. He was happy sometimes. He wasn't a saint, and he wasn't a sinner. He was just a normal human being who could have had a bigger ego than anybody. He never knew how big he was," McInerney insists.

When the funeral services ended, Judy McCarthy, wearing a touchingly symbolic green dress—with Martha McCarthy and all of the McCarthy children and grandchildren gathered around her—rose to leave the church alongside the beautifully elegant, unpretentious mahogany coffin. The large choir at the front of the church stood to sing with the musicians, and they began to serenade J.P. McCarthy as he was taken from the church, with a song that seemed to express what might be his very sentiment:

There's a tear in your eye
And I'm wondering why
For it never should be there at all.
With such power in your smile
Sure a stone you'd beguile,

So there's never a teardrop should fall.
For your smile is a part
Of the love in your heart
And makes even the sunshine more bright
You should laugh all the while
And all other times smile,
Now smile a smile for me.

For the springtime of life is the sweetest of all
There is ne'er a real care or regret;
And while springtime is ours
Throughout all of life's hours,
Let us smile each chance we get.
When Irish eyes are smiling
Sure it's like a morn in spring
In the lilt of Irish laughter
You can hear the angels sing.
When Irish hearts are happy,
All the world seems bright and gay.
And when Irish eyes are smiling,
Sure they steal your heart away.

"If funerals could be beautiful, it was the most beautiful," says Martha McCarthy.

Mourners climbed into their cars, to be led to the White Chapel cemetery in Troy by the Detroit Police motorcade arranged by McInerney in an appropriate thank-you for all McCarthy had done for the Detroit Police Athletic League. What occurred during that procession down Long Lake Road through Bloomfield Hills and Troy left a universally indelible impression on everyone in the funeral motorcade, as David Scott explains:

"There were people lined all the way down the road. People had watched the funeral on television, and walked down their driveways and just stood waving good-bye."

"What touched me most," says Trip Bosart, "is that as we went slowly by the people, there was a man and his son. The son was on his shoulders and they both had baseball caps on. The father took his cap off and kneeled down beside his son and told him to take his cap off and hold it over his heart. It shook me up," Bosart continues.

"Then over the hill, a lady runs across Long Lake Road, all alone, with tears streaming across her face and waving a little tiny Irish flag as hard as she could at the hearse. All the pall-bearers fell silent, and not another word was said until we got to the grave site."

Judy McCarthy remembers seeing the people on the road. "Joe would have been shocked at the people lining the road like a king or president had died. He would have said, 'What are all those people doing out here?' He never would have thought they were for him," she insists, "but they were a comfort."

"It made me both very sad and yet proud that they loved my dad that much," Kathleen McCarthy allows.

At the cemetery, final prayers were offered. A lone bagpiper brought the assembled mourners and full honor guard to attention, and J.P. McCarthy was laid to rest.

There was a reception given at Bloomfield Hills Country Club following the funeral. Touching pictures of McCarthy and his family were placed on display in the hallway.

Barry McGuire remembers running into Tom King on their way into the brunch. "King said, 'Get out of the way, McGuire, I've got to get a drink while McCarthy is still buying!' Wherever Joe was at that time, I'm sure he got a laugh out of that one!"

♣

One year later, in August of 1996, Mike Whorf sat down again with his pen, as he did with "Have you Ever Known an Irishman" and commemorated the one year anniversary of "the passing of this man."

They say that change is progress, and things can never be the same.
You'd be the first to know this in this fickle broadcasting game.
It's been a trying time down here, as if you didn't know.
I write these words to tell you—It ain't the same without you, Joe.

There's a whole new way of doing things, some of which you would approve.
The ruffled feathers of your friends are slowly being soothed.

Just Don't Tell 'Em Where I Am

They say that time's a healer. That to life there's ebb and flow.
Well, it's a pretty tough pill to swallow, cause it ain't the same
without you, Joe.

There's a whole new gang that's listening and new folks are on
the air
There's even a new McCarthy whose sitting in your chair
There's Paul and Ken and Mitch and some others that you'd
know
They're really very talented, but it aint' the same without you,
Joe.

Well, I guess it's all in retrospect to recall a talent true.
Your thoughts and insights, your well chosen phrases, the things
that made you you.
But something's missing in our lives as new folks come and go.
There's no place I'd rather be, but it ain't the same without you,
Joe.

In the course of time, as years pass by, we become dim memories.
But you have to take some pleasure to know there were thousands
that you pleased.
It's just the fact you're missed, my friend. Your smile, your
warmth, your glow.
We're all better to have known you, friend, but it ain't the same
without you, Joe.

Author's Note

Just a few months after his death, the J.P. McCarthy Foundation was established to help find a cure for Myelodysplastic Syndrome (MDS). The Foundation underwrites both basic laboratory research and clinical research into promising new methods of treatment of MDS and related diseases. It also promotes education about the disease and supports bone marrow donation with an annual registration drive. Additional information about the disease or programs supported by the Foundation may be obtained by contacting the Foundation office at 26261 Evergreen Road, Suite 180, Southfield, MI 48076, phone: 248/355-7575.